BIKING the GREAT NORTHWEST

20 TOURS IN
WASHINGTON
OREGON
IDAHO
& MONTANA

BIKING
the
GREAT
NORTHWEST

20 TOURS IN
WASHINGTON
OREGON
IDAHO
& MONTANA

JEAN HENDERSON
and Contributors

Maps by Ken Winkenweder

THE
MOUNTAINEERS

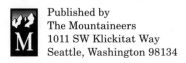
Published by
The Mountaineers
1011 SW Klickitat Way
Seattle, Washington 98134

8 7 6 5
5 4 3 2 1

Published simultaneously in Canada by Douglas & McIntyre, Ltd., 1615 Venables Street, Vancouver, B.C. V5L 2H1

Published simultaneously in Great Britain by Cordee, 3a DeMontfort Street, Leicester, England, LE1 7HD

Manufactured in the United States of America

Edited by Kris Fulsaas
Maps by Ken Winkenweder
Cover design by Dorothy Wachtenheim Design
Book layout by Word Graphics
Book design and typesetting by The Mountaineers Books

Cover photograph: Riding along Lake McDonald, Glacier National Park
(Photo: © Chuck Haney)
Frontispiece: Spectacular mountain scenery on the North Cascades Highway
(Photo: © Jean Henderson)

Library of Congress Cataloging-in-Publication Data
Henderson, Jean.
    Biking the great Northwest : 20 tours in Washington, Oregon, Idaho, and Montana : Jean Henderson and contributors.
        p.   cm.
    Includes index.
    ISBN 0-89886-425-9
    1. Bicycle touring--Northwest, Pacific--Guidebooks. 2. Northwest, Pacific--Guide-books. I. Title.
GV1045.5.N76H46   1995
796.6'4'0979--dc20   94-47654
                                                                            CIP

CONTENTS

◆

◆

OREGON

◆

IDAHO

◆

MONTANA

◆

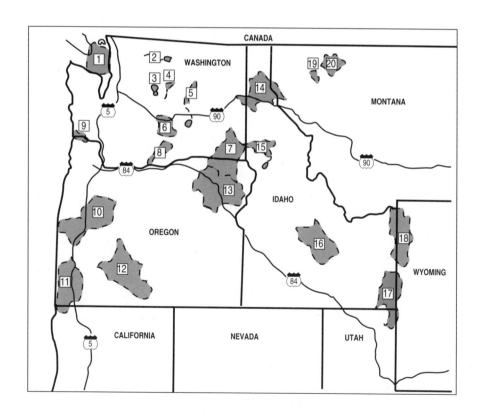

INTRODUCTION:
BICYCLE TOURING BASICS

◆

Launch a Northwest cycling adventure. Soon you will be lost in time on one of these bicycling tours—all favorites of a team of authors who in this book share their love of cycle touring. You will discover local history, geology, and legends while pedaling to some of the most scenic destinations in Washington, Oregon, Idaho, and Montana. Read about and try all twenty of the 2- to 9-day loops. Each is a great bicycling getaway with a distinct personality. Fly, train, drive, or bicycle to the starting point, pedal a fantastic loop with appealing side trips, alternative routes, and shortcuts. On your return, you usually travel a different route with new sights and scenery, but you also can add to the fun by connecting some of the loops or linking across a state by bicycle. Try one of these tours soon.

This book also explores beyond Washington, Oregon, Idaho, and Montana by including loops that nip into neighboring states and Canada. For example, Washington's tour 1, Puget Sound and Island Adventure, visits Vancouver Island, Canada, and Idaho's tour 18, Yellowstone and Grand Teton National Parks, loops through parts of Wyoming and Montana as well. Idaho's tour 17, Pioneer Historic Byway and Bear Lake Loop, includes a segment in Utah, and Oregon's tour 11, South Coast and Redwoods Loop, visits northern California. To locate specific cities, see appendix A, Tour Junctions. Appendix B lists the duration and mileage for each tour, and appendix C gives suggestions for linking the tours. Appendix D, Key Contacts, provides phone numbers of agencies that are useful for many of the tours.

To get you started, this introduction provides basics of bicycle touring. You can verify what to carry with the help of very detailed appendix E, Bicycle Touring Checklist.

PLANNING YOUR TOUR

Planning a tour is fun. It is also a tailoring process that will enhance your enjoyment later, on the road. Plan strategically and take advantage of the good kick-start provided by the information in this book.

Safety should permeate all aspects of your tour. To enhance it, thoroughly check potential changes in your chosen route before you leave home. To facilitate this, names of key agencies' phone numbers are included. Please read and heed information regarding availability of food and water. Contact tour information sources, determine each day's mileage and destination, and consider your options for accommodations.

Opposite: The Flathead Valley Loop captures the essence of this lovely valley. (Photo: Chuck Haney)

With minor, noted exceptions, the loops in this book are geared for indoor lodging, camping, or a combination of the two. Ranging from elaborate to primitive, suggested campsites are in U.S. Forest Service, state, county, and private campgrounds, or in commercial recreational-vehicle (RV) parks with tent sites. If you find that some campsites lack in amenities, balance their shortcomings with the quiet roads and stupendous scenery along the routes leading to them. Prices for lodging and campsites run the gamut, usually depending on luxuries and location. Again, readers are advised to check on availability and other specifics in advance.

If you are driving to the tour's beginning point, note conditions under which owner/managers of parking sites have agreed to allow overnight vehicles on their property. Safety and security were our primary concerns in selecting these sites, but the authors, publisher, and property owners accept no liability for loss or damage to vehicles parked there. Because changes do occur without notice, verify site availability in advance, and please honor the stated conditions for using them.

It is important to adopt a positive attitude before setting out on your tour. Touring will delight your senses and you will experience time rolling out like an endless carpet. Before you go, adopt these feelings and visualize idyllic days of smooth pedaling into constantly unfolding adventures. Dismiss thoughts of miserable weather and on-the-road challenges. On the road, if rain falls or the wind blows too fiercely, try to find a cozy spot and wait it out, or put on the appropriate gear, smile, and pedal forth. Often, major challenges, such as pedaling into a wind in "granny gear," become memorable highlights for a great story later. With an optimistic attitude, your enjoyment of a positively wonderful vacation will surely follow.

PHYSICAL PREPARATIONS

Train before the tour, not on the road. According to research at Ohio State University, overtaxed muscles can take up to six weeks to recover even half their original strength. Why risk soreness, vulnerability to challenging situations, and lack of endurance? Training is simply repetition, so ride often, adding miles and weight at regular intervals. You can increase miles and intensity gradually—at about 10 percent a week—by commuting to work or on errands and while enjoying bicycle social outings.

You can harden muscles and prepare for long periods in the saddle by training indoors or out, but you will gain valuable insight by riding the roads. Heat and hills affect saddle comfort. Weather conditions influence clothing choices. Maneuvering in traffic demands on-the-road practice.

ROUTE MAPS AND MILEAGE LOGS

For each tour's main route, you can rely on the descriptions and mileage logs in this book. Be aware that the maps are designed to be used in conjunction with other appropriate maps of the area. Also take advantage of other sources of information, some of which are available at little or no cost. Consult people who have been there, local bicycle clubs, travel literature and books, local visitors bureaus, state departments of transportation, state and city bicycling coordinators, and regional bicycle clubs.

A source for bicycle-specific information, accessories, tours, and maps is Adventure Cycling Association, Box 8308, Missoula, MT 59807. The country's largest recreational cycling association, founded in 1973 as BikeCentennial, Adventure Cycling's national bicycle route network encompasses more than 20,000 miles of backroads and trails.

For the best cycling-route detail, study United States Geological Survey (USGS) 7.5-minute maps. These are available in a large public or university library, or in a central reference location for each state. You can buy copies in individual sheets, in book form, or on CD-ROM disk.

Consult street maps printed with 24-hour traffic volumes to locate city routes carrying 20,000 or fewer cars daily. Highways with this density are best avoided, but city streets are okay, if a bicycle lane is provided. Ask bicycling coordinators or state transportation departments for this information.

Pay attention to mileages on tours that require carrying heavier loads (as for camping) and carefully study the elevation profiles provided in this book. You need not be daunted by profiles with teeth as jagged as a shark's. On paper, short, hilly tours often appear tougher than they are. It is true, however, that they demand muscle power in spurts. Most cyclists favor long, steady mountain grades where concentration can switch to scenery.

Take special note of long grades of 6 percent or higher. The average cyclist, with a load or at the end of a cycling day, tires quickly over this terrain. For uphill slogs of 15 percent or more, find a detour or plan to walk.

Heed prevailing winds, especially on the prairies, high desert, and unshielded roads. In a challenging head wind, alter the route, ride shorter miles, or gear down and flatten the pedaling profile.

ROUTE SELECTION

Choose a specific tour and your transportation to the starting point. Driving your car offers the greatest flexibility, but this book can facilitate connections by bicycle, train, or airplane as well. Connect tour routes or determine a car path to get there with the help of appendix C, Suggestions for Linking the Tours. Use key telephone numbers, including Amtrak, local chambers of commerce and visitors bureaus, state tourism offices, campgrounds, and others. These are included in each tour's summary and in appendix D, Key Contacts.

Factor in your personal energy flow patterns and consider specific daily cycling mileages for your tour. Review the tour summary for total mileage and elevation gain, take a look at the tour's elevation profiles, and consider the mileage log's daily mileages, shortcuts, alternatives, and side trips. The most appropriate tour should match your personal energy flow, preferences, and abilities. If not, choose another tour, change the starting point, or take a shortcut.

Think about how you will get your bicycle and gear to the starting point, what clothing choices will be needed, how to select a bicycle and gear appropriate for the tour, and whether a sag-wagon driver should be recruited. These and other topics are covered later in this chapter.

Review the tour description and mileage log to determine if the route is along mostly quiet backroads or in more-populated areas with busier highways. Choose what suits you, considering areas with more towns if you want to explore history, museums, cultural activities, or local festivals. If you prefer to completely get away, choose the more-remote tours. Be aware that some of the tours in this book may require camping, at least part of the time.

Determine the best season for your tour, with an eye to areas where searing heat, heavy rains, and prevailing winds are a prime factor. In recommending the seasons stated in each tour's summary, the authors considered all of these factors. For example, some tours are not recommended until later in the summer season, due to the possibility of snow on or near the roads.

Alter the starting time for each tour to suit your group and cycling style. Determine the number of miles to be ridden that day, the type of terrain to be covered, interesting sights along the way, the abilities of riders in your group, and normal traffic patterns on the route. Starting hours listed in each tour's summary are generally flexible, but a few are stated with specific reasons. For example, on tour 20, Glacier National Park, you must start early over Logan Pass in order to cross during the daily window when the road is open to cyclists.

Allow for stayovers in specific towns, travel fewer or more miles per day, or match personal energy flow patterns by changing a tour to suit you. Each tour is optimal when ridden as described, but most can be altered to suit your cycling style. Use the details in the mileage log to determine mileages between destinations and towns with services, then phone or write to the area chambers of commerce or visitors bureaus to verify your accommodation specifics.

Tour summaries also include "Points of Interest." Add to these significant highlights and, while you are at it, look into alternate activities for layover days at desired locations. For example, you could explore kayaking and whale-watching opportunities on tour 1, Puget Sound and Island Adventure, or ride a railroad and spend a day hiking on tour 13, Wallowas and Blue Mountains Loop.

Finally, plan with attention to the gravel sections noted in the mileage logs and tour descriptions, and to potential road construction along the route. Most gravel sections mentioned in this book are easily negotiable on a road bike (better on wider or knobby tires). To avoid them, take the alternative routes that are offered, when available. Checking on the status of road construction on a tour route is the reader's responsibility, but special consideration has been given to tour 14, The Idaho Panhandle. Due to a funding delay, paving near the top of Thompson Pass in Idaho will not be completed by the time this book is published. Choose this tour with this in mind, and please plan accordingly. If you want to try this tour before paving is completed, check the status of the roadway, using the telephone number provided under "Key Contacts" in the tour summary. Then allow additional time for riding that section or use a sag wagon on your tour.

Here are some general guidelines for tour planning:
• Adjust daily mileages on your tour to fit cycling abilities and preferences of the participants.
• Be aware of weather extremes common to your tour area (i.e., searing heat, prevailing high winds, heavy rain or thunderstorms) and time your tour if you wish to avoid them. For example, visit desert areas in September and rainy spots in late summer.
• Shorten daily mileages to allow for personal sightseeing interests, challenging terrain, limited daylight, and head winds.
• Allow for plenty of stops, or more leisurely riding, along especially scenic routes—just to drink it all in and enjoy.

- Satisfy a "morning" person by completing climbs early in the day.
- Think about what the area has to offer and plan accordingly. For example, arise to take in a sunrise ride or carry lights to ride at sunset.
- Take an occasional day off from touring, or an abbreviated one, to break the routine and facilitate shopping and laundry chores. This is especially important on tours that extend beyond a week in length.

SAG WAGONS

Carrying gear is not a cycle-touring requirement. You can widen tour opportunities with a "sag" wagon (car, truck, or van for carrying gear, and cyclists in an emergency). While desire for self-sufficiency precludes the use of a sag wagon for some, others may appreciate the options it allows.

To arrange a sag wagon, invite a non-cyclist to drive a tour, especially in remote areas. Often a spouse, other relative, or friend wants to tour, but cannot bicycle. Share the route maps and the gas, arrange to meet at specific locations, and provide alternative routes to bicycle trails. Encourage the driver to tour independently, and to use the vehicle for reconnaisance such as route checking and lodging arrangements, as well as picking up supplies and extending sightseeing.

A sag wagon allows you to customize your tour more easily. For example, you can avoid carrying heavy gear over a route that requires only a single night of camping (as in tour 7, Two-State Canyons Tour). Use two cars the first day while the riders cycle from the starting point. The drivers proceed to the first night's destination, carrying the gear. After the night of camping, one car—with the unneeded gear inside—is left at a safe, prearranged location. From then on, there is a single sag wagon for the cyclists. At the end of the tour, arrange to get the first driver back to the parked car and the camping gear back into its owners' hands.

You can also rent a car for all or part of a tour, making a tough tour section easier with a temporary sag wagon. Alternate driving duties and drop off the rental vehicle in a convenient location.

EQUIPMENT CONSIDERATIONS

SELECTING A BICYCLE

Match the bicycle frame to the selected route and the tour, then fit the bicycle frame to the rider, consulting experts, if desired. Fit is the key, even with more expensive models, because it means a comfortable, safe ride.

Bikes are categorized into touring, sport touring, racing, mountain, and commuting models. For well-balanced touring over long distances, choose either a touring or a sport touring frame. A touring frame is stretched out, giving a more comfortable ride, but is less responsive than the shorter sport touring model. The sport touring frame is more fun to pedal, but less comfortable on really bumpy roads.

Racing, commuting, or mountain bicycles generally should be used only for those specific uses. If used for touring, expect less comfort than touring frames offer over wide-ranging terrain and long distances. Sometimes, as in the case of the racing frame, they also are not designed to carry panniers or large loads.

To fit the bicycle to the rider, start with a 1- to 2-inch clearance between the top tube and the rider astride the frame. Then have the rider sit on the bicycle to check the reach to the handlebars and the saddle height (with one foot on a pedal at its lowest position, the knee should be *slightly bent,* not fully straightened). For long-distance riding, proper saddle height is critical in order to avoid unnecessary fatigue or even permanent knee damage.

BICYCLE PREPARATIONS AND TOOLS

Consider the gears in light of the selected tour's terrain. Wide-range gears are best for hauling loads up and over mountains or steep hills. It is possible to inch over a summit or up steep grades such as those in the Grand Tetons and Yellowstone or Washington–Oregon canyons, for example, with a "granny gear" that does not sacrifice efficient pedaling on the flat. An appropriate gear allows coverage of at least 90 inches of road with each pedal stroke. Spend time with a gear chart or an expert mechanic to determine what is appropriate for your bicycle, the desired route, and your cycling level.

To avoid mechanical blues on the open road, inspect your bicycle and all equipment thoroughly. Grease and adjust bearings, replace cables and brake pads, inspect wheels and gear cables, study all parts carefully for wear, and, above all, track down any "funny noise."

You can decrease the potential for flats by using new tubes and tires, even if your current ones are not worn. Carry two spare tubes. For thorn country, install Kevlar-belted tires. Plastic tire inserts also prevent punctures, but may increase rolling resistance.

Building a knowledge of bicycle tools and confidence in using them simplifies tool packing and eliminates weighty choices. To determine what tools to carry, consult appendix E, Bicycle Touring Checklist. Essentials are tire removal devices (tire irons), a pump, a spare tube and a patch kit, allen wrenches, pliers, and spare brake and gear cables—to fit your specific bicycle. For more remote locations, take an extra tube and a spare tire (folded ones are easier to pack), a chain tool, a freewheel remover, wire cutters, a screwdriver or an all-in-one, and a spoke wrench. Tape two or three spare spokes—that fit the bicycle wheel—to a fender stay, and tuck in a small rag and a hand cleaner that does double duty as a laundry aid.

BICYCLE RACKS AND BAGS

For touring, add sturdy racks to your bicycle, then panniers or other bags. For best road performance, balance the bicycle load and keep it low. Put approximately 60 percent of the weight behind the saddle, and maintain this low center of gravity by saving knapsacks for short jaunts. Be ready for emergencies or a change in plans by packing in bicycle bags, even if a sag wagon carries them.

- Rear rack. Consider a sturdy rear rack a touring essential. Most styles are standard, but a few bags require a customized rack, so shop for both at once. Look for quality and compatibility with your bicycle frame.
- Panniers (saddlebags). Select rear and/or front panniers that attach securely and detach easily for hands-free carrying. Well-designed styles feature pockets, quality and water-resistant fabrics, carrying handles, and some sort of light stiffening for stability. Verify that rear bags will not interfere when you rotate the pedals. Choose a smaller, matching version as front panniers if you plan to carry a lot of camping gear.

- Front rack and low rider. These two styles are distinguished by their placement on the bicycle. Front racks create of a platform over the front wheel that is handy for securing small tents and other gear. Low riders are racks that sit on braze-ons (eyelets built into the bicycle frame) midway down the front fork to provide stable, wind-resistant carrying capacity. The same type of pannier can be used for either the front rack or the low rider.
- Rack pack. This rests above the panniers and on top of the rear rack. It sits in the rider's slipstream to avoid energy loss from wind resistance and offers adaptable storage for both touring and day trips. Look for removable shoulder straps or carrying handles and at least one separated compartment.
- Handlebar bag. This provides accessible storage for eyeglasses and valuables, and an eye-level map holder. Because of its position on the bike, expect wind resistance. Check for interference with steering or the rolling of the front wheel. Handlebar bags vary in size and shape, and most include support racks. Seek compartments, a detachable map carrier, and pluses like a carrying handle and/or a snap-on purse.
- Waist pack. This can flatten to insert into another bag or be carried under the tent or sleeping bag while you are cycling. Use for hikes, city exploring, or grocery toting on foot. Some styles expand and include water-bottle holders.
- Knapsack. This is a favorite for short-term carrying capacity that does not add bulk or weight.

CYCLING ACCESSORIES

Enhance a tour with other special accessories:
- Helmet. Buy a helmet rated for safety by ANSI or Snell (or both). Let personal preferences guide your selection of style and color, but do not waver on fit.

For safety, always wear a helmet. (Photo: Allen Throop)

- Lock. Select a tiny deterrent lock and a medium-weight cable, or a stronger, U-shaped style of lock guaranteed against theft by the manufacturer. Weight varies and styles include either keyed or combination mechanisms.
- Cycle computer. Use this to keep track of miles and key into the mileage logs provided in this book. Look for easy installation and water resistance, then add features such as average and current speed, miles per hour, altitude, cadence, heart rate, elapsed time, and an alarm.
- Bell. Use it to signal pedestrians or danger. A bell is often required on trails or sidewalks.
- Lights. Carry lights for unplanned evening riding or foggy days. Communicate "cyclist" to motorists with a rear twinkle light. Use a battery-powered headlamp to add safety and see the road ahead. Choices include blinking lights for clothing or bags, tiny, valve-stem lights that illuminate wheels, and sophisticated dual, bright headlights with rechargeable battery packs.
- Rearview mirrors. Fit a handlebar mirror onto the bar end or fasten it onto the brake-lever mounts. While not always in the ideal position for seeing traffic behind you, they are reliable and stable. Helmet and eyeglass mirrors reflect traffic with a turn of the head. These are more fragile, and sometimes compatibility between helmets and glasses is an issue.
- Elastic shock cords. Attach a tent or a sleeping bag to your bike rack, hang out laundry to dry, or secure the bike on a ferryboat with these handy straps.
- Sunglasses. Pick eyewear with virtually 100 percent ultraviolet protection and shatterproof lenses. For touring, carry both dark and clear lenses to protect eyes from bugs, wind, and dust.

CLOTHING CHOICES

Clothing choices are as endless as pedal strokes. Focus on protection from the elements and remember to include non-bulky off-the-bike attire. Be a stickler for quality. For a more specific list, see appendix E, Bicycle Touring Checklist, at the back of this book.

Pack walking shorts and a T-shirt, and "dress-up" attire. Include a wrinkle-resistant shirt and pants, or shirt and skirt, in dark colors. For cycling, add black shorts and tights. This traditional clothing selection stems from cycling's early days when gear shifting required dismounting and reversing the rear wheel to access a different-sized cog. Black clothing was practical for accepting greasy hand wipes.

Make your laundry a downhill coast with easy-care, fast-drying fabrics. While ideal in hot, dry climates, cotton can be cold and usually will not dry overnight in coastal areas of the Northwest.

Seek performance and comfort in shoes. Carry walking shoes that coordinate with the wardrobe, and propel the bicycle effectively in a pair with recessed cleats. These can double as walking shoes. For non-cleated bicycling, choose a shoe with a hard, smooth sole and a narrow toe.

Go for protection in rain gear, but be aware of weight and bulk. Size a raincoat to top layers of your other clothing. Seek a bright color in guaranteed fibers that breathe (wick perspiration and provide a rain barrier). Add a pair of lightweight, thin booties that packs flat, to wear over bicycle shoes. Rain pants are usually worn only in severe conditions, or for added warmth off the bicycle, so tuck in an inexpensive, non-breathable pair.

Carry gloves with sufficient padding for cycling, plus a warm, long-fingered pair. Verify that seams will not create hand blisters, especially at the thumbs.

For headgear, use a bandanna, earband, or hat. A cotton bandanna is a touring asset that can be soaked as a helmet-liner in the heat. In cold weather switch to a hat or an ear insert in the helmet to retain up to 40 percent of body heat. Look for wool or high-tech fabrics.

Top everything with one extra layer of lightweight, non-bulky, high-tech-fabric clothing. It will be priceless in an emergency.

OTHER GEAR

When traveling and/or camping in isolated areas, be sure to carry the Ten Essentials:
- extra clothing
- extra food
- sunglasses
- knife
- firestarter
- first-aid kit
- matches in a waterproof container
- flashlight
- map
- compass

Be sure to carry a first-aid kit and know how to use it. Include large bandages, surgical tape, a knife or scissors, disinfectant, and aspirin or ibuprofen. Some incidentals that are a good idea are: insect repellent, suntan lotion, lip salve, and aloe vera ointment. The lotion and lip salve are valuable at high altitudes and in hot country, and the aloe vera ointment is useful as a versatile first-aid remedy for sunburn, bug bites, and saddle sores.

Campers should also include the basics of a tent, sleeping bag and pad, camp stove and fuel, and cooking gear.

PACKING STRATEGIES

Pack to balance the load and allow room for tour souvenirs and brochures picked up along the way. Lay out everything and sort it by categories. A good way to make the most of your available space is to tightly roll each item and secure it with a rubber band, then according to category either tuck it into small plastic bags or into a bag lining the pannier. Another space-saving method is to insert rolled items lengthwise and stuff the insides of shoes. If you may need an item during the day, keep it on top or in the smaller compartments of your panniers.

Place heavy items (except for the tent and sleeping bag) in the bottom of the rear panniers. Identify everything with legible, waterproof name tags, especially if public transportation will be used on any portion of your trip. If something later becomes a burden, you can simply mail it home.

SHIPPING THE BICYCLE ON PUBLIC TRANSPORTATION

If you plan to reach the tour starting point by plane, train, or bus, you will need to pack your bicycle. To lessen risk of theft and damage, use a box.

Remove only the pedals and loosen and turn the handlebars to position them parallel to the bicycle frame. Attach everything to the frame in case the box opens during transit. Protect your derailleur by attaching a U-shaped metal device to the rear axle, but check for compatibility with your bicycle's quick-release mechanism. In transit this derailleur protector will take the brunt of baggage loaded on top of the box. For easier reassembly of the bike, mark your preferred seat and handlebar positions with tape.

Inside the box, add padding and label everything with your name, flight or train number(s), and final destination. Attach a name tag to your bicycle seatpost and identify the outside of the box with a black marker. Panniers can either be snapped together as carry-on luggage, or secured to the frame as extra padding for the box. Before sliding your bike into the box, determine how you will transport the loaded carton to the public transit terminal.

Verify the bicycle as baggage on your train, plane, or bus. If the bicycle must go separately, ship it ahead via parcel post or an air freight service. Specify a receiver. Bicycle shops will accept and hold packed cycles and, for an additional fee, reassemble for pick-up. Ask baggage representatives or others representing your carrier to keep flattened, labeled boxes for your use on the return trip. This will save you the trouble of finding another suitable carton later.

To ship your bicycle you will need:
- Large box. Discarded boxes may be free after a major cycling event or near a train station or airport luggage areas.
- Packing tools. Carry allen, crescent, and pedal wrenches, plus a tape roll, knife, and marking pen.
- Fees. Bicycle handling and transport on domestic airline flights usually involves a charge. To get free bike transportation on specified airlines, contact the League of American Bicyclists or the Adventure Cycling Association (see appendix D, Key Contacts). They will require booking through their designated agents. Often, train or bus charges are limited to a fee for the box.

ON THE ROAD

SAFETY

Because safety should permeate all aspects of a bicycle tour, examine your bicycle carefully and replace worn and broken parts. Choose bright colors for cycling and be prepared for cold and wet weather that can dull thinking and affect road performance. Under these conditions, layer clothing and avoid cotton next to the skin. High-tech fibers and wool wick moisture away from the body to enhance warmth, even when wet. Carry a compact first-aid kit, personal identification, and an energy bar or two, and have cash available for emergencies. Mount a bell on your bicycle and carry emergency lights.

Practice safe bicycling habits by:
- allowing vehicles to pass if travel of five or more is impeded.
- riding as far to the right of the road as practicable. Think safety and ride the shoulder or bicycle lane, if available and hazard-free.
- communicating with motorists and fellow cyclists. Signal stops, turns, and road-hazard alerts with your hand. To signal a hazard, wave your lower right arm from side to side behind your back.
- wearing a helmet. For best impact protection, level the helmet all around your head and attach it snugly under your chin. Wear it at mid-forehead level and do not tip the helmet back to crown the back of your head.
- using a rearview mirror. Maneuver safely in traffic and be aware of oncoming hazards by using a rearview mirror on your handlebar, helmet, or glasses.

The author experiences one of the joys of bicycle touring, visiting with local residents. (Photo: Ken Winkenweder)

SOLO AND GROUP TOURING

Whether touring alone, with a friend or relative, or in a large group, keep these riding suggestions in mind:

- Before starting out, check your route maps and mileage logs to determine stops and the destination for the day. If others are with you, communicate these decisions to each person and make sure everyone has a map and/or mileage log for the route.
- In a group, space out along the road so that only three or four people are riding tightly together. Allowing traffic to flow easily around riders offers an extra buffer for your safety that may be critical in emergencies.
- Use both your left arm and your voice to signal stops, hazards, and turns to motorists and to fellow cyclists.
- Allow more breaks and longer stopping distances, and wear bright colors, in wet and low-light conditions.
- Anticipate having fun. A positive attitude is essential to a great tour.

FERRYBOAT COURTESY

Some of the tours in this book use ferryboats to link the roads. If ferry rides are a new experience for you, consider:

- using the provided rope or an elastic shock cord to help prevent damage to your bicycle or nearby vehicles. This is critical in rough waters because the rope secures your bicycle to a ferry railing or wall.

- arriving early, especially for the San Juan Islands in the summer. Line up at least 20 minutes before the departure time. You will most likely load and unload before the motor vehicles.
- moving between cars with your bicycle only if adequate room is available. If not, wait until after the attendant signals vehicles to move.
- removing valuables from the bicycle. Theft is rare on the ferries, but do not take a chance.

FOOD

To assure fuel for the approximately one-eighth horsepower it takes to move 16 miles per hour on the flat, eat at regular intervals. Concentrate on low-fat, high-carbohydrate foods. Graze on complex carbohydrates like bananas. They are a great source of potassium and did not become cyclists' staple for nothing. Bagels, muffins, low-fat cookies, fig bars, fruit, graham crackers, rice cakes, and gorp (a varied mixture of dried fruit and nuts often containing cereal, raisins, dates, and chocolate chips) are also delicious and effective choices.

Sports drinks are excellent for sagging cycle tourists, but they are not as much fun as eating. For on-the-road delays, carry concentrated drink powder or an energy bar or two. In remote areas it is a good idea to pinpoint food stops in advance, and to inquire often about facilities on the route ahead.

Because protein, the body's muscle builder, is harder to digest than carbohydrates, save protein for evening meals. Because fat is a less-efficient fuel that is digested by temporarily robbing your system of oxygen-rich blood, eat it after bicycling as well. Also be aware that you effectively prepare a ready supply of glycogen for your next day's ride by eating as soon as possible after today's pedaling. This quickly converts carbohydrates to body fuel. In short, tour with a different food attitude than for single-day rides: Eat often to supply tomorrow's fuel.

WATER

Cycling requires one to two quarts of water per hour, as much as a sedentary person needs all day. Carry at least two water bottles, keep them topped off, and sip regularly. By drinking water, you satisfy thirst, lubricate joints, regulate body temperature, and oxygenate cells. Foods cannot rehydrate you because they need fluid to be digested.

Crucial for both muscle glycogen and blood glucose, water prevents leg cramps, a severe headache, and intense thirst. Drink before you are thirsty and increase water consumption if your urine turns dark. This sign of too little water in your system should be heeded before it leads to dizziness, nausea, confusion, and/or fainting.

A good rule of thumb is to drink one standard bike bottle of water for every 45 minutes of pedaling. If you are cycling in the heat or wind, increase consumption significantly, and be sure to flood your cells before, during, and after riding. If bloating occurs the first few days of cycling (normal in hot climates), consume more water and shun coffee, tea, caffeinated sodas, alcohol, or other drinks that contribute to fluid loss.

EMERGENCY CONSIDERATIONS

For medical emergencies, carry a first-aid kit and know how to use it. In severe emergencies, flag down a passing motorist or ask someone to telephone authorities. Carry a bandanna, useful both as a flag and as a large bandage.

For mechanical emergencies, carry tools and equipment appropriate for the tour (see Equipment Considerations earlier in this chapter). If necessary, hitch a ride with a motorist, ask one to contact your sag-wagon driver (if he or she may be near a phone) or a bicycle shop. Other ideas are: flagging down the state patrol or scooting along on the bicycle by pushing off with one foot. It is possible to temporarily patch severe tire damage with roadside weeds and debris.

THE OPEN ROAD

Road conditions change without notice. Before embarking on a tour, ask about road construction and other travel interferences along your route. The authors and the publisher accept no liability for the safety of riders using the recommended routes in this book. Despite great care and detailed research, errors or changes may occur. If you find any, please notify the author or the publisher.

The team of cycling authors who have shared their favorite tours in this book dedicated a year to researching, writing, and assembling it in the sincere wish that you will find endless days of enjoyment using it on the open road. Bicycle touring is a feeling as carefree as the dancing breezes. Experience the yearning it creates, and yet satisfies, for new adventures. Your muscles and your senses will be honed to new refinement. Some of life's most basic pleasures, such as sleeping and eating, will become wonderful and more appreciated. Happy cycling.

A NOTE ABOUT SAFETY

Safety is an important concern in all outdoor activities. No guidebook can alert you to every hazard or anticipate the limitations of every reader. Therefore, the descriptions of roads, trails, routes, and natural features in this book are not representations that a particular place or excursion will be safe for your party. When you follow any of the routes described in this book, you assume responsibility for your own safety. Under normal conditions, such excursions require the usual attention to traffic, road and trail conditions, weather, terrain, the capabilities of your party, and other factors. Keeping informed on current conditions and exercising common sense are the keys to a safe, enjoyable outing.

The Mountaineers

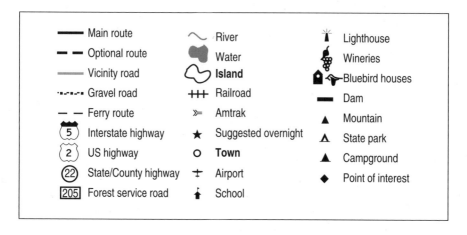

WASHINGTON

---

1. PUGET SOUND AND ISLAND ADVENTURE

Jean Henderson

Distance: 214 miles
Terrain: flat to rolling, with some short hills
Total cumulative elevation gain: 5,402 feet
Recommended time of year: April–October
Recommended starting time: 9:00 A.M.
Allow: 7 days; 1-plus layover days recommended
Points of interest: narrow-gauge train, life-size cutouts on buildings, Anacortes; historic homes, Port Townsend; lighthouse, gun batteries in Fort Worden State Park; marine exhibit, Port Angeles; Butchart Gardens, Empress Hotel, Victoria, B.C.; ferry cruises; American Camp, English Camp, and Roche Harbor, San Juan Island; Spencer Spit and Shark Reef, Lopez Island

PUBLIC TRANSPORTATION
Air: commercial airlines serve Seattle, about 75 miles southeast of Anacortes; arrange a shuttle to Anacortes or pedal a route described by Erin and Bill Woods in *Bicycling the Backroads of Puget Sound* (The Mountaineers, 1989).
Train: Amtrak serves Seattle or Everett, about 50 miles southeast of Anacortes

PRACTICAL INFORMATION
Key contacts: Anacortes Visitors Information, 360-293-3832; Fort Worden State Park, 360-385-4730; Port Townsend Visitors Information, 360-385-2722; Sequim–Dungeness Chamber of Commerce, 360-683-6197; Port Angeles Visitors Information, 360-452-2363; Black Ball Ferry from Port Angeles, 360-457-4491; Victoria Express (passengers only) from Port Angeles, 360-452-8088; Tourism British Columbia, Canada, 800-663-6000; Washington State Ferry Service, 800-84-FERRY; San Juan Islands Visitor Information Service, 360-468-3663

STARTING POINT
Washington State Ferry dock near Anacortes: From I-5 take Exit 230 to Highway 20 westbound. Continue approximately 12 miles into Anacortes, turning left on Twelfth Avenue and following signs to the ferry to the San Juan Islands. About 4 miles west of Anacortes, turn right to the ferry landing. Park and secure your car in one of three lots.

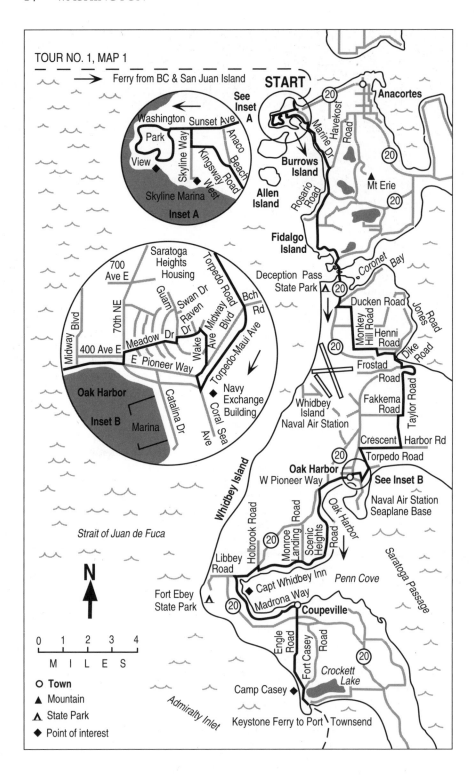

TOUR NO. 1, MAP 1

Ferry from BC & San Juan Island

START

See Inset A

Anacortes

Washington Park

Sunset Ave

Anaco Beach Road

Skyline Way

Kingsway West

View

Skyline Marina

Inset A

Burrows Island

Allen Island

Marine Dr

Havekost Road

20

Mt Erie

Rosario Road

Fidalgo Island

Coronet Bay

Deception Pass State Park

20

Ducken Road

Monkey Hill Road

Henni Road

Jones Road

Dike Road

Saratoga Heights Housing

700 Ave E

Torpedo Road

Guam

Swan Dr

Raven Dr

Midway Ave

Bch Rd

70th NE

Meadow Dr

Wake Ave

Torpedo-Maui Ave

Frostad Road

Midway Blvd

400 Ave E

E Pioneer Way

Fakkema Road

Taylor Road

Oak Harbor

Inset B

Marina

Catalina Dr

Coral Sea Ave

Navy Exchange Building

Whidbey Island Naval Air Station

Crescent Harbor Rd

20

Torpedo Road

Whidbey Island

Oak Harbor

W Pioneer Way

See Inset B

Naval Air Station Seaplane Base

Oak Harbor Road

Strait of Juan de Fuca

Holbrook Road

Monroe Landing Road

Scenic Heights Road

Saratoga Passage

N

Libbey Road

20

Capt Whidbey Inn

Penn Cove

Fort Ebey State Park

20

Madrona Way

Coupeville

0 1 2 3 4

M I L E S

Engle Road

Fort Casey Road

20

Crockett Lake

O Town

▲ Mountain

Λ State Park

◆ Point of interest

Camp Casey

Admiralty Inlet

Keystone Ferry to Port Townsend

Romantic Penn Cove is one of the many viewpoint stops on Whidbey Island.
(Photo: Ken Winkenweder)

Miles flow as effortlessly as the tides on this tour in the friendly, cool climate
of northwestern Washington. Experience wonder-filled bicycling amid dappled
sunlight, lush greenery, sparkling seas, tree-studded islands, bustling communities, and tranquil coves. Ferry hop to explore, riding to new destinations in
this archipelago of 172 islands. Adventures on tap encourage expanding the
suggested week-long tour to the maximum number of days you might have available. Make lodging reservations in advance, especially in the San Juan Islands,
the delicious icing on an already fantastic tour.

This tour begins not with a ferry ride, but with a two-wheeled cruise south
on Whidbey Island. Before pedaling away from the Anacortes ferry dock, however, turn back on Fidalgo Island, where it is located, to visit the city for which
it is named. Prowl the streets, investigating life-size cutouts on buildings. Climb
aboard the narrow-gauge mini-train that puffs along an abbreviated track in
the summer. It switches direction on the turntable at Ninth and Commercial,
and is housed near the dry-docked sternwheeler *W. T. Preston*.

Return to the Anacortes ferry dock, but continue to ignore the ferryboat.
Instead, meander past surprising views on a forested loop in Washington Park,
then pedal uphill to Highway 20 to cross the spectacular Deception Pass bridge.
Seething waters below mean mariners need to know when to enter for safe passage. Leave them to their charts, and roll past Deception Pass State Park to
pastoral landscapes on Whidbey Island. Zig and zag into Oak Harbor, a town
known for Navy aircraft flyers, and pop into the Captain Whidbey Inn, in ro-

mantic Penn Cove. Consider picturesque Coupeville for an overnight stay or dart instead across island farmland to a turn-of-the-century fort and the Keystone ferry. End Day One in Port Townsend where, before 1890, sea captains occupied the hilltop mansions that now serve as Victorian bed and breakfasts. Go over the crest into Fort Worden where the movie *An Officer and a Gentleman* was shot on location. Views are varied and fantastic, and facilities include campsites and refurbished officers' quarters.

On Day Two, take off on backroads flanked by salal, Oregon grape, ferns, and the state flower—the wild rhododendrons early explorers found blooming profusely. Roll around Discovery Bay in the shadow of the Olympic Mountains. In Sequim, wade knee-deep in spring wildflowers, or take an extra day to hike the 7-mile-long Dungeness Spit nearby. Rain is apt to fall anytime in the Northwest, but as little as 15 inches a year sprinkle sunny Sequim. On the opposite side of the towering Olympic Mountains, more than 240 inches drench the Olympic rain forest every year. End the day in the Sequim sunshine or roll into Port Angeles for a "big-city" experience or a side trip into Olympic National Park. Summer ferryboats to Canada depart three times daily.

On Day Three leave Sequim to glide in bewitching dawn light past blackberry patches and wheat fields into Port Angeles. Consider a 36-mile loop side trip up 5,230 feet to spectacular Hurricane Ridge. Then take a ferry across the Strait of Juan de Fuca to experience a touch of England, Canada style, with high tea in the stately Empress Hotel in Victoria, British Columbia. Watch hang gliders and sailing ships over Cadboro Bay, picnic in Beacon Hill Park, explore natural history at the British Columbia Provincial Museum, or ride a double-decker bus to the famous Butchart Gardens. **Note:** Plan a layover day in Victoria, if possible, to see its many sights.

On Day Four, pedal 30 shoreline miles to Sidney. Catch the Washington State Ferry, cruising into the San Juan Islands. Have a picnic aboard. First stop is Friday Harbor on San Juan Island. While cycling miles are abbreviated on the island, historic sites and breathtaking beauty are everywhere. The stage for the 1850s Pig War, San Juan Island was sought by both Britain and the United States. When a prize English pig was shot for uprooting an American farmer's potato patch, both sides set up armed garrisons that occupied the island for twelve years. Toward the end of the "war," however, they exchanged social invitations regularly.

In Roche Harbor on San Juan Island, experience history in the vintage Hotel De Haro and lime kiln relics. In 1886, realizing the potential of a ledge of 99.6 percent pure limestone, John S. McMillin based a thriving industry on the seemingly inexhaustible supply. Search out McMillin's Afterglow Manor mausoleum. Hidden in the trees is a marble dining table with what appears to be a missing chair. Overhead one of the pillars ends abruptly. The table reflects the squeezed formation for family dining that allowed each a view of Haro Strait below, and the column symbolizes life broken by death.

For the remainder of the tour, hop a ferryboat to Lopez Island, and plan additional side trips to Orcas or Shaw Island as well. With annual rain of less than 20 inches a year, the islands dazzle with more than sunshine. On Lopez Island delight in gentle landscapes first farmed by the Hudson's Bay Company, then spy on sea lions. See *Bicycling the Backroads of Puget Sound* by Erin and Bill Woods (The Mountaineers, 1989) for additional day trips in the San Juans.

Eventually, as your schedule demands, board the ferry bound for Anacortes. As the scenery en route to Fidalgo Island slips by, drink it in, then reluctantly close the book on an idyllic Puget Sound cycling adventure.

MILEAGE LOG
DAY ONE: ANACORTES TO PORT TOWNSEND—46.6 MILES

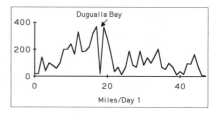

0.0   Washington State Ferry dock near Anacortes. Pedal uphill to **Sunset Avenue** (unmarked) and turn right at the Y intersection. Oakes Avenue is to the left.

0.6   Pass Skyline Way on the left and head into Washington Park (rest rooms, water, beach access on the right at Mile 1.2) straight ahead.

1.0   Bear left into Washington Park. Follow the one-way loop road through woods, up and over short rises, and past sweeping views. Watch for speed bumps and gravel troughs.

3.4   Exit the park as the loop ends. Right on **Skyline Way** almost immediately.

3.9   Left on **Kingsway**. Thread through a residential area. (**Note:** Services are straight ahead on Skyline Way.) Road name changes to **Kingsway West**.

4.9   Right on **Anaco Beach Road**. Enjoy island views as the road dips toward the bay.

5.2   Shift for a sudden, short uphill section where the road is renamed **Marine Drive** and narrows briefly.

7.1   Right, staying with **Marine Drive**, at a T intersection. On the left is Havekost Road, named for an early pioneer who donated the original site of Washington Park to the city of Anacortes.

8.2   Begin a short climb. Passing a sandy cliff, the road becomes **Rosario Road**.

10.2   Bear left to hug Rosario Road around a corner. Pass a road on the right that drops to Rosario Beach and the Walla Walla College Marine Station.

11.7   Pass a fishing access (pit toilet, hidden in woods) on the left.

11.8   Right on **Highway 20** at a T intersection. Pass Deception Pass State Park on the right. **Caution:** heavy traffic.

12.1   Pass two pullouts on the right, then cross the Deception Pass bridge, supported mid-span by tiny Pass Island. Use caution. Ride single file and watch for pedestrians. Pull off the road to enjoy views.

12.6   Bridge ends. Pass hiking trail access, rest rooms, water, and interpretative information on the right.

13.1   Pass the park's Cranberry Lake entrance on the right, and businesses and access to Coronet Bay Marina on the left.

13.5   Left on **Ducken Road**, and right on **Monkey Hill Road**.

15.8   Left on **Henni Road** at a three-way intersection with stop signs.

16.8   Right on **Imperial Lane**, and almost immediately left on **Jones Road** at a T intersection. View the bay and crops growing in the lowland delta.

17.5   Right on **Dike Road** at the foot of Dugualla Bay. Mount Baker and other peaks are to the left in the distance.

18.3 Left on **Frostad Road** at a T intersection.

18.6 Bend sharply right and continue on **Taylor Road** up and over short ridges.

20.6 Stay with Taylor Road as it bends right, then immediately turns a *sharp* left toward Crescent Harbor.

24.0 Right on **Crescent Harbor Road** at a stop sign. This road is busy for a short distance.

25.7 Left on **Torpedo Road** toward the Navy seaplane base. Enjoy a wide road with wide views of Crescent Harbor, Mount Rainier, and lower Whidbey Island.

27.5 Right on **Coral Sea Avenue** at the Navy Exchange Building and right again on Pioneer Way (unmarked) at the T intersection. Avoid going downhill by zigzagging left immediately on **Wake Avenue**. Wind through Saratoga Heights Housing, turning left on **Raven Drive**, left on **Guam**, and right on **Meadow Drive** to the exit.

29.3 Left on **70th Northeast Street** to enter Oak Harbor (all services). Right on **East Pioneer Way,** renamed West Pioneer Way shortly.

30.0 Pass 70th Southwest Street, with access to City Beach Park (rest rooms, water, picnic area) on the left.

31.0 Left on **Scenic Heights Road**.

31.6 Right on **Balda Road. Note:** This is a detour if Scenic Heights Road is barricaded. If open, continue on it, skipping to Mile 32.3 below.

32.3 Left on **Miller Road** and right immediately on **Scenic Heights Road**.

37.2 Right on **Holbrook Road** (just before a barricade) and immediately left on **Highway 20. Note:** The barrier can be bypassed, but entering the highway there is more dangerous.

38.4 Left on **Madrona Way**. Enjoy scenic cycling along the tree-lined shore.

39.1 Pass the historic Captain Whidbey Inn (restaurant, lodging) in a beautiful log cabin on Penn Cove on the left.

41.5 Enter Coupeville (all services) town limits (optional end to Day One).

41.8 Pass a picnic area on the left, and turn left immediately toward Coupeville's **Front Street** where waterfront buildings date to 1874. Right on **North Main Street** to climb out of the Island County seat.

42.2 Pass the Visitor Information Center on the right. Cross Highway 20 where the road name changes briefly to **South Main Street**, then to **Engle Road**, and continue west to the Keystone Ferry, passing access to Fort Casey and overnight lodging on the way.

45.9 Pass Camp Casey, operated by Seattle Pacific University, on the right. Enjoy a view of the bay and the Olympic Mountains.

46.1 Pass access to Fort Casey State Historical Park on the right. Gun batteries, camping, water, rest rooms, and views are up a short entry hill.

46.6 Keystone Ferry dock (ticket booth on the right with rest rooms and water immediately beyond). A park is further ahead. There is a restaurant across the road on the left. Board the ferry to Port Townsend.

46.6 Port Townsend ferry dock on Water Street. Turn left for the Visitor Information Center, about 0.5 mile. Follow marked circuits (indicated by seagulls painted on the pavement) past elegant homes and historic sites, now primarily bed-and-breakfast inns. Camping and lodging are offered in Fort Worden State Park about a mile northwest of the ferry dock.

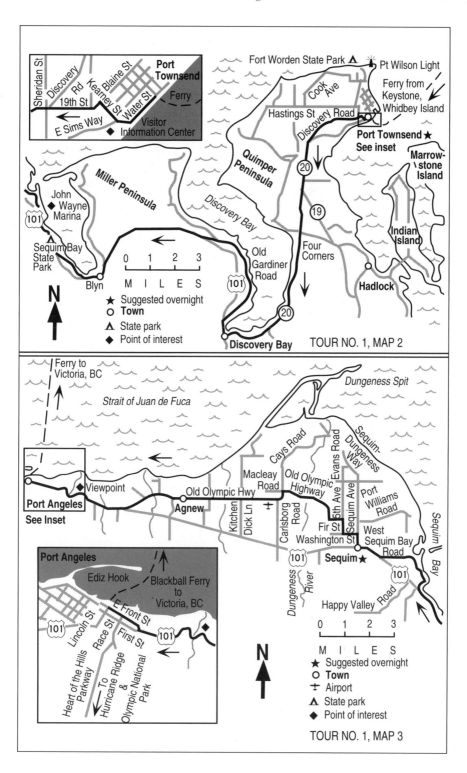

TOUR NO. 1, MAP 2

TOUR NO. 1, MAP 3

The Keystone ferry provides access to Port Townsend, a stop on the Puget Sound and Island Adventure. (Photo: Jean Henderson)

DAY TWO: PORT TOWNSEND TO SEQUIM—32.8 MILES

0.0   Port Townsend ferry dock. Left on **Water Street**, southbound, which briefly becomes Sims Way.

0.4   Right on **Kearney Street**. **Note:** The Visitor Information Center is immediately ahead on the left on Sims Way.

0.6   Left on **Blaine Street**, which becomes **Nineteenth Street** after dropping down the hill. Pass Kah Tai Lagoon Park on the left.

1.1   Cross Sheridan Street, where Nineteenth becomes **Discovery Road** and begins to probe woods of rhododendrons, ferns, fireweed, and madrona.

7.5   Right on **Highway 20** at a blinking light. Roll toward Port Angeles through trees with views of Discovery Bay below.

12.2 Pass a miniature stone village outside the abandoned Eaglemount Rockery on the left.

14.0 Right on **US Highway 101** at a T intersection at Discovery Bay (restaurants, store, other services).

15.0 Right on **Old Gardiner Road** at the end of a guardrail.

16.3 Pass Orcas Drive on the left (restaurant).

17.1 Right on the **US Highway 101** shoulder.

18.6 Right on **Old Gardiner Road**. Access the highway shoulder briefly at Mile 21.0 at a stop sign, then return to Old Gardiner Road.

22.2 Left on **US Highway 101** as Old Gardiner Road ends at the Clallam County line.

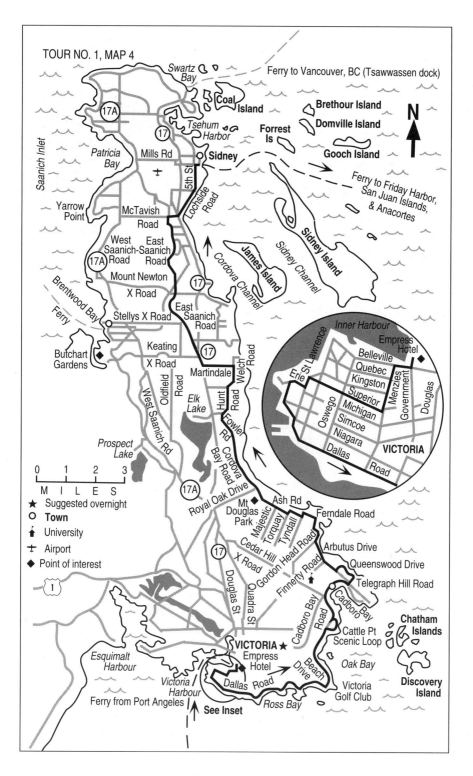

TOUR NO. 1, MAP 4

Swartz Bay

Ferry to Vancouver, BC (Tsawwassen dock)

Coal Island

Brethour Island

Domville Island

N

17A

17

Tsehum Harbor

Forrest Is

Saanich Inlet

Patricia Bay

Mills Rd

Sidney

Gooch Island

Ferry to Friday Harbor, San Juan Islands, & Anacortes

Yarrow Point

McTavish Road

5th St

Lochside Road

West Saanich-Saanich Road Road

East Road

17A

Sidney Island

Cordova Channel

James Island

Sidney Channel

Mount Newton X Road

17

Brentwood Bay

Ferry

Stellys X Road

East Saanich Road

Butchart Gardens

Keating X Road

17

Martindale

Welch Road

Inner Harbour

Empress Hotel

Oldfield Road

West Saanich Rd

Elk Lake

Hunt Road

Fowler Rd

Cordova Bay Road

Erie

St Lawrence

Belleville

Quebec

Kingston

Superior

Michigan

Oswego

Simcoe

Niagara

Dallas

Menzies

Government

Douglas

Road

VICTORIA

Prospect Lake

0   1   2   3
M I L E S

★ Suggested overnight
O **Town**
♁ University
✈ Airport
◆ Point of interest

1

17A

Royal Oak Drive

Mt Douglas Park

Ash Rd

Ferndale Road

Majestic

Torquay

Tyndall

Arbutus Drive

Queenswood Drive

Cedar Hill X Road

Gordon Head Road

Finnerty Road

Telegraph Hill Road

Douglas St

Quadra St

Cadboro Bay Road

Cadboro Bay

Chatham Islands

Esquimalt Harbour

VICTORIA ★
Empress Hotel

Cattle Pt Scenic Loop

Oak Bay

Discovery Island

Victoria Harbour

Dallas Road

Beach Drive

Victoria Golf Club

Ferry from Port Angeles

Ross Bay

See Inset

24.0   Right on the **Old Blyn Highway**.

25.3   Road angles left and name changes to **West Sequim Bay Road**. Ignore access to US Highway 101 on the left at the S'Klallam Indian Jamestown Village, operated by descendants of the original peninsula residents.

26.5   Right on **US Highway 101**. Pass a store at Mile 27.4.

27.8   Pass Sequim Bay State Park (rest rooms, water, camping, picnic sites) on both sides of the roadway.

28.4   Right on **West Sequim Bay Road**.

29.7   Right into the first parking lot of the John Wayne Marina (rest rooms, water, restaurant, picnic area ahead on the right). Exit by turning left, then right on **West Sequim Bay Road**.

32.8   Right on **US Highway 101** into Sequim (all services) where the road name changes to **Washington Street**.

DAY THREE: SEQUIM TO VICTORIA, B.C., CANADA—18.6 MILES

0.0   Intersection of Washington Street and Sequim Avenue in downtown Sequim. Right on **Sequim Avenue**, passing Sequim High School on the left.

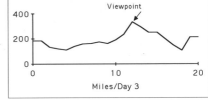

0.2   Left on **Fir Street**, and then right on **Fifth Avenue**.

1.4   Left on **Old Olympic Highway** as Fifth becomes Evans Road. Follow the highway as it bends right at Mile 1.9, passing houses and farms.

3.4   Cross the Dungeness River.

4.0   *Sharp* left with the highway as Cays Road comes in from the right. Macleay Road is straight ahead.

5.0   Pass the airport on the left.

9.0   Agnew (store).

12.0   Right on **US Highway 101** toward Port Angeles.

14.4   Right to enter a viewpoint (interpretative signs) of the Strait of Juan de Fuca and Hurricane Ridge. Exit right on US Highway 101 and sweep downhill into Port Angeles.

17.9   Stay with the roadway as it splits to become **East Front Street**. **Note:** A left turn at Race Street accesses an Olympic National Park ranger station in 1.5 miles. It offers information on a possible side trip to Hurricane Ridge.

18.6   Pass a viewpoint and turn right on **Lincoln Street** as US Highway 101 goes left. Immediately turn left on **Railroad Avenue** along the waterfront. Pass the Visitor Information Center on the right. Pier Park (rest rooms, water, viewing platform to climb, hands-on aquarium exhibit) is on the corner of Lincoln Street and Railroad Avenue. Board a ferry to Victoria, British Columbia. Two companies offer services and both carry bicycles. **Note:** Carry personal identification and do not take fruit into Canada.

18.6   Inner Harbour, Victoria, British Columbia (all services). Obtain bicycle route and visitor information from Tourism Victoria on Government Street, across from the Empress Hotel.

DAY FOUR: VICTORIA, B.C., CANADA TO FRIDAY HARBOR—30.1 MILES

0.0   Victoria, British Columbia. With the Empress Hotel before you and your back to the Inner Harbour, turn right on **Government Street**. Then immediately turn right again on **Belleville Street**, and left immediately on **Menzies Street**.

0.7   Right on **Superior Street**, left on **St. Lawrence Street**, and right on **Erie Street**.

0.9   Left on **Dallas Road** at a T intersection.

3.9   Enter a residential area.

4.3   Half-right on **Ross Street** at a stop sign. This quickly becomes **Crescent Road**, then **King George Terrace**, then overlooks the shoreline and mountains.

5.4   Stay with the shoreline as the road name changes to **Beach Drive** at a stop sign and passes through a golf course at Mile 6.2.

7.1   Pass the Oak Bay Marina on the right.

8.4   Enter the gates of the Uplands, a residential area, and turn right almost immediately on the **Cattle Point Scenic Loop**.

9.0   Right on **Beach Drive** as the loop ends at a memorial statue. In spring heather blooms here.

10.3   Enter the municipality of Saanich, where the road name changes to **Cadboro Bay Road**. Then enter the Cadboro Bay village center (services).

11.2   At the village edge, the road name changes to **Telegraph Hill Road**. Continue with it briefly, then turn left on **Lockehaven Drive**. It quickly becomes **Queenswood Drive** and heads into woods.

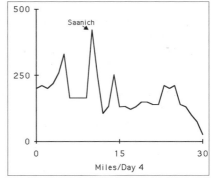

12.7   Right on **Arbutus Road** and stay right at Mile 13.1 when it meets Finnerty Road.

13.7   Right on **Gordon Head Drive** as Arbutus ends, then left on **Ferndale Road** and stay with it through a sharp right turn.

15.1   Left on **Tyndall Avenue** as Ferndale ends, then right at the next corner on **Barrie Road**, left on **Torquay Drive**, and right on **Ash Road** at the stop sign.

16.0   Right on **Cordova Bay Road** as Ash Road ends at Mount Douglas Park. Enter a woods and follow the road right and past a signal light.

18.4   Pass the Parkview Store on the right and continue into a small community (store, bike shop, bakery, other services).

19.3   Stay right past Mattick's Farm, bearing right as the road name changes to **Fowler Road**.

20.2   Right on **Hunt Road** as Fowler becomes Sayward Road and immediately ends. Hunt Road becomes **Welch Road** and continues straight ahead through horse country.

22.1   Left on **Martindale Road** as Welch Road heads toward a dead end.

23.1   Right on **Highway 17**. Exit left immediately on **East Saanich Road**.

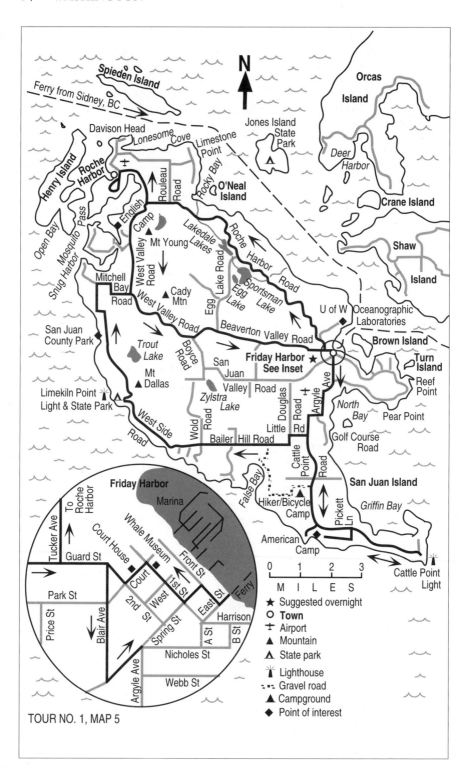

TOUR NO. 1, MAP 5

Climb a short hill and stay with East Saanich at the Mount Newton crossing.

27.1   Enter the municipality of North Saanich (limited services).

28.4   Right on **McTavish Road** (store).

28.8   Cross over Highway 17, continuing past the signal light to a stop sign. Left on **Lochside** (unmarked) to trace the shoreline into Sidney, where the road is renamed Fifth Street.

29.9   Right on **First Street** (may be unmarked) toward the Sidney–Anacortes ferry. **Note:** Sidney (all services) is straight ahead at this intersection. From town there are several access roads to the ferry.

30.1   Right to the ticket booth and ferry dock. Board the ferry to Friday Harbor on San Juan Island (a crossing of 1 hour, 40 minutes).

30.1   Disembark in Friday Harbor (all services).

DAY FIVE: FRIDAY HARBOR–ROCHE HARBOR– ENGLISH CAMP LOOP, SAN JUAN ISLAND–22.9 MILES

0.0   Friday Harbor, San Juan Island ferry dock. Right on one-way **Front Street**, and immediately left at the fountain on **Spring Street**. This street is aptly named because the fountain at its foot is built over a spring.

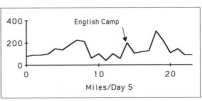

0.1   Right on **First Street**, immediately passing the Whale Museum on the right, where fascinating sights, sounds, and history of the orca whale pods in this area are offered for a small fee.

0.3   Pass two sides of the San Juan County Courthouse by turning left on **Court Street** and immediately right on **Second Street**, which is renamed **Guard Street** in the next block as it bends left.

0.5   Right on **Tucker Avenue** toward Sportsman Lake, Lakedale Lakes, Lonesome Cove, and Roche Harbor.

0.9   Stay left at an unmarked Y intersection where the road name changes to **Roche Harbor Road**. To the right approximately 1 mile is the University of Washington Laboratories, generally open only to authorized visitors or students in classes.

1.3   Continue straight ahead with Roche Harbor Road when a road sign finally appears.

4.7   Pass Egg Lake Road on the left; access to Egg Lake, Lakedale Lakes, and Sportsman Lake.

7.5   Continue straight ahead as Rouleau Road, leading to Lonesome Cove and Limestone Point, comes in on the right.

8.0   Bear right on Roche Harbor Road (toward Roche Harbor) as West Valley Road merges from the left.

9.3   Pass the Roche Harbor Airport on the right.

9.5   Right at the Roche Harbor Resort archway, and immediately left up an unmarked roadway. Right immediately on an unmarked dirt trail, noting a small, faded "mausoleum" sign high in the trees. Continue 0.25 mile.

9.7   Afterglow Vista Mausoleum, the final resting place for the John S. McMillin family. The surrounding area is private property. Please respect rights.

9.9   Exit the mausoleum, turning left and downhill on the unmarked, paved road, and immediately right on another unmarked road to pass the Roche Harbor archway on the left.

10.1   Right immediately into the **Roche Harbor Resort**. Bear left along the shore. **Caution:** pedestrians, children, cyclists.

10.4   Pass the 1880s church and the Hotel De Haro on the left. Enter a cyclists' walk zone. Now Catholic, the church was built by McMillin for Methodist services.

10.8   Bicycle parking area. To exit, keep the lime kiln remnants on your left. Make an almost 180-degree left turn at the T intersection and crank up a short, steep unmarked road with former limestone rock quarries on the right.

The vintage Hotel De Haro in historic Roche Harbor on San Juan Island (Photo: Heidi Emam)

11.3 Right at the archway on **Roche Harbor Road**.

12.8 Right on **West Valley Road**.

14.0 Right on a hard-packed dirt road, entering English Camp. Parking lot is 0.3 mile down the hill. **Note:** Watch for a trail crossing the road just before the turn into English Camp. To the left this short trail leads to Mount Young (650 feet) and an island panorama. Soldiers who served during the Pig War are buried there.

14.3 English Camp (interpretative exhibits, bicycle racks, pit toilet). To exit, backtrack to **West Valley Road** and turn right.

16.0 Pass **Mitchell Bay Road** on the right. **Alternative:** Here you have the option of combining this loop with the one touring the island's west side (see Day Six).

19.4 Bear left past Boyce Road where the road is renamed **Beaverton Valley Road**.

22.3 Left to stay with Beaverton Valley Road. It shortly passes the San Juan Island Library and is renamed **Guard Street** in Friday Harbor.

22.8 Right on **Blair Street** in Friday Harbor.

22.9 Spring Street in the Friday Harbor city center.

DAY SIX: FRIDAY HARBOR–AMERICAN CAMP–WEST SIDE LOOP, SAN JUAN ISLAND–31.3 MILES

0.0 Friday Harbor, Spring Street and Argyle Avenue. Leave town on **Argyle Avenue**.

1.3 Left to remain on Argyle Avenue at a T intersection, sticking with it when Golf Course Road comes in from the left at Mile 2.1.

2.6 Continue left as the road name changes to **Cattle Point Road** (unmarked.)

5.8 Bear left at a Y intersection where the road name changes to **American Camp Road**. **Note:** A right turn here leads directly into American Camp headquarters.

6.2 Pass the Jakle's Lagoon trailhead on the left. The island's only nature trail, this moderate to strenuous walking route leads to the lagoon, Mount Finlayson (295 feet), and Third Lagoon along the shoreline.

7.2 Stay with American Camp Road, watching for whales, seals, ships, eagles, and rabbits.

10.0 Enter the Cattle Point Interpretative Area (interpretative signs, lighthouse, pit toilets). Sea lions frequent the channel rocks. (Shark Reef on Lopez Island is visible across the channel.) The U.S. Navy Compass Station helped guide area ships in the 1920s. After exploring the area, backtrack 1.3 miles on **American Camp Road**.

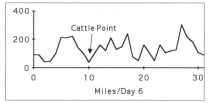

11.3 Left on unpaved **Pickett Lane**, then immediately right at the top of the hill on an unmarked, dead-end road.

12.2 Follow a path, watching for rabbits, to American Camp headquarters (rest rooms, water, interpretative displays, helpful personnel).

13.1   Right to exit the headquarters parking area on **Cattle Point Road**.

13.2   Left on **American Camp Road**, which shortly is renamed **Cattle Point Road**.

15.5   Left on **Little Road**.

16.0   Left on **Douglas Road** at a T intersection that immediately bends right to become **Bailer Hill Road**.

18.6   Pass Wold Road on the right. Continue straight ahead when Bailer Hill Road is renamed **West Side Road**.

18.6   **Alternative:** Cut 6.8 miles from the route by returning to Friday Harbor on Wold Road. Turn right at mile 18.6. It is renamed Boyce Road at Mile 20.3. Turn right at Mile 21.0 on San Juan Valley Road at a T intersection. As it enters Friday Harbor at Mile 24.5, the road becomes Spring Street.

21.8   Pass the entrance to Lime Kiln Point State Park (pit toilets). Pods of resident and migrating whales frequent this coast. A whale-watching area is a short walk away. After exploring the area, backtrack and turn left at the park exit to climb a short hill on West Side Road.

21.8   Pass San Juan County Park (limited hiker-biker campsites, sandy beach, pit toilet).

23.6   Right on **Mitchell Bay Road**. Snug Harbor marina and resort are to the left.

25.0   Right on **West Valley Road**. **Note:** If you wish to combine this loop with the loop to English Camp (see Day Five), it is 1.5 miles to the left.

28.4   Bear left to **Beaverton Valley Road** as Boyce Road comes in from the right.

31.3   Pass the San Juan Island Library as the road becomes **Guard Street** in Friday Harbor.

DAY SEVEN: LOPEZ ISLAND LOOP—31.2 MILES

0.0   Friday Harbor, San Juan Island ferry dock. Board the ferry for Lopez Island.

0.0   Lopez Island ferry landing. Head south on the only road from the dock.

0.4   Pass Odlin County Park on the right.

1.3   Left on **Port Stanley Road**.

3.8   Left on **Baker View Road** toward Spencer Spit State Park, a triangular wedge of sand that encloses a saltwater lagoon.

5.0   Spencer Spit State Park (rest rooms, picnic area, campsites). At the end of the sandy spit is a historic cabin and a popular boaters' passageway. After exploring the park, backtrack to Port Stanley Road and turn left to continue on the main route.

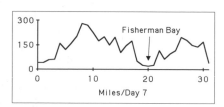

6.2   Left on **Port Stanley Road**.

8.1   Left on **Lopez Sound Road**, as Port Stanley Road goes right.

9.6   Right on **School Road**, as Lopez Sound Road turns left.

10.6   Left on **Center Road** at a T intersection.

12.1   Right on **Fisherman Bay Road**, and right on **Richardson Road**.

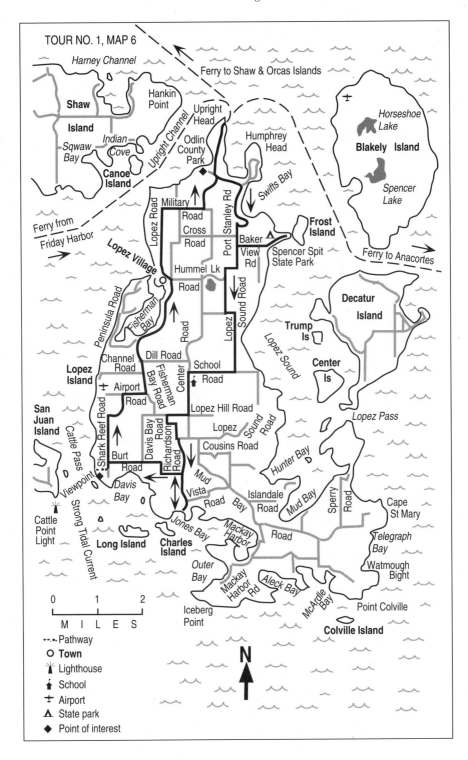

TOUR NO. 1, MAP 6

Harney Channel

Shaw

Island

Sqwaw
Bay

Indian
Cove

Canoe
Island

Hankin
Point

Upright Channel

Upright
Head

Odlin
County
Park

Ferry to Shaw & Orcas Islands

Humphrey
Head

Swifts Bay

Blakely Island

Horseshoe
Lake

Spencer
Lake

Ferry from
Friday Harbor

Lopez Road

Lopez Village

Military

Road
Cross
Road

Hummel Lk
Road

Port Stanley Rd

Baker
View
Rd

Frost
Island

Spencer Spit
State Park

Ferry to Anacortes

Peninsula Road

Fisherman Bay

Dill Road

Channel
Road

Lopez
Island

Airport
Road

San
Juan
Island

Cattle Pass

Shark Reef Road

Strong Tidal Current

Cattle
Point
Light

Viewpoint

Fisherman
Bay Road

Center
Road

School
Road

Lopez Hill Road

Road

Lopez

Sound Road

Sound Road

Lopez Sound

Trump
Is

Decatur
Island

Center
Is

Lopez Pass

Davis Bay
Road

Burt
Road

Richardson
Road

Lopez

Cousins Road

Davis
Bay

Mud
Vista

Road

Bay

Islandale
Road

Mud Bay

Hunter Bay

Sperry

Road

Cape
St Mary

Long Island

Jones Bay

Charles
Island

Mackay
Harbor

Road

Telegraph
Bay

Watmough
Bight

Outer
Bay

Iceberg
Point

Mackay
Harbor Rd

Aleck Bay

McArdle
Bay

Point Colville

Colville Island

0   1   2

M I L E S

N

- - - Pathway
O Town
Lighthouse
School
Airport
State park
Point of interest

12.1   Side Trip: Continue 2 miles to the end of Richardson Road to look out over Jones Bay and the Strait of Juan de Fuca. Once the busiest port in the islands, Richardson featured a store that burned to the ground in 1990. When you've finished exploring, backtrack on Richardson Road and rejoin the main route at Davis Bay Road.

13.1   Left on **Davis Bay Road**, following it right, then left.

16.6   Continue straight on **Burt Road**, as Davis Road turns right.

17.6   Left on **Shark Reef Road**. Continue 500 feet to a bicycle rack on the right. Walk 0.5 mile on a trail to the beach above Cattle Pass. Leisure boats ply these waters, but the name originated when cattle were unloaded here, possibly in the Hudson's Bay Company era. For an exceptional vista into the Strait of Juan de Fuca, walk south. After their lunch on neighborhood salmon, sea lions sleep on the rocks in the channel. Return to the bicycle rack and ride north on Shark Reef Road.

20.6   Right on **Airport Road**, then left on **Fisherman Bay Road** (restaurants, bike shop, lodging).

21.6   Left on **Lopez Road** into Lopez Village (store, bakery, other services).

29.0   Follow Lopez Road as it turns right, and changes name to **Military Road**.

28.9   Left on **Ferry Road** toward the ferry landing. Continue uphill, passing Odlin County Park (rest rooms) on the left.

31.2   Lopez Island ferry landing. No ticket required when sailing eastbound. Board the ferry to Anacortes and your parked car. End of tour.

Alternative: Additional day loops on Orcas Island and/or Shaw Island can also be made, either from Friday Harbor as a base, or staying on a different island each night (note that Shaw Island has very few services). On Orcas Island, experience hills and divine views, and pump up 2,409-foot Mount Constitution for a sweeping scene of islands before the distant, blue Olympic Mountains. Stop to admire shipbuilder Robert Moran's empire at Rosario, begun in 1904 when he thought he would die within six months. He built the resort surrounded by the sea, forest, and a lake, donated the land for Moran State Park, and lived another thirty-nine years. On Shaw Island, relax along a route with few commercial facilities. See *Bicycling the Backroads of Puget Sound* or *Bicycling the Pacific Coast* (The Mountaineers Books, 1989 and 1990) for routes on these islands as well as additional tours on Lopez and San Juan islands.

◆

2. NORTH CASCADES HIGHWAY

Roger Aasen

Distance: 130 miles
Terrain: hilly to mountainous; not recommended for novice cyclists
Total cumulative elevation gain: 9,355 feet
Recommended time of year: late June–early September

Recommended starting time: 9:00 A.M.
Allow: 2 days
Points of interest: Seattle City Light Tours, Diablo; Diablo Lake; Ross Lake;
Washington Pass Overlook; Shafer Museum, Winthrop

PUBLIC TRANSPORTATION

Air: none available
Train: none available

PRACTICAL INFORMATION

Key contacts: Seattle City Light Tours, 206-684-3030; Winthrop Central Reservations, 800-422-3048

STARTING POINT

Colonial Creek Campground on Highway 20, approximately 4 miles east of Diablo Dam: From I-5 take Exit 230 at Burlington, then follow Highway 20 east through Marblemount, and on to Colonial Creek Campground. Park in the day-use area or check with the ranger for the best place to leave your vehicle overnight.

For pure enjoyment of spectacular mountain scenery, this 130-mile weekend tour is hard to beat. Opened in 1972, seventy-nine years after it first was proposed, the North Cascades Highway makes for delightful bicycle touring. The joy is heightened in the autumn when big-leaf maple trees turn golden yellow and vine maples are often a brilliant red. Enjoy good shoulders and smooth pavement over most of the route. Because facilities are almost nonexistent along the route, carry everything that may be needed. Water is usually available at the Washington Pass Overlook, but there are no supplies after that until the small store at Mazama at Mile 51.7. Extra clothing layers, including rain gear, are recommended. The area is subject to sudden weather changes.

Before you head to Colonial Creek Campground, reserve space on a Seattle City Light Skagit Tour in Diablo. Reap geological, historical, and topographical background for the bicycle tour, ride the incline railway, and enjoy a picnic lunch. Tiny Diablo is the last place to buy supplies before crossing the North Cascades.

Pedal away from Colonial Creek Campground, the largest and nicest campground along the highway, feeling the tour's tone almost immediately. Climb the steep 1.5-mile hill to overlook Diablo Lake and Dam and marvel at Thunder Creek, hanging glaciers on Pyramid and Colonial peaks, and Davis Peak to the west. This magnificent panorama spreads above Diablo Lake. Its jade hue is created by suspended glacial flour in the water. Beyond this point, the route's terrain moderates somewhat, interjecting an occasional downhill, but mostly it ascends all the way to Rainy Pass.

At the Ross Lake and Dam viewpoints (located 0.2 mile apart), look west into North Cascades National Park, and east into the Pasayten Wilderness. Visible on a clear day is the sharp tip of Hozomeen Peak, reaching 8,080 feet skyward in the distance. Directly below is Ruby Arm, a portion of Ross Lake, the reservoir behind the third Seattle City Light dam on the Skagit River. The North Cascades Highway, one of the first proposed in Washington State, never

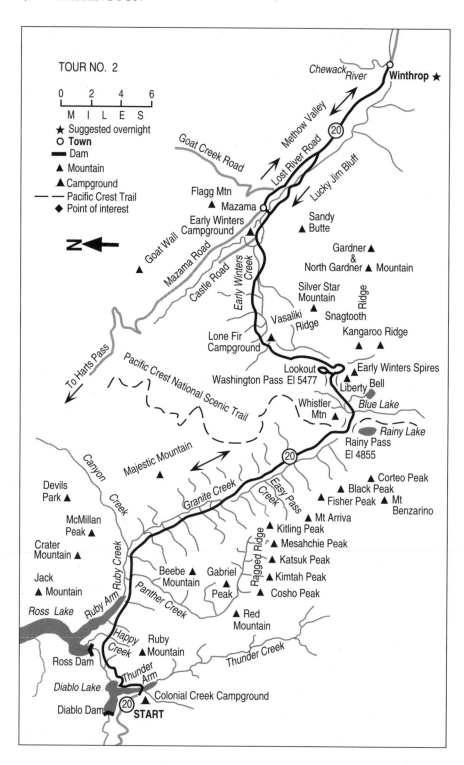

TOUR NO. 2

0   2   4   6
M I L E S

★ Suggested overnight
O Town
▬ Dam
▲ Mountain
▲ Campground
— Pacific Crest Trail
◆ Point of interest

N

Chewack River   **Winthrop ★**

Methow Valley
Lost River Road
Goat Creek Road
Lucky Jim Bluff

20

Flagg Mtn
▲ Mazama
Early Winters
Campground ▲
Goat Wall
Mazama Road
Castle Road
Early Winters Creek

Sandy
▲ Butte

Gardner ▲
&
North Gardner ▲ Mountain

Silver Star
Mountain ▲
Snagtooth Ridge

Vasaliki
Ridge
Snagtooth
Kangaroo Ridge

Lone Fir
Campground ▲
▲   ▲

To Harts Pass
Pacific Crest National Scenic Trail

Lookout
Washington Pass El 5477
Early Winters Spires ▲
▲ Liberty Bell

Whistler
Mtn ▲
Blue Lake

Rainy Lake
Rainy Pass
El 4855

20

Majestic Mountain
▲

Canyon Creek
Granite Creek
Easy Pass Creek

Corteo Peak ▲
Black Peak ▲
Fisher Peak ▲   ▲ Mt Benzarino

Devils
Park ▲

McMillan
Peak ▲

Crater
Mountain ▲

Jack
▲ Mountain

Mt Arriva ▲
Kitling Peak ▲
Mesahchie Peak ▲
Katsuk Peak ▲
Kimtah Peak ▲
Cosho Peak ▲

Beebe ▲
Mountain
Gabriel
Peak ▲
Ragged Ridge

Ross Lake
Ruby Arm   Ruby Creek
Panther Creek

Red
Mountain ▲

Ruby
▲ Mountain

Happy
Creek

Thunder Creek

Ross Dam

Diablo Lake
Thunder
Arm

Colonial Creek Campground ▲

Diablo Dam
20 **START**

enters North Cascades National Park. It straddles a narrow corridor through the Ross Lake National Recreation Area and enters the Okanogan National Forest. Many peaks visible to the south and west are in the national park's southern segment.

On the final approach to Rainy Pass, prepare for tougher pedaling. The Pacific Crest hiking trail, which stretches from Canada into Mexico, crosses the highway at the Cascade Crest summit (4,860 feet). The road then descends steeply for about 1.5 miles. The next 3.5 miles is another challenging climb up and over Washington Pass. At 4,477 feet, Washington Pass comes within 99 feet of the top of Sherman Pass, the state's highest highway crossing. Divert attention from burning thighs by spotting mountain goats on the nearby mountainsides.

At Washington Pass you can take a side road north to the overlook and rest area. A short trail leads to a viewpoint on a high bluff overlooking the highway. To the south, the view is dominated by the massif of Liberty Bell Mountain (7,720 feet), with the Early Winters Spires (7,807 feet) beyond. Far below, the highway serpentines toward Mazama in a 7-mile run dropping away from Washington Pass. After the drop the route moderates, but continues mostly downhill to the turnoff for Mazama. In Mazama are a small cafe and inn. Campgrounds along the route offer alternatives to the recommended overnight in Winthrop.

From Mazama, enjoy terrain that levels out and widens to dramatically reveal the typical eastern Washington topography of dry rolling hills and ranch lands. When the pseudo-Western town of Winthrop is finally reached, cross the Chewack River and turn to roll down the abbreviated main street past mock-frontier storefronts and rough plank boardwalks. Surroundings hint at a long history, but Winthrop is relatively young. It was founded by a Harvard-educated teetotaler in 1891. In the heart of town, modern shops, including restaurants, stores, motels, a bakery, and a sporting goods store, buzz behind frontier exteriors.

Explore the Shafer Museum, immediately east of the main street. The 1897 log cabin in which it is located was the original home of the town's founder, Guy Waring. Tour the national fish hatchery, 1 mile south of town, or learn about fire-fighting techniques and aircraft at the smokejumpers' base, about 5 miles further east near Twisp. If time allows, prowl the assortment of mountain-bike trails in the Sun Mountain and Rendezvous areas.

On Day Two, retrace the route on the North Cascades Highway back to your vehicle. While the roadbed may be the same, the tour in reverse takes on an entirely different personality. On the 7-mile grind up to Washington Pass, admire the deeply fissured Liberty Bell Mountain and contemplate how this area's hard rock sabotaged multiple attempts to extract gold ore from the North Cascades. After Rainy Pass, roll almost effortlessly back to Colonial Creek Campground. The Diablo Lake Overlook hill, so tough to pedal when muscles were warming up yesterday, now evokes a smile. It is icing on the weekend and a deserved, great payoff for all the climbing that preceded it.

MILEAGE LOG

DAY ONE: COLONIAL CREEK CAMPGROUND TO WINTHROP—65.1 MILES

0.0   Colonial Creek Campground on Highway 20 east of Diablo Dam. Turn right (east) on **Highway 20** out of the campground. Proceed toward the bridge over the Thunder Arm section of Diablo Lake and head uphill. This is probably the steepest climb of the day.

1.7   Pass Diablo Lake Overlook on the left. A panorama of mountains is complemented by the jade of the lake.

4.7   Pass Happy Creek forest walk (pit toilet on the right).

5.2   Pass Ross Lake and Dam Overlook on the left.

8.6   Cross Panther Creek bridge.

15.7   Enter Skagit County.

18.4   Cross Granite Creek.

21.8   Pass Easy Pass trailhead on the right.

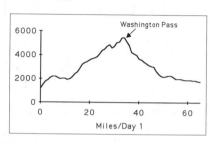

24.2   Pass a viewpoint on the right. Several large peaks are generally visible to the west. These include Mount Arriva (8,215 feet), Black Peak (8,970 feet), Mount Benzarino (7,765 feet), and Fisher Peak (8,040 feet).

27.9   Rainy Pass Summit (4,855 feet), with picnic facilities and hiking trail access. Cross the Pacific Crest Trail. Start down a 5.5 percent grade.

29.2   Bottom of the hill. Begin to climb up to Washington Pass.

32.8   Washington Pass summit (5,477 feet). Turn left on **Overlook Road** for a scenic, 1-mile round trip to the rest area (rest rooms, water, scenic overlook, short hiking trails).

33.8   Left on **Highway 20** from Overlook Road toward Winthrop. Start down a 7.5 percent grade for 7 miles.

40.0   Pass the Lone Fir Campground on the right.

49.3   Pass Early Winters Campground. Pass the Forest Service Information Center on the left.

51.2   Left toward Mazama.

51.2 Alternative: For a shorter (by 0.7 mile) and less hilly route into Winthrop, continue straight ahead on Highway 20. This rejoins the main route when it merges with Lost River Road at Mile 57.0.

51.7   Cross the bridge and turn right on **Lost River Road** (may be unmarked) in Mazama (lodging, restaurant, store on the left where the road heads into the wilderness and up to Hart's Pass). The Hart's Pass road was built for the 1890s mining boom when hundreds of prospectors flooded the area.

57.0   Pass a junction with Highway 20 on the right. Lost River Road merges with Highway 20 and continues down the narrow valley toward Winthrop.

65.1   Winthrop (restaurants, shops, stores, overnight accommodations). Cross the Chewack River and immediately turn right on **Riverside Drive** (unmarked). This is Winthrop's main street and the continuation of Highway 20 toward Twisp. **Note:** To visit the Shafer Museum, continue straight ahead and uphill for one block on Bridge Street. Turn right on Castle Street and proceed to the museum.

Good shoulders, smooth pavement, and superb scenery characterize the North Cascades Highway. (Photo: Jean Henderson)

DAY TWO: WINTHROP TO COLONIAL CREEK CAMPGROUND—64.4 MILES

0.0   Winthrop, intersection of Riverside Drive and Bridge Street.
Head west on **Highway 20**,
crossing the Chewack River.
Retrace the Day One route.

8.1   Bear left, staying with Highway
20 at a junction with Lost River
Road, then backtrack on the Day
One route over the passes.

64.4   Left into Colonial Creek Campground. End of tour.

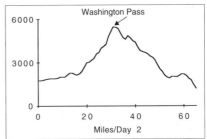

3. LEAVENWORTH LOOPS

Jean Henderson

Distance: 82 miles
Terrain: flat to rolling with a few short hills
Total cumulative elevation gain: 3,337 feet
Recommended time of year: April–October
Recommended starting time: 9:00–10:00 A.M.
Allow: 2 days
Points of interest: Leavenworth Bavarian Village; Aplets and Cotlets Factory, Cashmere; Cashmere Pioneer Village Museum; Chumstick Valley; Lake Wenatchee

PUBLIC TRANSPORTATION
Air: commercial airlines serve Wenatchee, about 20 miles from Cashmere, but the bicycle may have to be shipped
Train: Wenatchee is served by Amtrak, but no baggage is loaded or unloaded there; ship the bicycle and pick up the described route in Cashmere

PRACTICAL INFORMATION
Key contacts: Leavenworth Chamber of Commerce, 509-548-5807; Cashmere City Hall, 509-782-3513; Cougar Inn at Lake Wenatchee, 509-763-3354; Lake Wenatchee State Park, 509-763-3101

STARTING POINT
Leavenworth city center adjacent to Highway 2: Make overnight parking arrangements at a motel or campground.

Escape from city life to a Bavarian-style village and an exquisite mountain lake. Erin and Bill Woods of Redmond, Washington designed this route to visit an old-time-America community, sample unusual candies, and enjoy a wide variety of cycling in orchards, through woods, and along rivers. With just enough climbing to keep the riding interesting, this 82-mile weekend tour will become a favorite.

Begin in the ersatz Bavarian village of Leavenworth on Highway 2. In the heart of the Cascade Mountains, charming Leavenworth is growing like the evergreens that surround it. For accommodations, consider one of the many facilities with a hot spa. One adds breakfast in a spacious second-story dining room while a properly costumed Bavarian balances on the narrow railing to sound notes on a gigantic Alpenhorn.

To energize the sagging local economy, Leavenworth became Bavarian in the 1960s. Originally a Great Northern Railway village, it had a second life as a sawmill town. The dam on the Wenatchee River was constructed during that period to form a booming ground for logging activities. Now the town perks with several annual festivals that keep tourist dollars rolling in like logs down the deep canyon walls. Stroll the streets and probe the Icicle Creek area to enjoy a

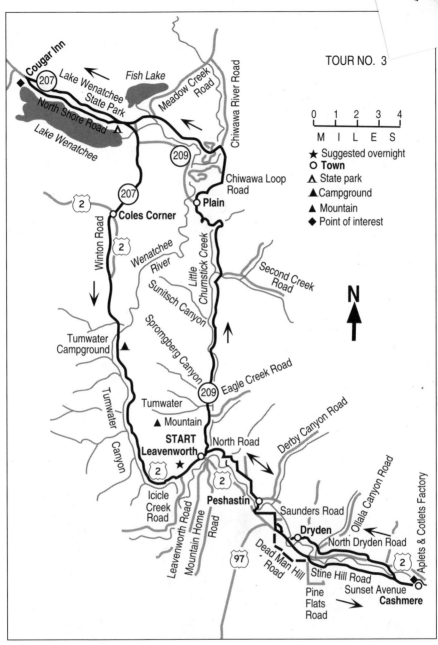

Cougar Inn

207

Lake Wenatchee
State Park

Fish Lake

Meadow Creek Road

Chiwawa River Road

North Shore Road

Lake Wenatchee

TOUR NO. 3

0 1 2 3 4
M I L E S

★ Suggested overnight
O **Town**
▲ State park
▲Campground
▲ Mountain
◆ Point of interest

209

2

207

Coles Corner

Chiwawa Loop
Road

Plain

Winton Road

2

Wenatchee
River

Little Chumstick Creek

Sunitsch Canyon

Second Creek
Road

N

Tumwater
Campground

▲

Spromgberg Canyon

Eagle Creek Road

209

Tumwater
Canyon

Tumwater
▲ Mountain

Derby Canyon Road

START
Leavenworth
★

North Road

Ollala Canyon Road

2

Aplets & Cotlets Factory

Icicle
Creek
Road

Leavenworth Road

Mountain Home Road

Peshastin

Saunders Road

Dryden

North Dryden Road

97

Dead Man Hill Road

Stine Hill Road

Sunset Avenue

2

Cashmere

Pine
Flats
Road

fish hatchery, hiking trails, and a goodie from the bakery's wood-fired ovens. Add a night in the area to fully explore the sparkling shores of Lake Wenatchee.

From Leavenworth, quickly dart into orchards surrounding tiny Peshastin on the Wenatchee River. Ride Highway 2 briefly, passing through teensy Dryden with its towering stacks of fruit crates. Continue into Cashmere, seeking the backroads and views away from buzzing traffic. Tree-lined Cashmere streets hark back to old-time America's manicured lawns spread before houses with broad porches. Founded in 1892 as a Catholic site for educating Native Americans, Cashmere's name honors the beautiful Vale of Kashmir in northwestern India. Look for Mount Cashmere, rising 8,500 feet, west of town. Pass huge apple sheds and along quiet streets, then wander into the Aplets and Cotlets factory to sample old-fashioned hospitality and delicious, fruit-based candies. Tours are available. Before returning to Leavenworth over a different route, visit the local museum, a pioneer village near Highway 2. On the water, sight the flotillas of rafts filled with eager tourists seeking a thrill on the Wenatchee River.

On Day Two, pedal west from Leavenworth to Lake Wenatchee. The longer of the two loops, it probes the Chumstick Valley and forests around Lake Wenatchee, pausing briefly in Plain, where a few businesses cling to life. Early settlers had their eyes on the area's huge red cedar groves. They intended to cut them down and ship them out when the Great Northern Railway came. It never did, so enjoy the shade of these big trees. Near the lake's western tip, revel in the spectacular setting at the Cougar Inn.

Complete the forested loop, then desert the backroads to roll along the Wenatchee River as it swirls and falls beside Highway 2 in the scenic Tumwater Canyon. Pedal with overhead glances to catch sight of agile rock climbers that frequent the canyon walls just north of the roadway. As Leavenworth again comes into view, the stresses of everyday life seem very far away.

Orchards and evergreens surround Leavenworth, a central Washington theme town. (Photo: Jean Henderson)

MILEAGE LOG
DAY ONE: LEAVENWORTH–CASHMERE LOOP–29.5 MILES

0.0 Leavenworth city center. Pedal east on **Front Street**, following it as it bends left toward Highway 2.

0.4 Cross Highway 2 as Front Street ends, continuing on **Highway 209**.

0.9 Bear right on **North Road**.

5.0 Pass through the Peshastin business district and turn right under the railroad trestle on **Main Street**, as Derby Canyon Bypass continues on.

5.3 Left on the left shoulder of **Highway 2**, and left immediately on **Saunders Road**.

7.3 Left on **Highway 2**, this time moving to the right shoulder.

    7.3 Alternative: Avoid 1.3 miles of highway riding by crossing over to Dead Man Hill Road. Rejoin the main route at Mile 9.4.

8.6 Bear right on a side road exit, then left on a frontage road where Johnson Road continues uphill.

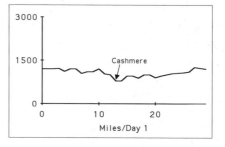

9.2 The road bends right to become **Stine Hill Road**.

12.1 The road is renamed **Sunset Avenue** as it enters Cashmere.

13.4 Left on **Division Street** in Cashmere as Sunset Avenue ends. The Aplets and Cotlets factory is on the right immediately across the railroad track on Mission Street. Town center is one block further on. Tour the old-fashioned neighborhoods with pleasant, wide streets. The museum is a mile to the right on Cottage Avenue (the main street) near the railroad track and Highway 2.

14.0 Backtrack on **Division Street** to **Sunset Avenue** and turn right.

14.9 Right on **Goodwin Road**.

15.2 Cross the Wenatchee River, circle left under the bridge with the traffic pattern, and turn left on the **Highway 2** shoulder.

16.6 Right on **North Dryden Road**.

20.2 Cross the railroad tracks and turn left on **Main Street** in Dryden.

20.4 Right on **Alice Avenue**, then right again on the **Highway 2** shoulder.

21.1 Bear right at the exit and turn left on **Motel Road**. Continue straight ahead when road name changes to **Saunders Road**.

22.8 Right on **Highway 2**.

23.1 Go under the railroad trestle and turn right with **Main Street**. Cross the Wenatchee River into Peshastin. The road is renamed **North Road** as it leaves town.

27.5 Left on **Highway 209** as North Road ends.

28.0 Cross Highway 2 and continue into Leavenworth on **Front Street**.

29.5 Leavenworth city center.

DAY TWO: LEAVENWORTH–LAKE WENATCHEE LOOP–68.2 MILES

0.0 Leavenworth city center. Proceed on **Front Street**, bearing left with it as it meets Highway 2.

0.4   Cross over Highway 2 as Front Street ends, and continue on **Route 209** past the Leavenworth High School.

13.4   The settlement of Plain (limited services).

14.4   Continue straight on **Chiwawa Loop Road** toward Chiwawa River Road as Highway 209 swings left.

22.8   Bear right at a Y intersection toward Highway 207 North.

23.2   Right on **Highway 207**.

28.2   Pass **North Shore Drive** and turn left into the Cougar Inn driveway. After enjoying the view and the inn, backtrack on **Highway 207**, turning right almost immediately on **North Shore Drive**.

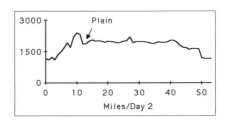

32.9   Right on **Highway 207** as North Shore Drive ends.

34.1   Pass the Lake Wenatchee Village (limited services) on the left.

34.7   Pass the entrance to Lake Wenatchee State Park.
Side Trip: There is a 2-mile loop through the park.

37.9   Cross Highway 2 (restaurants, limited services) at Coles Corner. Although unmarked, the route is now **Winton Road**.

40.3   Right on **Highway 2** as Winton Road ends.

48.7   Begin pedaling adjacent to an expansive view of the Wenatchee River tumbling through Tumwater Canyon. Spot rock climbers and survey ravages of recent forest fires on the canyon walls above.

52.7   Leavenworth city center. End of tour.

---

4. WENATCHEE APPLE LOOP

Jean Henderson

Distance: 98 miles
Terrain: flat with a few steep climbs
Total cumulative elevation gain: 2,816 feet
Recommended time of year: April–October
Recommended starting time: 9:00 A.M.
Allow: 2 days
Points of interest: North Central Washington Museum, Wenatchee; Columbia River; Lake Chelan; Earthquake Point; Rocky Reach Dam

◆ ◆ ◆

PUBLIC TRANSPORTATION

Air: commercial airlines serve Wenatchee; verify that a bicycle can go as baggage
Train: Amtrak serves Wenatchee, but bicycles are not loaded or unloaded there

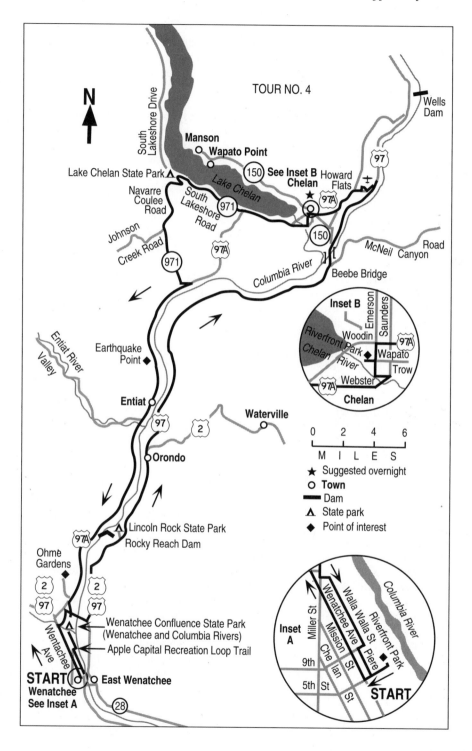

TOUR NO. 4

N

South Lakeshore Drive

Wells Dam

Manson
Wapato Point

Lake Chelan State Park

97

See Inset B   Howard
Chelan   Flats

150

Lake Chelan

Navarre
Coulee
Road

South
Lakeshore
Road

971

97A

150

Johnson
Creek Road

971

97A

Columbia River

McNeil Canyon Road

Beebe Bridge

Inset B

Emerson
Saunders

Riverfront Park
Chelan

Woodin

97A

Wapato

River

Trow

Webster

97A

Chelan

Entiat River Valley

Earthquake
Point

Entiat

97

2

Waterville

Orondo

0   2   4   6

M I L E S

★ Suggested overnight
○ **Town**
▬ Dam
▲ State park
◆ Point of interest

97A

Lincoln Rock State Park
Rocky Reach Dam

Ohme
Gardens

2

97

2

97

Wenatchee Confluence State Park
(Wenatchee and Columbia Rivers)
Apple Capital Recreation Loop Trail

Wenatchee Ave

START   ○ ○ **East Wenatchee**
Wenatchee
See Inset A

28

Inset
A

Miller St

Walla Walla St

Wenatchee Ave

Riverfront Park

Columbia River

Mission St

Chelan St

Piere

9th

5th St

St

START

PRACTICAL INFORMATION

Key contacts: Wenatchee Visitors Bureau, 800-57-APPLE; North Central Washington Museum, Wenatchee, 509-664-3340; Chelan Visitors Bureau, 800-4-CHELAN; Lake Chelan State Park, 509-687-3710

STARTING POINT

Wenatchee, Riverfront Park on Fifth Street and the Columbia River: From Highway 2, exit on Wenatchee Avenue, then turn left in about 2 miles to the foot of Fifth Street. Overnight parking is available nearby in either the Convention Center Complex at the foot of First Street or in a pay lot at Palouse and Mission streets.

For a mere 98 miles total, this tour packs a real wallop. A perfect weekend getaway, the loop offers central Washington sunshine, apple orchards, and glistening Lake Chelan with its opportunities to cruise into remote Stehekin. In addition, this tour's proximity to Cashmere on the west (see tour 3, Leavenworth Loops) and Grand Coulee or Potholes on the east (tour 5, Grand Coulee and Potholes Sunshine Loops) makes it easy to link with some of the other Central Washington explorations in this book. Simply connect by bicycle or car.

Begin in Wenatchee, the central Washington hub where orchards grace the hillsides above the Columbia River. Rooted in a Native American description, Wenatchee means "robe of the rainbow." A short distance downstream, the area's first bridge carries bicycle/pedestrian traffic across the Columbia. It was built in 1908 for the irrigation pipeline from the main canal to orchards on the east plateau. Apples are the primary crop. Washington produces more than half of the nation's fresh apples, about 10 billion annually.

From Wenatchee, trace the mighty Columbia River 43 miles upstream, then twist and turn through orchards into Chelan. The "Recreational Hang-Gliding Capital of the World," Chelan has natural beauty and hot summer thermals for soaring high above the wheat fields and the Columbia River. At Sky Park on 3,800-foot Chelan Butte is the jumping-off point for glider pilots. Below, on the shores of Lake Chelan, the town fans out from the landmark Campbell's Lodge, established in 1901. Stunning snow-topped peaks reach up 7,000 feet behind 55-mile-long Lake Chelan, which is 1,500 feet deep, up to 2 miles wide in places, and fed by twenty-seven glaciers and fifty-nine streams.

Amid such extraordinary scenery, campsites and lodging require advance reservations. Consider booking more than one night to fully explore Chelan and environs. Parasailing, swimming, apple shed and museum tours, and horseback riding await. Remote Stehekin and North Cascades National Park, 55 miles uplake, also beckon. Forget television and phones. Stehekin has changed little in the last century. Only the single pay phone, installed by the National Park Service in 1993, is available. Ferry service, launched in 1888, departs Chelan daily.

On Day Two, hug the Lake Chelan shore for a while longer before climbing into the glacier-gouged Navarre Coulee where bucolic and pine scents mix. Near the end of the 9-mile road, these give way to more orchards. Exit near Ribbon Cliff, where a violent 1872 earthquake split the mountain, sending a massive rock slide to dam the Columbia River for several hours. Tag along with the Columbia through more fruit-producing communities. Stop at the Rocky Reach Dam to watch migrating salmon negotiate an exceptionally long ladder, or linger at the outdoor picnic tables.

At Entiat, look for hints of the alpine Ohme Gardens decorating rocky cliffs above the route, then begin the final trek into Wenatchee. Meander parks, trails, and back streets of the area. Then pass through mountains of apple crates that signal the conclusion of a marvelous central Washington tour and the beginning of pleasant, warm memories.

MILEAGE LOG
DAY ONE: WENATCHEE TO CHELAN—53.2 MILES

0.0   Wenatchee, Riverfront Park, foot of Fifth Street on the Columbia River. Exit the park on **Fifth Street**, riding under the overpass.

0.7   Right on **Wenatchee Avenue**/Truck Route.

3.4   Exit on **Easy Street**, then veer right to **Highway 2/97**. Ignore the turn-off toward Entiat on Highway 97A (Alternate). This will be the return route.

4.4   Cross the Columbia River.

5.4   Left on **Highway 2/Highway 97N** at a T intersection, heading toward Spokane.

10.0   Pass the turnoff for Rocky Reach Dam and Lincoln Rock State Park (camping, picnicking, swimming, rest rooms, water) on the left.

16.5   Enter Orondo, a settlement dedicated to orchards and fruit shipping. It bears the name of the chief of the legendary people who operated copper mines in the Lake Superior region. Purportedly, the mythical miners had escaped the sinking of the lost continent of Atlantis.

17.3   Continue straight ahead on **Highway 97** as Highway 2 goes right toward Spokane.

19.7   Pass the Orondo River Park on the left (rest rooms, water).

23.0   Pass the Daroga State Park Group Camp on the left.

23.6   Pass Daroga State Park on the left (water, rest rooms, camping).

38.5   Pass Beebe Bridge Park on the left (water, rest rooms).

38.7   Cross the Beebe Bridge over the Columbia River and bear right to continue northbound on the Highway 97 shoulder.

44.0   Left on **Highway 97A** toward Chelan.

45.4   Right on **Howard Flats Road** toward the Chelan Airport. Wander through the orchards and among stacked crates.

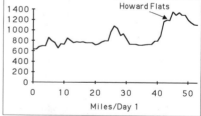

47.3   Left on **Howard Flats Northeast** at a T intersection.

47.8   Left again on **Howard Flats Road** at a T intersection.

49.4   Right on **Highway 97A** toward Chelan at a T intersection.

52.4   Enter Chelan (all services) where the highway becomes **Woodin Avenue**. Campbell's Lodge is at the end of the street near the lake. A half block from it is St. Andrew's Episcopal Church, possibly Washington's oldest log church in continuous use. Its first service was held on Christmas eve, 1898.

53.1   Left on **Emerson Street**.

53.2   Right into Chelan Riverfront Park (water, rest rooms).

DAY TWO: CHELAN TO WENATCHEE—45.2 MILES

0.0   Chelan, Riverfront Park. Ride south out of the park on **Emerson Street**, which shortly is renamed **Trow Street**.

0.2   Right on **Webster Street**/Highway 97A (unmarked) at a stop sign. Cross the Chelan River.

3.7   Bear left at a Y intersection with Woodin Avenue. Continue on **Highway 97A**, passing through the Lakeside area of Chelan. Until 1956, Lakeside was a separate community. In 1927 a section of it was flooded when a dam raised the lake level 21 feet. Lakeside Park is at the foot of Millard Street, which takes off toward Sky Park, turning to dirt on the way.

5.0   Road is renamed **South Lakeshore Road**. Continue along Lake Chelan on Highway 971 when Route 97A goes left into Knapp Coulee.

9.5   Pass an entrance to Lake Chelan State Park (water, rest rooms, camping, limited commercial services) on the right.

9.6   Left on **Navarre Coulee Road**/Highway 971 North toward Wenatchee. A short climb leads through pine-scented forests and farms, finally dropping into the orchards.

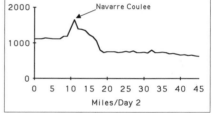

18.6   Right on **Highway 97A South** as Highway 971 ends at a T intersection.

23.4   Pass Earthquake Point. A historical marker on the right indicates that Ribbon Cliff, with its lava-filled fissures, is above. Split in 1872 when a violent earthquake hit the area, the mountain issued a slide that stopped the Columbia River's flow for several hours.

25.1   Enter Entiat (rest rooms, water, fruit sheds, cafes).

37.9   Pass the entrance to Rocky Reach Dam (water, rest rooms, picnic area) on the left. Visitors can enjoy self-guided tours, educational exhibits, and fish viewing.

41.1   Pass Ohme Garden Road on the right. Hints of the garden's alpine beauty dangle over the cliff above. Covering nine acres on what was once a dry, desolate hill, it has sweeping views and tours (fee).

41.4   Bear left toward East Wenatchee, passing under Highway 2 and an overhead sign.

41.9   Pass the Washington Apple Commission's Visitor Center (rest rooms, water, information) on the right.

42.1   Bear left on **Euclid Avenue** at a Y intersection with Penny Avenue. Cross the railroad tracks, following signs to the Wenatchee Confluence State Park.

42.6   Left into Wenatchee Confluence State Park (rest rooms, water, camping), and immediately turn right on the **Apple Capital Recreation Loop Trail**. At the end of the bridge across the Wenatchee River is an information kiosk. The nature trail described on the kiosk is not open to bicycles.

43.5 Exit the park, turning left on **North Miller Street** at a T intersection (unmarked). Follow it to the right, ignoring an opportunity to re-enter the park when it appears on the left.

43.9 Left on **Walla Walla Street**. Apple crates are stacked high.

44.2 Pass the entrance to Walla Walla Point City Park (water, rest rooms) on the left.

44.6 Right on **Ninth Street**, immediately left on **Piere Street**, and left on **Fifth Street** at a T intersection.

45.2 Enter Wenatchee Riverfront Park. End of tour.

Side Trip: To visit the 1908 footbridge, continue south a short distance along the Columbia River on the city's designated bicycle route. Backtrack to Riverfront Park from Bridge Street.

5. GRAND COULEE AND POTHOLES SUNSHINE LOOPS

Jean Henderson

Distance: 184–236 miles
Terrain: flat to moderate, with occasional rolling hills
Total cumulative elevation gain: 7,990 feet
Recommended time of year: April–October
Recommended starting time: 8:00 A.M.
Allow: 3–4 days
Points of interest: Sun Lakes State Park; Grand Coulee Dam; Dry Falls Park and Interpretative Center; Lenore Caves; Summer Falls State Park; Drumheller Channels; Potholes Reservoir and State Park; Columbia National Wildlife Refuge

◆ ◆ ◆

PUBLIC TRANSPORTATION
Air: none available
Train: none available

PRACTICAL INFORMATION
Key contacts: Sun Lakes State Park, 509-632-5291; Grand Coulee Dam Area Chamber of Commerce, 509-633-3074; Grant County Visitor and Information Center (Washington only), 800-992-6234; Grant County Visitor and Information Center, 509-765-7888

STARTING POINT
Sun Lakes State Park on Highway 17 in central Washington: The park is 3 miles south of Highway 2 near Coulee City. Park near your cabin or tent in the state park.

Discover mind-boggling geology in central Washington's Columbia Basin. Where geologic forces greater than any other ever documented once ravaged the land, Grand Coulee Dam, one of the world's largest concrete structures, now sits. Approximately ninety different times during the last Ice Age, a natural dam in what is now northern Montana gave way to pressure from a 2,000-foot-deep lake. It sent water equal to ten times all the earth's rivers thundering across the Northwest. Traveling in excess of 65 miles per hour, water torrents ripped up to 200 feet of topsoil from 50 cubic miles of earth. Then the exposed layers of tilted, solidified lava were ravaged by more floods and scoured by glaciers.

The three loops in this tour envelop 184 miles of amazing geology, warm sunshine, and cheerful bird serenades that prompt adding to the basic 3- or 4-day itinerary. Unlike most of the book's tours, this is a series of loops linked by a 52-mile connector. The connector can be cycled, but driving is recommended, to take full advantage of the most interesting parts of the tour. Cycle under a big sky, protected from the wind and sun by towering 700-foot-high coulee walls. Traffic is generally light, allowing the melodies of red-winged and yellow black-birds, meadowlarks, and robins to fly on the wind. Swallows dart overhead, marbled marmots scurry in the rocks, beavers surface in the pools, and cotton-tails hop through the grass.

On Day One visit Grand Coulee Dam, but prepare for the long cycling day by leaving extra gear behind. Get an early start from Sun Lakes State Park for the ride through the sagebrush and wheat fields. Jumbo towers marching like erect soldiers to carry electricity to hundreds of cities and towns in several states guide the way. Follow them north and down into the 50-mile-long coulee where 550-foot-high Grand Coulee Dam sits with blue, elongated Roosevelt Lake before it. From above, the gigantic dam seems dwarfed until autos on top appear as toys. Besides mile-wide concrete, the dam supports to some extent the economies of several area cities with similar names, including Coulee City, Grand Coulee, Electric City, and Coulee Dam. Drop swiftly into the community of Grand Coulee, the oldest in Grant County, and continue toward the $1.6 million circular Visitor Arrival Center.

The Eighth Wonder of the World, Grand Coulee Dam is an engineering feat begun in 1933 during the Great Depression. It had been a dream since the turn of the century. Take the self-guided tour, then return to Sun Lakes State Park within the gaping jaws of the protective coulee, along the 27-mile shoreline of Banks Lake. Water pumped 283 feet up from Roosevelt Lake fills Banks Lake, a primary partner in the Columbia Basin Federal Reclamation Project that converts about a half million acres of scrubland into arable farmland.

Turn west at Coulee City and roll into the Dry Falls Interpretative Center to solve the amazing detective story of the Columbia Basin's geologic history. It unreels on a brief videotape. Exhibits include a baby rhinoceros re-created from the actual mold found with its bones near here. Scientists conjecture the animal lay dead in a small pond slowly filling with molten lava. Gaze at the 400-foot cliffs of Dry Falls. The last Ice Age's repeated flooding, sending onslaughts of water racing across the vast desert in 48 hours, gnawed the 3.5-mile face of the falls. This also forced the Dry Falls cliffs to retreat about 20 miles from their original location near present-day Soap Lake. Finish the day's ride at Sun Lakes State Park.

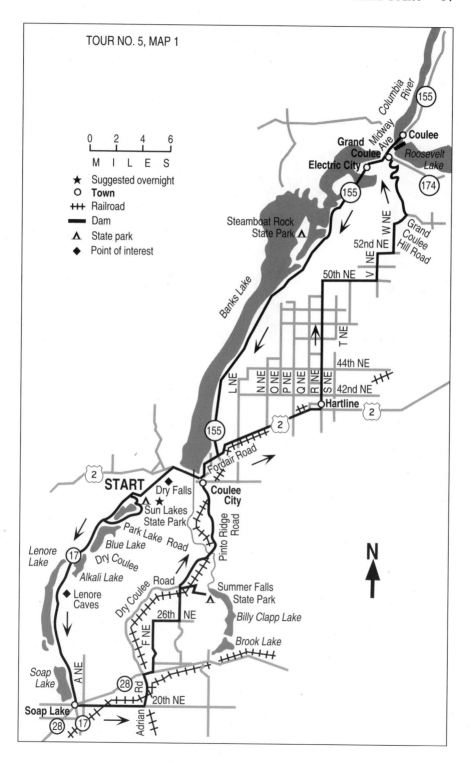

TOUR NO. 5, MAP 1

0   2   4   6
M I L E S

★ Suggested overnight
○ **Town**
+++ Railroad
—— Dam
▲ State park
◆ Point of interest

Columbia River

○ **Coulee** 155

Midway Ave

Grand Coulee

Roosevelt Lake

Electric City ○

174

155

W NE

V NE

Grand Coulee Hill Road

Steamboat Rock State Park ▲

52nd NE

50th NE

Banks Lake

T NE

44th NE

L NE   N NE   O NE   P NE   Q NE   R NE   S NE   42nd NE

○ **Hartline**   2

2   2

155

Fordair Road

2

START

◆ Dry Falls
Sun Lakes State Park ▲ ★

Coulee City ○

Park Lake Road

Pinto Ridge Road

Lenore Lake

17

Blue Lake

Dry Coulee

Alkali Lake

Dry Coulee Road

◆ Lenore Caves

Summer Falls State Park ▲

Billy Clapp Lake

26th   NE

F NE

Brook Lake

Soap Lake

A NE

28

Rd

20th NE

Soap Lake ○

28   17

Adrian

N

The route along Banks Lake is protected from wind and sun by towering coulee walls. (Photo: Jean Henderson)

Saddle up on Day Two for a shorter cycling loop. Skim the shores of Park and Blue lakes, then head to bubbling Soap Lake. Try a healing soak in the sixteen natural chemicals that made this a world-famous spa in the 1930s and 1940s. Still soothing and beneficial, the lake has lost only its allure. Along the way take a side trip to peek into Lenore Caves, where prehistoric hunters found shelter. Carry food for a pleasant picnic in Summer Falls State Park, where Billy Clapp Lake is a tribute to a turn-of-the-century dreamer who envisioned Grand Coulee Dam. The 165-foot falls are meek when canal water from Banks Lake and Dry Falls Dam is diverted for irrigation. The day's loop brings you back for a second night in Sun Lakes State Park.

On Day Three, link to the Potholes Reservoir area by car or by bicycle to explore a Swiss-cheese landscape with irrigation waters seeping through. Elevating the water table with the Columbia Basin Federal Reclamation Project had an odd effect on the ancient lava beds and sand. Located near the heart of the project, Potholes Reservoir collects and distributes water for thirsty farms and ranches farther south. Irrigated circles of grain, orchards, and enormous sheds of potatoes along the route testify to the results. Depending on whether you ride or drive this connector route, either stay the night at Potholes State Park and cycle the final loop on Day Four, or combine Days Three and Four in one day.

On Day Four, from Potholes State Park continue past commercial resorts, neatly furrowed rows, and orchards thick with blossoms or fruit. Witness another chapter of nature's central Washington drama in the unique channeled scablands below the Drumheller Viewpoint.

Picnic in the Columbia National Wildlife Refuge, a mixture of federal, state, and private lands. Birds, local history, and natural beauty blend for a pleasant retreat at McManamon Lake. Cheer on fishers of all types and ages, including the terns that seem to fall from the sky, then leave them to their lunch and pedal back into the Potholes Reservoir. As the scenery passes, reflect on the incredible phenomena that built the vast stage for this tranquil central Washington tour.

MILEAGE LOG
DAY ONE: SUN LAKES STATE PARK–GRAND COULEE DAM LOOP–
77.7 MILES

0.0   Sun Lakes State Park entrance on Park Lake Road. Turn right on **Highway 17** at the park exit.

2.0   Pass the Dry Falls Interpretative Center on the right.

4.0   Right on **Highway 2 East** at an intersection with Highway 17 (restaurants, store). Cross the Dry Falls Dam.

6.0   Pass Coulee City on the right and the Coulee City Community Park and marina (camping, rest rooms, picnic area) on the left. Continue straight ahead on Highway 2. Coulee City began in 1881 as McEntee's Crossing.

6.5   Left on **Road I.8 Northeast**.

7.2   Road bends right and the name changes to **Fordair Road**. Ride through sagebrush and irrigated wheat fields while negotiating a gentle climb.

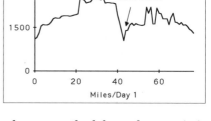

7.6   Road bends slightly right and crosses J Road Northeast.

8.3   Cross Highway 155 to continue on **Highway 2** toward Spokane. Climb a short hill, noticing the magnificent wall of the coulee across the lake and green, irrigated fields on the plateau lands.

12.3   Cross a railroad track that is angled and in poor condition.

16.6   Left on **Road R Northeast** toward Hartline. Road name changes briefly to **Range Street** as Hartline is entered.

17.0   Left on **Willard Street** in Hartline (limited services).

17.2   Hartline City Park (rest rooms, water) on the left. After visiting the park, backtrack one block on Willard Street.

17.4   Left on **Main Street** at the Hartline Post Office.

17.6   Right on an **unmarked road** at a T intersection. (A sign exists, but lettering is obliterated.)

17.8   Left on **Road R Northeast** at a T intersection. Climb a series of low ridges.

21.5   Revel in the first view of the mountains surrounding this area. Towering power standards march across the desert to deliver electricity.

26.1   Road bends right to become **Fiftieth**. Sign may appear to designate the opposite of what is true. Numbered roads run east–west.

30.2   Left on **Road V Northeast** as the pavement ends for Fiftieth Northeast, and terrain becomes more gentle.

32.2   Road bends right and is renamed **Fifty-second Northeast**.

33.2   Route continues on **Road W Northeast** as Fifty-second Northeast becomes gravel.

36.3   Left on **Grand Coulee Hill Road** (approaching from the right) at a stop sign as Road W Northeast merges with it. Proceed downhill.

39.0   Pass a sign warning truckers to use low gear. Check brakes for the drop into the coulee. **Caution:** hairpin curves. Grand Coulee Dam's backside comes into view almost immediately, with Roosevelt Lake in the foreground.

40.3   First of two extremely sharp curves. Pavement may be rough in places.

41.1   Bear left on **State Highway 174**/Truck Route. As it crosses the highway, Grand Coulee Hill Road is renamed **Spokane Way**. Follow it, immediately turning right to continue dropping into Grand Coulee.

41.6   Right on **Midway Avenue**/Highway 155 in Grand Coulee toward Grand Coulee Dam. Spokane Way intersects with Midway Avenue and Seaton Street.

42.6   Pass a scenic overlook of Grand Coulee Dam, 151-mile-long Roosevelt Lake, and environs. The dam began operating in 1942, contains 12 million yards of concrete, and is about twelve city blocks in length.

43.2   Pass another viewpoint on the right.

43.6   Right into the lower parking area of the circular Visitor Arrival Center for Grand Coulee Dam (rest rooms, water, picnic area, self-guided tours and videos). This was opened in 1978.

43.6   Left on **Highway 155** from the lower parking area of the Visitor Arrival Center. After visiting the exhibits, retrace your route into the community of Grand Coulee.

43.9   Pass a viewpoint on the left, touting the area's attractions on flags atop blue-capped posts.

45.5   Road name changes to **Midway Avenue** as it enters Grand Coulee (all services). Visitor information is available in the Chamber of Commerce/City Building on the right in the next block.

45.9   Continue south on **Highway 155** as Midway Avenue intersects with Highway 174 and continues uphill toward Electric City.

46.2   Pass the Gehrke Windmills on the right. This unique compound of colorful homemade windmills features household items that are usually discarded.

46.3   Right into **North Dam Park** (rest rooms, water, picnic area). To see the feeding canal for Banks Lake, cross the 0.3-mile dam. A dozen pumps each bring 720,000 gallons of water per minute up from Roosevelt Lake.

46.5   Right on the **Highway 155** shoulder.

47.1   Enter Electric City (all services).

48.1   Begin passing the shores of Banks Lake. Watch for fish, beaver, marmots, and birds.

48.9   Pass the Grand Coulee Airport access road on the right.

51.1   Pass a campground entrance on the right (pit toilets at the end of the unpaved road).

52.9   Pass the entrance to Steamboat Rock Rest Area (rest rooms, water), about 0.5 mile down a paved road.

53.9   Pass a gravel pullout with an interpretative sign on the right.

56.2   Pass the access road to Steamboat Rock State Park (camping, water, rest rooms, swimming, concession) on the right. Steamboat Rock, a 700-foot-high basalt cliff, was an island in the ancient Columbia River.

62.9   Pass a campground (pit toilets) entrance on the right and begin a short climb.

64.2   Pass a fishing access (pit toilet) on the right, as the downhill run ends.

68.8   Pass the junction of Highway 155 and Highway 2 East (small store, take-out restaurant). Coulee City is ahead on the right.

68.9   Right on **Fordair Road**. **Note:** The rest of today's ride backtracks on the route from Sun Lakes State Park.

70.0   Left on **Road I.8 Northeast** as Fordair ends.

71.2   Right on **Highway 2**.

71.7   Pass Coulee City on the left, and cross the Dry Falls Dam.

73.7   Left on **Highway 17** toward Dry Falls Interpretative Center and Sun Lakes State Park.

75.7   Pass the Dry Falls Interpretative Center (open daily, free) on the left. Exhibits and video interpret the dramatic geological events that have shaped this area.

77.7   Left on **Park Lake Road** into Sun Lakes State Park.

Day Two: Sun Lakes Park–Summer Falls Loop—48 miles

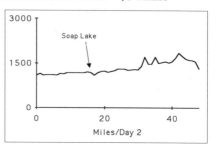

0.0   Sun Lakes State Park, intersection immediately north of the park store. Turn right on **Park Lake Road** and cross to the opposite shore of the lake, following **Park Lake Road**.

2.7   Pass Sun Village Resort on the left. Road bends right to meet Highway 17.

3.0   Left toward Soap Lake on **Highway 17** at a stop sign.

3.2   Pass an interpretative sign on the left. An ancient Indian trail that was used from 1859 to 1868 as the Caribou Cattle Trail ran through here. Today Highway 97 roughly approximates the trail that was more than 500 miles long. In Dry Coulee 0.5 mile to the east, the main wagon road used by homesteaders in the early 1900s is still faintly visible.

10.1   Pass on the left the access road to Lenore Caves.

   10.1   **Side Trip:** To visit the caves, turn to the left and continue 0.4 mile south to a parking area, then hike 0.25 mile into the caves. Backtrack to Highway 17 to rejoin the main route.

11.0   Pass the entrance to Lenore Lake and campground (pit toilets) on the right. At this point the highway passes over an ancient lava fold.

14.5   Pass a commercial campground on the right. Immediately begin passing Soap Lake on the right. Soap Lake was a nationally acclaimed spa in the l930s and l940s.

16.8   Enter Soap Lake (all services), where Highway 17 is renamed **Daisy Street**. Pass the town center and the lakefront on the right.

17.6   Left on **Third Avenue Southeast**.

17.8   Right on **Elder Street South**. Pass a city park on the left.

18.2   Left on **Sixth Avenue Southeast**, following it around bends to unmarked Highway 28. **Note:** Look for a sign a few yards to the left to verify the road name.

20.0   Cross Highway 28 and bear left on **Twentieth Northeast**.

21.1   Pass an apiary (bee hives) on the left and continue east alongside the fields of alfalfa, grasses, and sagebrush.

21.7   Cross a railroad track with an amiable rubberized surface.

24.5   Left on **Adrian Road**, just before a short hill. The surface is rough in places as it passes through a small settlement labeled Adrian (no services) at the train track.

25.2   Cross a rough railroad track and climb a short hill.

27.0   Right on **Highway 28** (unmarked) as primitive Dry Coulee Road begins across the highway.

27.5   Left on **F Road Northeast**.

28.0   Right on **Twenty-sixth Northeast**.

30.0   Left on **Pinto Ridge Road**, continuing north toward Coulee City.

32.0   Right toward **Summer Falls State Park**. Watch for the cattle guard on this downhill run over hard-packed gravel.

33.3   Enter Summer Falls State Park (rest rooms, water). The power plant was built in 1984. Enjoy a picnic on Billy Clapp Lake, then backtrack to Pinto Ridge Road.

34.6   Right on **Pinto Ridge Road**.

43.2   Cross the railroad tracks and enter Coulee City (all services). Coulee City was a watering hole on the Caribou Trail.

43.8   Left on **Main Street**.

44.3   Right on **Sixth Street**, and immediately left on **Walnut Street**, which bends right to become **I Northeast**.

44.7   Left on **Highway 2**, and cross Dry Falls Dam.

44.9   Left on **Highway 17**.

47.0   Pass the Dry Falls Interpretative Center on the left.

48.0   Left on **Park Lake Road** into Sun Lakes State Park.

DAY THREE: SUN LAKES STATE PARK TO LIND COULEE FISHING ACCESS, POTHOLES RESERVOIR—52 MILES

0.0   Sun Lakes State Park. Drive or pedal this connector route to Lind Coulee Fishing Access near Moses Lake. Turn left on **Highway 17** out of the park and continue toward Soap Lake.

16.8   Enter Soap Lake.

18.0   Pass through an intersection with Highway 28, staying on Highway 17. Notice the erratic rocks in the fields on the left. These relics of the geological

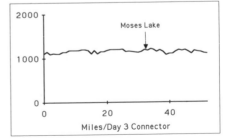

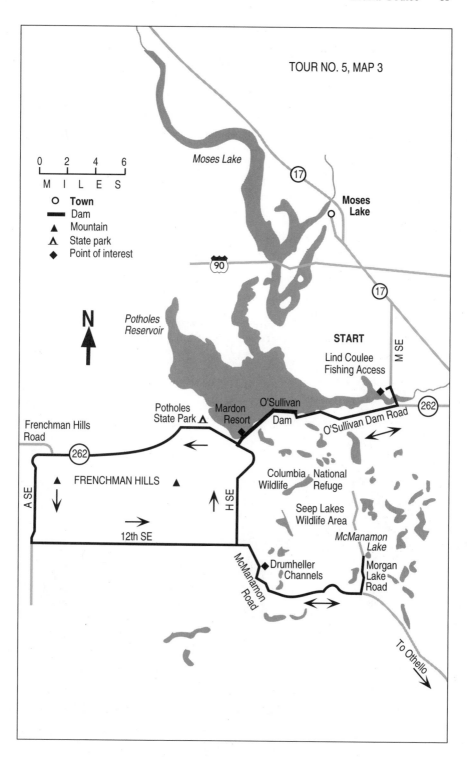

TOUR NO. 5, MAP 3

Moses Lake

17

**Moses
Lake**

0   2   4   6
M I L E S

○ **Town**
━ Dam
▲ Mountain
△ State park
◆ Point of interest

90

N

Potholes
Reservoir

17

M SE

START

Lind Coulee
Fishing Access

Potholes
State Park ▲   Mardon   O'Sullivan
Resort   Dam

262

Frenchman Hills
Road

262   O'Sullivan Dam Road

Columbia   National
Wildlife   Refuge

A SE   ▲ FRENCHMAN HILLS   ▲

H SE

Seep Lakes
Wildlife Area

McManamon
Lake

12th SE   McManamon
Road   Morgan
◆ Drumheller   Lake
Channels   Road

To Othello

upheaval in this area were carried here by raging floods or left by re-
treating glaciers.

25.8   Left to stay with Highway 17 as Highway 282 merges from the right.
Climb a series of short ridges.

34.2   Pass McConihe Road, a route to the northern reaches of Moses Lake, on
the right. Access to Moses Lake State Park (day use) is from I-90.

37.1   Divided highway begins.

39.3   Pass under a pedestrian crossover, continuing on Highway 17, and over
Parker Horn, an arm of Moses Lake.

40.8   Pass Broadway Avenue, an access route into the community of Moses
Lake. **Note:** From here to Nelson Drive, you can cycle a parallel section
of highway frontage to the right.

42.3   Left with Highway 17.

43.3   Cross I-90.

45.7   Right on **M Road Southeast**.

52.0   Right into the **Lind Coulee Fishing Access** parking area, just before
a bridge.

*The Potholes Reservoir area takes its name from ancient lava beds that have
been perforated by seeping water.* (Photo: Ken Winkenweder)

DAY FOUR: LIND COULEE FISHING ACCESS–
MCMANAMON LAKE LOOP–
57.8 MILES

0.0   Potholes Reservoir, Lind Coulee Fishing Access. Turn right on **M Road Southeast** to exit the parking area. Cross a bridge over the Potholes Reservoir and turn right on **O'Sullivan Dam Road** at the T intersection. **Note:** Rocks, fossils, and bones of prehistoric animals found in the Lind Coulee are exhibited in the Adam East Museum in Moses Lake. Featured is one of the largest single collections of Indian artifacts in Washington. Most originated with natives who inhabited the basin area.

2.5   Cross O'Sullivan Dam (rest rooms on the right).

6.0   Pass the Mardon Resort (store, cafe, water, rest rooms) on the right.

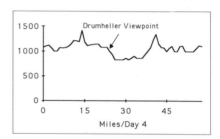

7.6   Pass H Street Southeast on the left. This turnoff leads to Royal City or Othello. **Note:** The return route is via H Street Southeast.

8.3   Pass a small resort (store, deli).

8.4   Pass the entrance to Potholes State Park campground on the right (potholes, fishing, camping, water, rest rooms).

15.2   Pass a turnoff to Royal City and Ephrata (road is signed Frenchman Hill) on the right. O'Sullivan Dam Road is renamed **Highway 262**. Stay with it.

15.5   Road turns sharply left and is renamed **A Southeast**. Panorama of variegated hues and shapes blends irrigated crops and with a blue canal threading through.

17.0   Left at a stop sign on **Twelfth Southeast** (unmarked) as A Southeast hurries to an intersection with Highway 26.

21.8   Continue straight ahead into Adams County. Road name changes to **McManamon Road** as it crosses H Street Southeast.

24.4   Pass a winery on the left.

24.9   Left into Drumheller Channels, a national scenic overlook. A few yards down the pathway is a dramatic overview and interpretative panel on the channeled scablands.

25.3   Enter the Columbia National Wildlife Refuge.

29.2   Pass a sign indicating the end of the wildlife refuge. Continue following McManamon Road. Because this land is a mixture of state, federal, and private properties, the sign refers to the road only. The refuge is to the left.

29.6   **Left on Morgan Lake Road.**

30.1   Pass Deadman's Bluff on the left. An interpretative sign tells the unfortunate demise of a youngster herding cattle in the dark.

30.6   Pass Para Homestead information sign on the left. This family's holdings are part of the private lands here.

31.0	Right into the parking area for McManamon Lake (unmarked). This is a pleasant lunch stop where diving terns and other birds generally provide entertainment.
31.0	Left on **Morgan Lake Road** to backtrack the above route past the Drumheller Channels.
32.4	Right on **McManamon Road** toward the Potholes Reservoir.
35.1	Pass the Drumheller Channels Overview on the right.
36.4	Cross into Grant County.
36.6	Right on **H Southeast**. (The road to the left is labeled May Street.)
41.4	Right on **O'Sullivan Dam Road** at a T intersection.
41.8	Pass the Mardon Resort on the left. Backtrack to the fishing access on the route above.
57.6	Left on **M Road Southeast** toward Moses Lake.
57.8	Left into Lind Coulee Fishing Access parking area. End of tour.

6. NORTHERN EXPOSURE LOOP

Susie Stephens

Distance: 209 miles
Terrain: moderate with some hills
Total cumulative elevation gain: 4,874 feet
Recommended time of year: May–October
Recommended starting time: before noon; early start especially recommended for Day Two
Allow: 3 days
Points of interest: *Northern Exposure* backdrops, Roslyn; Roslyn cemeteries; State Telephone Museum, Cle Elum; 1883 Thorp Grist Mill; Ginkgo Petrified Forest and Museum; petroglyphs near the Columbia River; Wanapum Dam and Indian Heritage Museum; Yakima River Canyon

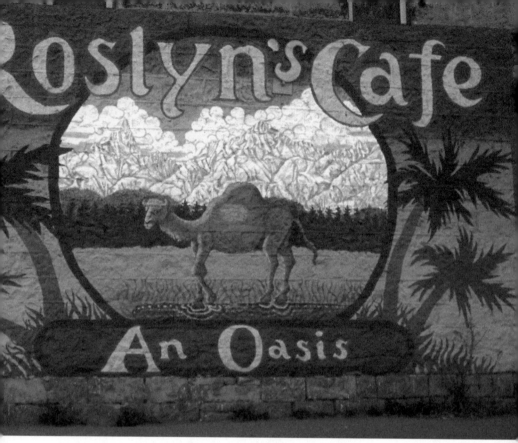

Roslyn, start of the Northern Exposure Loop, attracts star chasers like bicycle tires attract thistles. (Photo: Susie Stephens)

◆ ◆ ◆

PUBLIC TRANSPORTATION
Air: none available
Train: none available

PRACTICAL INFORMATION
Key contacts: Cle Elum–Roslyn Visitor Information, 509-674-5958; Ellensburg Visitor Information, 509-925-3137; Wanapum Dam Tour Center, 509-754-3541, ext. 2571; Yakima Tourist and Convention Bureau, 800-221-0751

STARTING POINT
Roslyn–Cle Elum Middle School on Highway 903: From I-90 eastbound, take Exit 80 toward Roslyn and proceed 3 miles on Bullfrog Road. Turn right on Highway 903 at a T intersection (unmarked) and immediately right again into the school parking area. Request permission for overnight parking in advance from Roslyn–Cle Elum Middle School, 509-649-2393.

Experience central Washington on this 209-mile tour of spreading farms, expansive desert, and awe-inspiring canyons. Although the cycling along this

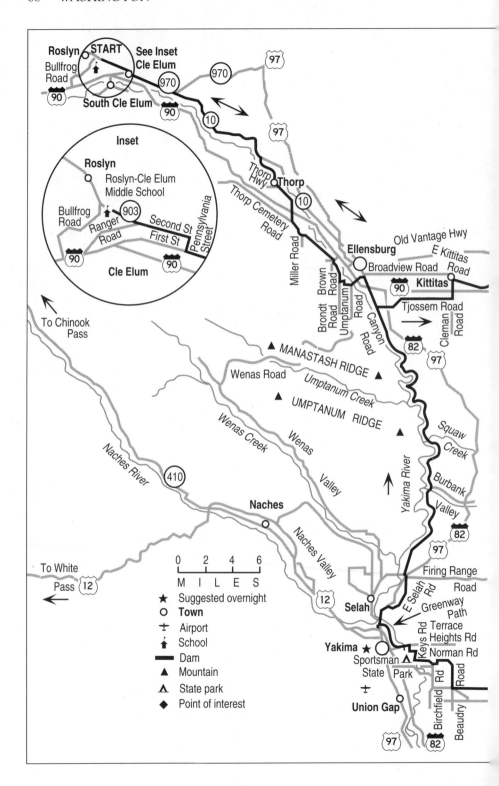

Roslyn
START
See Inset
Cle Elum
Bullfrog Road
South Cle Elum
90
970
970
97
97
10

Inset

Roslyn
Roslyn-Cle Elum Middle School
Bullfrog Road
903
Ranger Road
Second St
First St
Pennsylvania Street
90
90
Cle Elum

Thorp Hwy
Thorp
10
Thorp Cemetery Road
Miller Road
Old Vantage Hwy
E Kittitas Road
Ellensburg
Broadview Road
Kittitas
90
Tjossem Road
Cleman Road
Brown Road
Brandt Road
Umptanum Road
Canyon Road
82
97

To Chinook Pass

MANASTASH RIDGE
Wenas Road
Umptanum Creek
UMPTANUM RIDGE
Squaw Creek

Wenas Creek
Wenas
Wenas Valley
Yakima River
Burbank Valley
82

Naches River
410
Naches
Naches Valley
97

To White Pass
12
Firing Range Road

0   2   4   6
M I L E S

★ Suggested overnight
○ **Town**
✝ Airport
🏠 School
▬ Dam
▲ Mountain
△ State park
◆ Point of interest

Naches Valley
12
Selah
E Selah Rd
Greenway Path
Keys Rd
Terrace Heights Rd
Yakima ★
Sportsman State Park
Norman Rd
Birchfield Rd
Beaudry Road
Union Gap
97
82

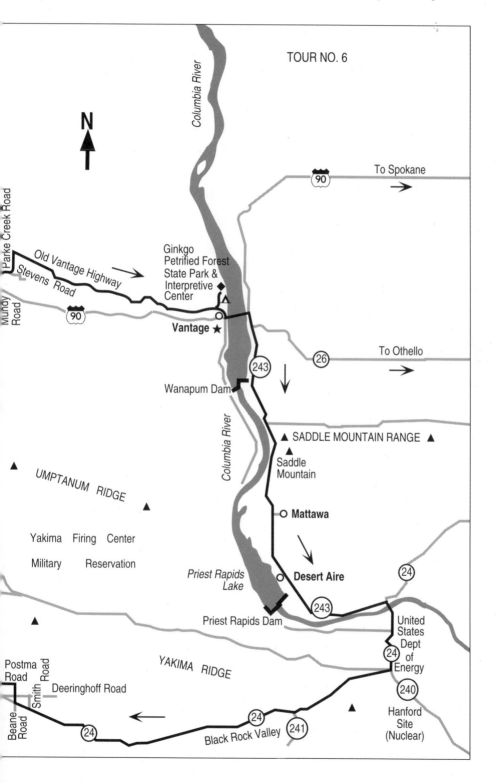

route can be challenging, the paybacks are wonderful drops down into the canyons. This loop offers a wide variety of scenery and fascinating places to learn more about Native American and geological history, and you can add to the tour's 3 days by staying over in Yakima. This bustling city offers much to explore, including museums, vast vineyards, and local cultural events.

Expect to begin this tour with company. Star chasers are attracted to Roslyn like thistles to a bicycle tire. They wander about hoping to glimpse a favorite star from *Northern Exposure*, a Roslyn-based television series, but the actors are more likely to be taping in a Seattle-area warehouse. Sitting on its black gold—coal—Roslyn boomed in the 1880s, but its charm still rubs off in the museum, unique cafes, and the oldest operating saloon in the state. To grasp the ethnic diversity of the coal-mining era, visit the twenty-six Roslyn cemeteries, a fascinating array of headstones and memorials near town.

In nearby Cle Elum, a bakery pumps alluring aromas from the same building in which it opened in 1906. The state's last operator-assisted telephone facility, deeded to the city in 1966, invites investigation. Picnic in Thorp, 20 miles into the tour, near a grist mill on the National Register of Historic Places. A feed and flour mill from 1883 to 1946, it now features industrial artifacts and a multimedia presentation during the summer.

By the time you reach Thorp, the Cascade foothills have totally given way to the fertile and often windswept Ellensburg plain. Refresh at the seasonal stands, brimming with treats such as apples, peaches, and pears. Feel the cool breezes approaching from across a golden and green sea of irrigated farms accented with barns, cows, goats, and orchards. Ellensburg roars with a traditional Labor Day rodeo and hums with education year-round in Central Washington University, founded in 1891. In the ornate downtown district, pedal among brick survivors of an 1889 fire and an 1893 national economic depression. Originally spelled Ellensburgh, the community's name honors the founder's wife, Mary Ellen (Mrs. John) Shoudy. (The "h" was dropped in 1894 to simplify mail delivery.) For a short time the mansion at Fifth Avenue and Kittitas Street was the Shoudy home.

Pedal onto the thirsty desert where birds and reptiles are the primary residents. Thrill at the expansive backdrop of Mount Stuart and the Cascade Mountains. From the vantage point of your bicycle saddle, the mountains will stand out more and serve as a measure of the distance you have traveled. Climb the old Vantage Highway, preparing for an incredible payback: a 2,000-foot plunge into the Columbia River Valley and the community of Vantage.

Once green and swampy, the desert near the Columbia River is now a dry gold and red. See solid evidence of this dramatic climate shift in nearby Ginkgo Petrified Forest State Park. Approximately 200 varieties of trees from 200 million years ago lie petrified here, testifying to how lush the landscape once was. A half mile northwest of Vantage, living Ginkgo trees with their distinctive unribbed, fan-shaped leaves mark the route to petroglyphs on the river side of the museum and gem shop. These are ancient, hand-painted messages rescued from the lapping backwaters of dams on the mighty Columbia River below.

Begin Day Two early to assure a pleasant crossing of the Columbia River, free from heavy high-speed traffic. The busy bridge at Vantage replaced a two-car barge ferry in the early 1920s. Flow south with the river to Wanapum Dam, which in 1965 blocked the 20-foot Priest Rapids and flooded a dozen Wanapum villages near prolific fishing grounds. An area at the dam's west end is now the

Awe-inspiring canyons offer great downhill runs on the Northern Exposure Loop. (Photo: Scott Stevens)

Wanapum village and its story is told in the Heritage Center. Also learn how crackling hydroelectricity here supplies public and private uses in Washington and Oregon. End your day with a long, delicious descent through rich apple orchards and grape vineyards into Yakima.

Yakima, with 300 days of sunshine annually, is a fertile agricultural area where apples, mint, winter pears, hops, and wineries flourish. If you yield to the temptation to explore the valley and the city of Yakima, spend an extra day before resuming the tour. Among the diversions are winery tours, trolley rides, and a museum that is a tribute to a renowned Yakima son, the late Supreme Court Justice William O. Douglas. For other sightseeing in the valley, see tour 8, Central Washington Bluebird Loop.

On Day Three, follow the canyon of the snaking Yakima River 25 miles into Ellensburg, then backtrack on the first day's route to Roslyn. Despite the earth's crust buckling around it over millions of years, the Yakima River has stead-fastly maintained its winding course through this striking canyon of stark basalt cliffs and long talus slopes. You can enjoy the roll along the river, knowing that most of the vehicle traffic is to the east on I-82, leaving the canyon road for slower-paced travelers and sightseers. Watch the river for inner-tubing and fishing activities and keep an eye overhead for birds of prey as well as human-powered flyers. This is a parapente training area where lightweight parachutes are used like hang gliders to descend from the canyon's walls.

MILEAGE LOG

DAY ONE: ROSLYN TO VANTAGE—61.9 MILES

0.0 Roslyn–Cle Elum Middle School on Highway 903, halfway between the two communities. Turn right toward Cle Elum on **Highway 903**.

   0.0 Side Trip: To visit Roslyn town center and the cemeteries, turn left on Highway 903 and proceed 1.2 miles to Pennsylvania Avenue. Turn left. To rejoin the main route, backtrack on Highway 903 to the school.

1.6 Enter Cle Elum where the road name changes to **Second Street**.

1.8 Right on **Pennsylvania Street** at the stop sign and immediately left on **First Street** (bakery, groceries, restaurants). Pass the Telephone Museum at 221 East First Street on the left.

4.1 Continue straight ahead as First Street becomes **Highway 970**.

6.2 Right on **Highway 10** toward Ellensburg, passing a rest area (portable toilets; no water) on the left.

7.3 Begin the first climb. The road rolls over hills, following the Yakima River.

15.3 Right on **Thorp Highway**, descending quickly to cross the Yakima River.

18.3 Enter Thorp and pass the Thorp Grist Mill on the left. A picnic area (portable toilet; no water) is adjacent to the old mill's lade behind the building.

20.3 Cross I-90 and continue straight ahead. Pass a vendor of antiques and fruit on the left. During the summer and fall, fresh local fruit is featured.

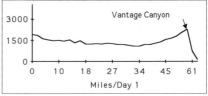

21.6 Photo opportunity: red-and-white-trimmed farmhouse with cast-iron bridges over the irrigation canal, fountains, statues of cherubs, a gazebo, plastic ducks, and swans.

25.5 Right on **Hanson Road** and left immediately on **Brown Road**.

27.9 Left to remain on **Brown Road** as the route straight ahead is renamed Brondt Road.

28.3 Left at the stop sign on **Umptanum Road**, then cross the Yakima River. Pass Rinehart River Park (portable toilets; no water) on the left, a popular fly-fishing spot with shady picnic areas on the river. Bicycles are not allowed on the many walking trails.

39.5 Right on **Canyon Road** (restaurants; stores 0.25 mile to the left). Downtown Ellensburg is 1.5 miles to the left. **Caution:** The next 2 miles are busy with traffic entering and exiting I-90. The shoulders are narrow.

31.2 Left on **Tjossem Road**. Views of the Stuart Range to the left.

32.3 Cross I-82. There are more mountain views here.

36.9 Left on **Cleman Road** at a stop sign, then cross I-90.

38.4 Enter Kittitas (cafe, store), a town with a short but scenic Old West main street. This is across the Iron Horse Trail, the former railroad grade now a pedestrian, mountain bicycle, and horse trail. The lawn in front of the old train station offers a nice picnic spot. Turn right on **Main Street** and immediately left on **First Street**, which becomes **East Kittitas Road**, then **Parke Creek Road** after leaving town.

40.9   Stay left on **Parke Creek Road** as Mundy Road comes in from the right.
41.7   Stay left on Parke Creek Road as Stevens Road goes right.
44.2   Right on the **Old Vantage Highway**.
48.5   Summit (microwave tower). Begin a 2,000-foot descent into Vantage.
59.5   Pass the Ginkgo Petrified Forest State Park (rest rooms, water).
61.4   The Ginkgo Museum and Gem shop is 0.25 mile farther on the left.
61.9   Enter Vantage (campsites, motels, groceries, cafes). **Note:** More rugged bicycle tourists can continue across the Columbia River about 3 miles (to Mile 2.9 of Day Two) for a primitive campsite with plenty of soft sand, but no rest rooms or water. Sunsets are spectacular. Nearest groceries are in Vantage.

DAY TWO: VANTAGE TO YAKIMA—82.3 MILES

0.0   Vantage, KOA Campground in town center. Turn left on the **Old Vantage Highway**, following signs to I-90.

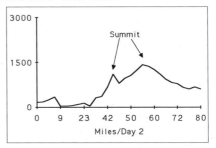

0.3   Cross **I-90**, then turn right on the eastbound entrance to I-90 toward Spokane. There is a shoulder until the Columbia River bridge. **Caution:** An early start avoids heavier traffic.
1.7   Right on **Highway 26** at Exit 137.
2.8   Right on **Highway 243** toward the Vernita Bridge and Richland.
2.9   Primitive campsite (no rest rooms, no water).
6.9   Pass the road to Wanapum Dam on the right. A picnic area (rest rooms, no water) is located on the Wanapum Dam Road just off the highway. Located 1 mile down Wanapum Dam Road is the Native American Heritage Center and Museum. Tours are available. The museum opens at 10:00 A.M.
17.3   Pass the road to Mattawa (store, nice park with rest rooms, water) on the left, which is uphill 0.6 mile. The name means "what is it?" in Wanapum.
21.4   Pass the community of Desert Aire on the right (store, snack bar, ice cream parlor, barber shop).
22.8   Pass the entrance to Priest Rapids Dam (rest rooms, water).
31.4   Right on **Highway 24**. Cross the Columbia River. There is a very pleasant rest area (rest rooms, water, shade) on the right just after the bridge.
35.5   Summit, the first of two climbs before Yakima.
37.2   Right to stay with Highway 24 at the junction with Highway 240. Sign reads 40 miles to Yakima.
43.0   Top a false summit (1,100 feet). Continue along the Yakima Ridge.
45.3   Cafe (open Sundays during summer). Bear right to stay with Highway 24 as Highway 241 goes left to Sunnyside.
55.7   Yakima Ridge Summit (1,420 feet).
60.0   View of Mount Rainier straight ahead.
67.3   Right on **Beane Road**.
68.8   Left on **Postma Road**.
73.2   Right on **Beaudry Road**.

75.2   Beaudry becomes **Norman Road**. Follow Norman Road through curves.

76.9   Right on **Gun Club Road**.

77.9   Junction of Gun Club Road and Keys Road. Sportsman State Park (water, hot showers) is straight ahead. (To continue to hotels in Yakima, turn right on Keys Road.) Inexpensive bicycle campsites are available in the state park's primitive area. Friendly skunks wander around at dusk.

78.3   Railroad crossing.

79.6   Left on **Terrace Heights Road**.

80.1   Cross the Yakima River. Turn right immediately after the bridge to enter the bicycle trail following the river.

81.6   Bicycle trail passes under two I-82 bridges. Continue under the bridges. Note the ramp between the bridges leading up to the bike crossing over the river. The route for Day Three begins here just outside the community of Selah.

81.9   Continue straight on **Gordon Street** as the trail ends. Follow Gordon Street under the bridge, curving left, then right.

82.3   Left on **Tamarack Street**. It is a block to First Street (motels, restaurants, markets).

DAY THREE: YAKIMA TO ROSLYN—64.9 MILES

0.0   Yakima, Yakima Greenway Trail (backtrack to Mile 81.6 of Day Two). Proceed over I-82, taking the bicycle trail ramp (unmarked) that leads up between the two bridges over the river. This narrow, separated trail crosses the I-82 bridge northbound. **Note:** At first this trail access appears to be a freeway entrance ramp.

0.5   Right as the bike trail ends at the **Selah Road** I-82 crossing. Cross I-82, following the green bike route signs toward Ellensburg. There is a pleasant picnic area (rest rooms, no water) on the right.

0.6   Left on the shoulder of **I-82 North** toward Ellensburg.

2.0   Right at **Exit 29, East Selah**, from I-82. Fruit stand.

4.8   Left on **Firing Range Road** at the stop sign. Cross I-82. After the bridge, this becomes **Canyon Road** and continues toward Ellensburg.

11.0   Summit (1,100 feet).

12.0   Pass a rest area (portable toilets, no water) on the left.

17.4   Pass Squaw Creek Rest Area (portable toilets, no water) on the left.

26.8   Pass a picnic area (no facilities) on the river on the left.

32.0   Continue with Canyon Road as it passes under I-90.

34.1   Left on **Umptanum Road**.

46.4   Thorp Grist Mill (portable toilet, no water).

48.8   Cross the Yakima River.

49.6   Left on **Highway 10**.

58.7   Left on **Highway 970**. Pass a rest area (portable toilets, no water) on the right.

60.8   Enter Cle Elum (all services).

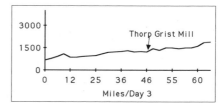

63.1   Right on **Pennsylvania Street**, then left in one block on **Second Street**. As it leaves Cle Elum, this becomes **Highway 903**.

64.9   Roslyn–Cle Elum High School and Middle School on the left. End of tour.

The grist mill in Thorp is on the National Register of Historic Places. (Photo: Susie Stephens)

7. TWO-STATE CANYONS LOOP

Jean Henderson

Distance: 368 miles
Terrain: flat to rolling, punctuated with deep canyons; not recommended for novice cyclists
Total cumulative elevation gain: 24,116 feet
Recommended time of year: April–early June, September

TOUR NO. 7, MAP 1

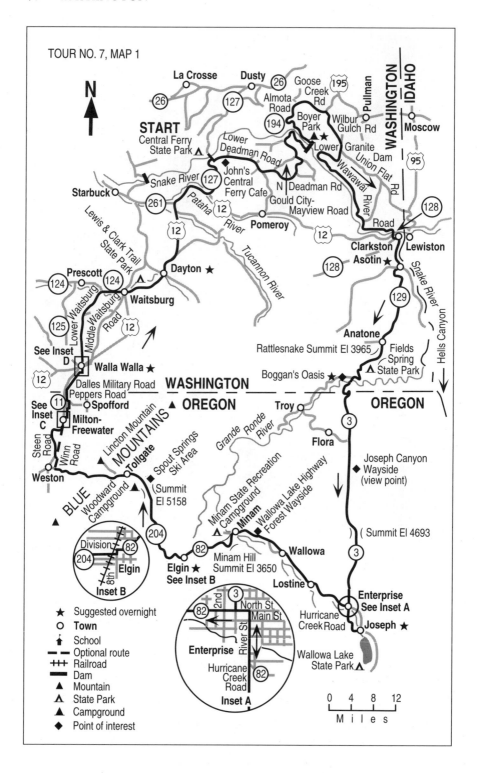

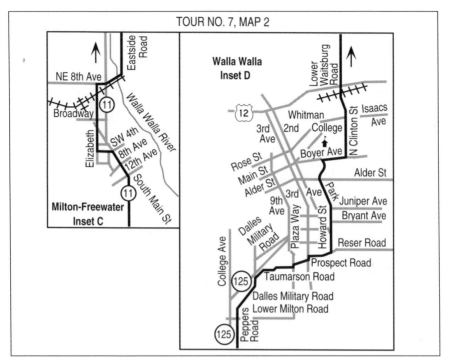

Recommended starting time: before 2:00 P.M. the first day
Allow: 8 days
Points of interest: Lower Granite Dam; Fields Spring State Park, Puffer Butte; Wallowa Lake; Elgin Courthouse, Elgin; Frazier Pioneer Farm, Milton-Freewater; Whitman College, Walla Walla; Whitman Mission and other historic sites, Walla Walla; Preston-Shaffer Mill site, Waitsburg; Washington's oldest courthouse, circa 1887, Dayton; 1881 train depot, Dayton

PUBLIC TRANSPORTATION
Air: commercial airlines serve Lewiston, but may not carry bicycles; pick up the tour route on Day Three if you fly to Lewiston
Train: none available

PRACTICAL INFORMATION
Key contacts: Central Ferry State Park, 509-549-3551; John's Central Ferry Store and Cafe, 509-843-1715; Boyer Park and Marina, 509-397-3208; Asotin Visitor Information, 800-933-2128; Boggan's Oasis, Anatone, 509-256-3372; Joseph, Oregon, Visitor Information, 503-432-1015; Walla Walla Visitor Information, 509-525-0850

STARTING POINT
Central Ferry State Park on the Snake River and Highway 127 in southeastern Washington: From Dusty on Highway 26, take Highway 127 south-

west for 17 miles. Check with the park ranger on site regarding parking. A small fee may be charged. Parking is also available for a daily fee, approximately 2 miles farther on the described route, at John's Central Ferry Store and Cafe.

Views are as expansive as the population is sparse on this eight-day tour of southeastern Washington and northeastern Oregon. Spring adds another dimension. Bright green landscapes brushstroked with flowering purple lupines and bunches of yellow balsamroot seem to race toward summer. Even the rivers rush in a futile attempt to forestall the time when all will be thirsty and brown.

Enjoy backroads to rural charms. Delight in yesteryear's elegant homes, courthouses, and train depots, and relish delicious, homemade pancakes and pies offered in typical hometown style. In planning this route, Loretta Goetsch of Seattle took advantage of her own early-morning energy to start most days with a climb. After the work comes the play, featuring gentle glides over flat grasslands, rolling hills, and a thrilling dive down into a spectacular canyon for the next day's climb. Do not let the remote nature of the route preclude getting advance reservations. Tiny Joseph, Oregon, attracts tourists like honey lures bears, and Boggan's Oasis is the sole facility in the Grande Ronde Canyon.

Begin the adventure on the Snake River near Deadman Creek where two ill-fated gold seekers were found after the snowy winter of 1861–62. On the river, lidded grain barges sit loaded for world markets. Once cargo arrived at the river on tramways from the fields above. Roll toward Boyer Park, plunging 1,600 feet to Lower Granite Dam where a fascinating story of salmon unfolds. Salmon leave here in trucks, but find their way back for spawning by sensing information in river water transported with them to immediately below Bonneville Dam. To prevent "the bends" in returning fish, nitrogen is forced from river water rolling over the dam. If the river is not high for your visit, imagine Lower Granite, the last in a series of eight dams on the Snake and Columbia rivers, bombarded with surges of enormous logs. When sucked into the lock with the ship traffic, logs tip barges, spilling semi-truck–sized containers like toothpicks. Lentils swell to the size of dinner plates and toilet tissue balloons while divers risk peril to clear the unpredictable lock contents.

Camp the first night in nearby Boyer Park. You can lighten your load for the rest of the loop by stowing gear for later pickup, and recruiting a driver for a sag wagon. On Day Two climb up and sail back down to the Snake River in a 32-mile exercise that progresses a mere 3 miles toward Clarkston. Hear whirring wheels echo off the 3,000-foot Snake River canyon walls as your legs spin toward Idaho. In Clarkston, pick up a parkside bicycle path to tiny Asotin and the end of the day's pedaling. Asotin is a tiny county seat named for river eels.

On Day Three, climb away from Asotin and to within a few miles of the granddaddy of all canyons. Beyond the farm tablelands, Hells Canyon severs the distant landscape, but hurry on to pie and coffee in Anatone. At Fields Spring State Park, hike up 4,450-foot Puffer Butte, wading in wildflowers and watching for woodpeckers. Look down 3,000 feet into the Grand Ronde Canyon where this day's ride concludes, then mount up and whisk to the waiting river.

On Day Four there is no way to go but up and around the seventy-four Buford Grade curves. Pedal up 2,500 feet in 10 miles, leaving Washington's remote southeastern corner and entering the hills once roamed by Chief Joseph's band of Nez Perce Indians. Cross a 4,693-foot summit to approach Enterprise, Oregon, while marveling at the distant Wallowa Mountains. With bright green

The 1887 Columbia County Courthouse is the oldest still in use in Washington. (Photo: Ken Winkenweder)

grasslands and tiny Joseph below, they tower above at 8,200 feet. As Wallowa Lake enters the already dazzling picture, feel the growing urge to linger.

On Day Five, backtrack to Enterprise, wend through tiny communities, and cross gurgling streams. Climb through forests into Elgin, a petite community with a 1912 combination city hall, opera house, and jail on the National Register of Historic Places. See the handpainted mountain backdrop, recently rediscovered after forty years in the rafters, and peek through the curtain signed in the 1930s by the Carter Family.

On Day Six stop by the 1868 Frazier farmhouse in Milton-Freewater, then cross the border and enter the Blue Mountains, Washington's most productive elk area and a favorite haunt of mushroom lovers. Pedal through the onion fields to Walla Walla. Its Nez Perce name means "many waters" but, from turn-of-the-century buildings along an old-time main street to the state's oldest newspaper, college, and bank, Walla Walla is Northwest history. Complete the day's route on the Whitman College campus, but continue to explore. The 1836 site of Marcus and Narcissa Whitman's mission, the common grave of the 1846 massacre victims, and a section of the original Oregon Trail are 7 miles away.

Discover an abandoned grist mill on the Touchet River on Day Seven. Established in 1865 by Sylvester Wait, it is easily missed in Waitsburg, the state's only community operating under its territorial charter. In Dayton hark back to

the 1870s. Tour the state's oldest courthouse, an 1887 classic Italianate building with a 22-foot-high tower. Then seek souvenirs in the attractive 1881 but-
terscotch-colored building of the state's oldest existing rail depot.

On Day Eight pass sheds and sight the yellow helmets on the bobbing heads
of workers preparing asparagus and peas for market. Overhead, crop-dusting
biplanes swerve low as the route slides up and over the golden grain fields.
Bypass tiny Pomeroy, the sole community in Garfield County, forgoing terrain
that requires wheat combines with special leveling capabilities. Delight instead
in a fairly gentle route that soon plunges to the Snake River to complete its
probes of magnificent Washington and Oregon canyons.

MILEAGE LOG

DAY ONE: CENTRAL FERRY STATE PARK TO BOYER PARK—40.4 MILES

0.0   Central Ferry State Park on
      Highway 127 in Garfield
      County. Turn right out of the
      park and cross the Snake River.

0.9   Bear left on **Lower Deadman
      Road**, following signs to Lower
      Granite Dam.

2.7   Pass John's Central Ferry Cafe
      and Store (restaurant, store,
      campground) on the right. **Note:**
      This facility offers an alternate starting point for the tour, depending on
      your parking arrangements.

11.3 Stay left with Lower Deadman Road at an intersection with Wild Horse
      Hill Road.

12.9 Bear left at a Y intersection on **Gould City–Mayview Road** (unmarked)
      toward Lower Granite Dam.

14.8 Stay right with **North Deadman Road** at the Gould City–Mayview Y
      intersection.

20.0 Left on the **Kirby–Mayview Road**. Road name shortly changes to
      Casey Creek Road (unmarked).

27.3 Check bicycle brakes, then fly about 1,600 feet down to the Snake River.
      The road name changes to **Almota Ferry Road** (unmarked) and traces
      the river upstream to the Lower Granite Dam.

37.4 Lower Granite Dam. Cross the dam. Turn left on **Almota Road**/Highway
      194 toward Boyer Park.

 37.4 Side Trip: To visit the fish transportation area, interpretative
      exhibits, or spillway, turn left before crossing the dam (rest rooms,
      water). Lower Granite is named for a rock outcropping about 6
      miles upriver. Backtrack to cross the dam and rejoin the main
      route.

40.4 Left into **Boyer Park** (restaurant, camping, showers, store, marina).
      Ship traffic locking through the dam provides all-night entertainment.

DAY TWO: BOYER PARK TO ASOTIN—68.6 MILES

0.0   Boyer Park. Turn left on **Almota Road**/Highway 194, following the
      Snake River downstream.

6.0   Almota Summit (1,678 feet).

8.0 Right to stay with Highway 194/**Goose Creek Road** at a T intersection.

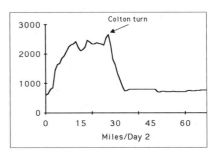

15.0 Stay with Goose Creek Road as it passes through stately pines and drops over Union Flat Creek to be renamed **Wilbur Gulch Road**. After double Y intersections, go right and begin dropping back to the Snake River.

27.0 Right at a T intersection (unmarked) at a stop sign where a sign points left to Colton. Drop back to the Snake River on **Wawawai Grade Road**.

32.7 Pass Wawawai County Park (rest rooms, picnic area, camping, swimming, bird sanctuary) on the right. Wawawai translates to "council grounds" for this site, which originally was an Indian village and later a homestead. Now submerged beneath the dam's backwaters are orchards that once made this the Snake River's largest fruit-shipping port.

33.4 Cross railroad tracks as the road bends left to become **Wawawai River Road**. Boyer Park is 3 miles downstream from this spot.

41.4 Blyton Landing (boat launch, pit toilet).

50.0 Right at a T intersection to stay with Wawawai River Road toward Lewiston.

60.0 Right on **Highway 128** into Clarkston (all services).

60.5 Right immediately at the end of the bridge to access the bicycle path underneath. Keep the Snake River on your left.

61.3 Right at **Fourteenth Street**, and immediately left on **Fair Street**.

62.3 Continue straight on the bicycle trail at a stop sign where Second Avenue goes right.

68.6 Enter Asotin (all services) where the bike path ends in Chief Looking Glass Park. Asotin, the county seat, predates both neighboring Clarkston and Lewiston.

DAY THREE: ASOTIN TO BOGGAN'S OASIS—33.5 MILES

0.0 Asotin, town center and Highway 128. Head south toward Hells Canyon.

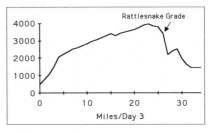

0.4 Right on **Highway 129**/Washington Street, passing Asotin's historical churches on the right.

0.9 Pass the Asotin Fairgrounds on the right and ascend through the desert to farm tablelands.

18.8 Enter Anatone (services), population 51. Named for a local Indian woman, this town bustled as a trading post on the 1860s gold trail.

19.2 Pass the Anatone Cafe, with cyclist-tested, homemade pies, on the left.

20.8 Pass through a pine forest on Highway 129. Watch for deer.

22.5 Rattlesnake Summit (3,965 feet).

23.1 Left into **Fields Spring State Park**. Both the park and Puffer Butte are named for homesteaders. At least eight species of woodpeckers have been identified here.

23.8   Enter the picnic area (rest rooms, water). A mile-long trail to Puffer Butte opens a 4,450-foot view into three states and the 3,000-foot Grande Ronde Canyon. In the spring the park is resplendent with wildflowers. After your hike up the butte, get back on the bike and roll down to the park entrance.

24.4   Left on **Highway 129**. Whisk past Rattlesnake Grade's 110 guardrailed curves, dropping to the river.

33.5   Cross the Grande Ronde River. On the right is Boggan's Oasis, the only commercial facility here (lodging, cafe). **Note:** Through Boggan's Oasis you can make advance arrangements to stay overnight at Boggan's Ranch, with meals and a car shuttle included. Boggan's Ranch is located beside the Grande Ronde River on the unpaved road, immediately north of the river.

DAY FOUR: BOGGAN'S OASIS TO JOSEPH, OREGON—55.1 MILES

0.0   Boggan's Cafe on Highway 129. Continue south toward Oregon, riding up and around Buford Grade's ninety-seven guardrailed curves.

4.0   Cross into Wallowa County, Oregon, where the road becomes **Highway 3**.

10.3   Leave the Grand Ronde Canyon, rolling down through a pine-scented forest.

13.5   Pass a junction for the communities of Flora and Troy.

13.9   Pass the Rimrock Inn Restaurant and Trailer Park (seasonal) on the left.

17.5   Left into the Joseph Canyon Wayside. Visualize the Nez Perce Indians who once roamed the lands below.

25.5   Pass the Sled Springs Stage Station site.

27.5   Crest a summit (4,693 feet).

31.0   Begin a 1.5-mile dive through the trees. The distant 8,200-foot Wallowa Mountains come into view.

32.5   Pass access to trailheads and camping on the left. Highway 3/11 continues to Enterprise, threading through a wide valley.

46.4   Enter Enterprise (all services), population 2,020. Highway 3 becomes **West First Street** and intersects **Highway 10/82** (North Street) at a stop sign. Turn left and immediately right on **River Street** to pass the Wallowa County Courthouse on the left.

46.7   Bear right on **Hurricane Creek Road** toward Joseph at a Y intersection with Highway 82. Pedal through a sharp, green landscape with the snow-topped Wallowa Mountains jutting up behind.

53.0   Bear left with **Airport Lane** at the Hurricane Creek Grange. Hurricane Creek becomes gravel at this Y intersection.

55.1   Enter Joseph (all services).

55.1   **Alternative:** Camping and lodging are also available on Wallowa Lake in 3 miles. Turn right on Main Street (Highway 82/251) and continue on the Wallowa Lake Highway. Pass Old Chief Joseph's gravesite on the right, just at the edge of town.

The stunning Wallowa Mountains come into full view on the approach to Enterprise. (Photo: Ken Winkenweder)

DAY FIVE: JOSEPH, OREGON TO ELGIN, OREGON—52.7 MILES

0.0   Joseph, intersection of Main Street and Airport Lane (Hurricane Creek Road). Following Day Four's mileage log, backtrack 8 miles to Enterprise, bearing right at the grange hall at Mile 2.1.

8.0   Enter Enterprise where the road name changes to **River Street**.

8.5   Left on **Highway 10/82** (North Street).

8.6   Bear left with **Highway 10/82**.

9.5   Pass the Wallowa–Whitman National Forest Visitors Center (rest rooms, water, information) on the right.

18.1   Enter Lostine (services), population 270.

18.4   Right to stay on Highway 82 at a Y intersection with Lostine Campground Road.

25.6   Enter Wallowa (services), population 670. Shortly enter Water Canyon, tracing the river on your left.

26.6   Bear right toward Elgin at a Y intersection. You may get a chuckle over the three signs near the same spot—each indicating a different distance to Elgin.

33.6   Pass a rest area (rest rooms) on the right.

35.6   Pass the Wallowa Forest Wayside on the left.

39.1   Enter Minam, a former mill site, now a store and motel on the river. Pass over a bad rail track, then cross the Wallowa and Minam rivers.

39.5   Pass access to the Minam Store (in sight) and Minam State Recreation

The tiny town of Joseph is an especially charming setting for a stayover.
(Photo: Ken Winkenweder)

Campground (2 miles away). There is a cool rest area (pit toilet) under
the bridge. You can watch rafters splash in the river while you picnic.

40.1   Enter Union County and continue to climb.

44.3   Summit of Minam Hill (3,650 feet).

52.2   Enter Elgin (all services), population 1,710, settled in 1882.

52.7   Bear left with **Highway 82**, which is renamed Albany Street. Directly
ahead is the 1912 combination city hall, opera house, and jail; tours on
request.

DAY SIX: ELGIN, OREGON TO WALLA WALLA—62.5 MILES

0.0   Elgin, intersection of Albany
Street and Division Street/High-
way 204. Head toward Spout
Springs on **Highway 204**.

5.3   Enter the Umatilla National Forest.

13.5   Pass Summit Road on the left.
The terrain appears to level
slightly.

17.2   Summit of the Blue Mountains (5,158 feet).

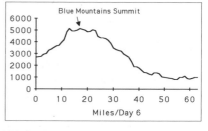

18.3   Pass the Spout Springs ski area (mountain bike rentals, restaurant—opens at 11:00 A.M.).

21.0   Community of Tollgate.

21.5   Leave the Umatilla National Forest.

22.2   Pass an old well site at Tamarack (store, cafe) on the right.

25.5   Pass Lincton Mountain (store on the right).

40.3   Right on **Winn Road**.

42.4   Cross Highway 11 toward Blue Mountain Station. Road name changes to **Steen Road**.

    42.4 Alternative: Turn right and continue into Milton-Freewater on Highway 11. Rejoin the main route at Mile 48.6.

42.6   Pass through a short tunnel. Highway 11 buzzes on the hillside above.

47.9   Left on **Highway 11** toward Milton-Freewater at a T intersection.

48.6   Enter Milton-Freewater (all services), population 5,530. Frazier Farmstead Museum (small entrance fee) is three blocks to the right at Fourteenth and Chestnut. Built in 1868, it features a house and furnishings in mint condition, and farm implements.

49.7   Continue north on Highway 11/**South Main Street** in Milton-Freewater.

49.8   Left on **Southwest Fourth Avenue**, and immediately right on **South Elizabeth Street**. Cross Main Street to continue on **North Elizabeth Street**.

50.8   Right on **Northeast Eighth Avenue**, and cross Highway 11 on a bridge.

51.1   Cross a waterway and bear left on **Eastside Road**, following the irrigation ditch.

52.1   Pass the bell-topped former Umatilla schoolhouse on the left. Wind through orchards with wheat fields in the background.

53.4   Left on an unmarked road toward Walla Walla at a Y intersection. (Spofford is a mile to the right.)

53.8   Right toward Walla Walla at a T intersection (unmarked).

54.1   Pass the bell-topped Tumalum School, circa 1911, on the right.

55.5   Right on **Peppers Road**, crossing over an unmarked bridge.

57.1   Cross **South Ninth Street**.

57.8   Continue on **Dalles Military Road** at a stop sign. Intersect with Highway 125, but keep it on your left, even after route name becomes **Taumarson Road**.

59.4   Left on **Ninth Avenue (Plaza Way)**, and immediately right on **Prospect Road** to enter the Walla Walla city limits (all services).

59.9   Left on **Third Avenue** at a stop sign, and immediately right, to stay with **Prospect**.

60.5   Left on **Howard Street** at a four-way stop. Pass the Oddfellows Cemetery on the left.

61.9   Bear left on **Park Street**.

62.5   Boyer Avenue; Whitman College Campus. For city center, follow Boyer to Main Street and turn left.

DAY SEVEN: WALLA WALLA TO DAYTON—27 MILES

0.0   Boyer Avenue and Park Street on the Whitman College campus. Head east on **Boyer Avenue**.

0.4   Left on **North Clinton Street**.
0.9   Cross a diagonal railroad track
      and cross Highway 12.

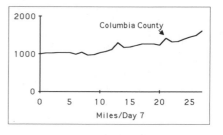

1.2   Bear left on **Lower Waitsburg Road** at a Y intersection with Middle Waitsburg Road.
6.0   Bear left at an unmarked Y intersection (after a downhill) to stay with Lower Waitsburg Road. A sign on the right points to the Howard Smith Ranch.
14.2 Right on **Highway 124** toward Waitsburg at a T intersection where the Lewis and Clark Trail goes left.
19.2 Enter Waitsburg (all services). Near city center, Highway 124 merges into Highway 12. Continue toward Dayton, passing the historic Preston-Shaffer Mill site. Immediately west of the Main Street bridge on the river, the mill's first stones, brought in a sailing ship around Cape Horn, are displayed in Coppei Park (Second and Coppei).
19.8 Pass the state's oldest grange, circa 1873, on the right.
20.3 Enter Columbia County.
22.7 Pass Lewis and Clark Trail State Park (campground, interpretative kiosk, bird-watching trail, water, rest rooms).
27.0 Enter Dayton (all services), population 2,600. Town center is a mile further. Dayton is the site of the state's first territorial high school, and the state's oldest train depot and courthouse.

DAY EIGHT: DAYTON TO CENTRAL FERRY STATE PARK—28.6 MILES

0.0   Dayton, Columbia County Courthouse. Continue north on Highway 12.
6.7   Begin a 3-mile, 6 percent downhill grade.
9.7   Cross the Tucannon River.
14.4 Pass Highway 261, the turnoff to Starbuck, on the left.

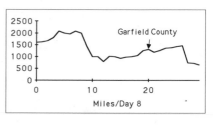

20.7 Enter Garfield County.
22.7 Cross the Pataha River and climb a short rise, bearing left on **Highway 127** (toward Colfax and Central Ferry State Park). About 20 miles to the right is Pomeroy, the seat and sole community of Garfield County.
23.7 Top Kuhl Ridge and sail down a 5 percent grade. Rollers continue for almost 5 miles, then the terrain drops to the Snake River.
27.7 **Alternative:** If you parked at John's Central Ferry Cafe and Store, turn right on Lower Deadman Road. Do not cross the Snake River.
28.1 Cross the Snake River.
28.6 Left into Central Ferry State Park. End of tour.

◆

8. CENTRAL WASHINGTON BLUEBIRD LOOP

Jean Henderson

Distance: 152 miles
Terrain: rolling hills with a mountain pass and a steep canyon
Total cumulative elevation gain: 7,976 feet
Recommended time of year: April–October
Recommended starting time: 9:00 A.M.
Allow: 3 days
Points of interest: Yakama Nation Cultural Center, Toppenish; American Hop Museum, Toppenish; Railroad and Steam Museum, Toppenish; Simcoe & Western Train Excursions, Toppenish; Goldendale Observatory State Park, Goldendale; Presby Mansion, Goldendale; bluebird houses; Yakima Valley vineyards

PUBLIC TRANSPORTATION
Air: several airlines serve Yakima, 17 miles from the starting point; travel the Yakima Valley Highway (12) to Toppenish
Train: none available

PRACTICAL INFORMATION
Key contacts: Yakima Valley Visitors and Convention Bureau, 509-575-1300; Goldendale Chamber of Commerce, 509-773-3400

STARTING POINT
Toppenish, intersection of Highway 97 and Highway 22: Request overnight parking at a nearby motel.

A little-known community where the bluebirds outnumber the residents, a giant telescope for celestial viewing, and bountiful orchards and vineyards spread before glacier-capped mountain peaks are featured on this 3-day, 152-mile central Washington tour.

Begin the adventure in Toppenish, first trading your bicycle for a mule-drawn Conestoga wagon and a narrated tour of the vast murals that paint this town with 1850–1920 history. Every June famous Western artists create another outdoor mural to add to the thirty that already decorate town walls. Take a local train into White Swan, passing hop fields on the way, or explore history in the American Hop Museum and the Rail and Steam Museum. Celebrate Native American history in the Yakama (traditional Indian spelling) Nation Cultural Center.

Pedal out of Toppenish onto the high plateau. The 49 miles toward the Columbia River Gorge should drop to Goldendale, but in reality they roll over hills

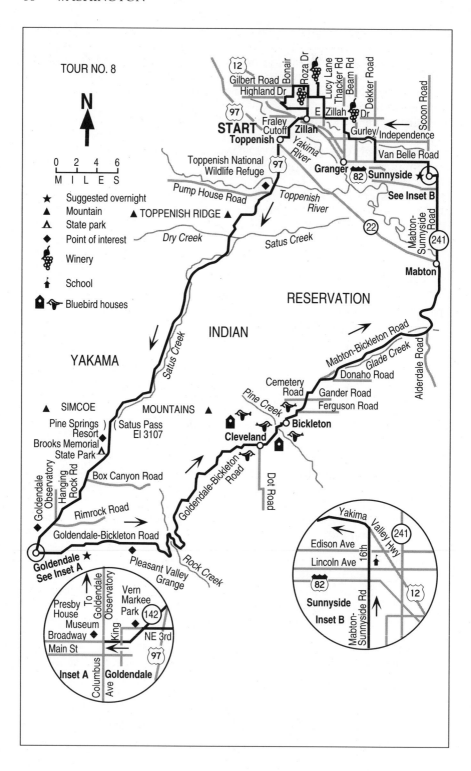

TOUR NO. 8

N

0   2   4   6
M I L E S

★   Suggested overnight
▲   Mountain
△   State park
◆   Point of interest
🍇   Winery
✝   School
🏠🐦   Bluebird houses

▲ TOPPENISH RIDGE ▲

12
97
START
Toppenish
Gilbert Road
Highland Dr
Fraley
Cutoff
Zillah
Bonair
Roza Dr
Lucy Lane
Thacker Rd
Beam Rd
Dekker Road
Scoon Road
E Zillah Dr
Gurley
Independence

Toppenish National
Wildlife Refuge
97
Granger
82 Sunnyside ★
See Inset B
Van Belle Road

Yakima
River

Pump House Road
Toppenish
River

Dry Creek
Satus Creek

22
241
Mabton-
Sunnyside
Road
Mabton

RESERVATION

INDIAN

YAKAMA

Satus Creek

Mabton-Bickleton Road
Glade Creek
Alderdale Road

▲   SIMCOE

Pine Springs
Resort
Brooks Memorial
State Park

MOUNTAINS   ▲

Satus Pass
El 3107

Cemetery
Road
Gander Road
Ferguson Road
Donaho Road
Bickleton

Cleveland

Pine Creek

Goldendale Observatory
Hanging Rock Rd

Box Canyon Road

Rimrock Road

Goldendale-Bickleton Road

Goldendale-Bickleton
Road

Dot Road

Goldendale
See Inset A ★

Pleasant Valley
Grange

Rock Creek

See Inset A

Presby
House
Museum
Broadway ◆
Main St

To Goldendale
Observatory

King
Columbus Ave

Vern
Markee
Park
142
NE 3rd
97

Inset A   Goldendale

Yakima Valley Hwy
241

Edison Ave
Lincoln Ave
16th

82

Sunnyside
Inset B

Mabton-
Sunnyside Rd

12

and climb 3,100-foot Satus Pass. Visit an unusual state park, 1.5 miles north of Goldendale, where casual visitors and amateur astronomers can peer into a 24-inch reflecting telescope. View the constellations or enjoy a daytime panorama of the mountains. On the way peek into the gracious 1902 Presby House where twenty rooms billow with well-preserved furnishings, and include photos of ancient Indian fishing grounds at now-flooded Celilo Falls on the Columbia River.

On Day Two strike out for Bickleton, the world's bluebird capital. Watch for fluttering wings because about 1,500 bluebirds return here annually from their winter in Mexico. Volunteers over a 150-square-mile area refurbish the distinctive blue-roofed houses atop fence posts, in trees, or on buildings. From Valentine's Day to late October, red-breasted Western and all-blue Mountain Bluebirds happily fill the wide-open countryside with delightful melodies. Bickleton residents annually join their neighbors in Cleveland in dusting off the wooden horses of a rare, 1928 carousel that runs on a track at the Pioneer Picnic.

Climb gradually into Bickleton, enjoy a 1,075-foot drop into Rock Creek Canyon, and expect a reward for the long, 2,100-foot pump up the other side. Collect after Bickleton when the route crosses the Horse Heaven Hills where wild mustangs once roamed, then plunges suddenly into the broad, irrigated Yakima Valley. On the plateau anticipate surprises like undulating seas of desert grasses and wild sage scents on a brisk tail wind.

Finish the tour on Day Three, passing through vineyards, hop farms, asparagus fields, orchards, and livestock areas. Above the green patchwork landscape, Mount Adams and Mount Rainier wear their glacier coats. A few low ridges punctuate the gentle terrain. Linger in the sunshine or at local wineries to treasure the scenery. Admire the 1914 Zillah Community Church with its beautiful stained-glass windows, then end the day by crossing the Yakima River to Toppenish and one more look at its remarkable murals.

MILEAGE LOG
DAY ONE: TOPPENISH TO GOLDENDALE—48.9 MILES

0.0 Toppenish, junction of Highway 97 and 97N and Highway 22. Proceed south on **Highway 97** toward Goldendale.

3.7 Pass through the Toppenish National Wildlife Refuge.

4.5 Pass Pump House Road on the right. This is an unimproved road to the refuge headquarters.

27.6 Enter Klickitat County.

33.0 Enter a forest thick with ponderosa pine and scrub oak.

34.0 Crest Satus Pass (3,107 feet).

36.5 Pass Pine Springs Resort (restaurant, store, gift shop) on the right.

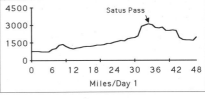

36.6 Pass the Brooks Memorial State Park entrance, nestled in the Simcoe foothills.

46.2 Bear left to stay with Highway 97 as Hanging Rock Road comes in on the right. Columns of lava frozen by time hang overhead.

47.2 Pass a rest area access on the left. A unique house on the right has a pedestrian bridge in back and buffalo in the field beside it. A sign ahead welcomes you to Goldendale.

47.9   Right on **Highway 142 West** toward Goldendale.

48.1   Pass Northeast Third Avenue on the left where the Day Two route begins. On the right is Vern Markee Park (information kiosk). Road name changes to **Broadway** as it enters Goldendale (1,635 feet), the Klickitat County seat.

48.9   Goldendale Junction. Turn left to reach the city center. Or cross Columbus Avenue for a side trip to the Presby House Museum, fairgrounds, and the Columbia Gorge. Turn right for a short side trip to the Goldendale Observatory.

DAY TWO: GOLDENDALE TO SUNNYSIDE—71 MILES

0.0   Goldendale, intersection of East Broadway/Highway 142 West and Columbus Avenue. Backtrack on **Broadway**.

0.8   Right on **Northeast Third Avenue** toward Bickleton. After leaving town, the road is renamed the **Goldendale–Bickleton Road**.

2.0   Look back to views of Mount Adams and Mount Hood.

11.5   Pass the Pleasant Valley Grange on the right.

14.4   Start dropping into the Rock Creek Canyon.

16.4   Pass a picnic area by the river in the bottom of the canyon.

30.0   Begin passing distinctive bluebird houses on fence posts, in trees, and near houses and barns.

32.6   Keep straight, passing Dot Road from the Columbia Gorge on the right. Enter Cleveland, where the Pioneer Picnic carousel is stored. It was purchased from a Portland, Oregon, amusement park.

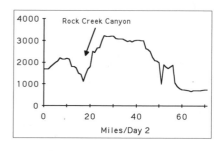

33.1   Pass the Cleveland Cemetery on the left. It appears large for the population density, but serves the entire plateau.

35.2   Cross Pine Creek bridge. Detailed doodling on the road's surface indicates light traffic density.

36.0   Enter Bickleton (store, cafe, post office), 100 residents and 1,500 migrating bluebirds. The tavern is in one of the state's oldest buildings (1882). Road name changes to **Pleasant Valley Road** as it leaves town.

36.7   Left on the **Mabton Highway** at Bickleton High School.

40.1   Enter Yakima County.

41.4   Stay straight as the road name appears to change to **Glade Road**.

49.0   Pass through an unidentified, sleepy settlement (no services).

54.2   Keep straight toward Mabton. On a windy day the aroma of sagebrush wafts through the air.

54.9   Enjoy a view into the irrigated Lower Yakima Valley, then drop down a big hill, passing through cherry orchards, then hop fields.

61.9   Enter Mabton (all services), population 1,250.

62.2   Left on **Highway 22 West** toward Sunnyside (unmarked) at a stop sign adjacent to a pedestrian overpass.

Mount Adams, wearing its coat of glaciers, appears in the distance above the beautiful Yakima Valley. (Photo: Jean Henderson)

62.3   Right on **Highway 241**, immediately after crossing a series of railroad tracks. As it leaves Mabton, this road becomes **Mabton–Sunnyside Road**.

65.7   Pass Wanita Grange on the left and cross I-82.

69.2   Enter Sunnyside (all services), population 11,000.

69.5   Cross Lincoln Avenue at a stoplight. The road name changes almost immediately to **Sixteenth Street** and passes the high school.

70.3   Left on **Yakima Valley Highway (Highway 12)** toward Granger.

71.0   Stop light with city center to the left. Founder Ben Snipes's cabin and the city museum are nearby in Central Park.

DAY THREE: SUNNYSIDE TO TOPPENISH—31.6 MILES

0.0   Sunnyside, junction of Sixteenth Street and Yakima Valley Highway. Proceed out of town on the **Yakima Valley Highway (Highway 12)**.

0.3   Right on **Scoon Road** (labeled First Avenue on the opposite side of the highway).

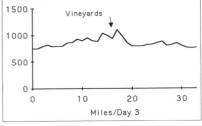

1.3   Left on **Van Belle Road**.

5.5   Enjoy a nice view of the fields and both Mount Rainier and Mount Adams.

6.4   Right on **Dekker Road**.

8.3   Cross an irrigation canal and immediately turn left on **Gurley Road** (Independence Road). Enter a cattle-producing area.

10.4   Cross Beam Road, riding up and down low ridges through orchards and hop farms, then pass Lincoln Grange and a winery.

11.2   Right on **Thacker Road**. Immediately cross the Sunnyside Irrigation Canal (unmarked) and bear left briefly on **Eaker Road**, which bends right and becomes Thacker again.

13.2   Left on **East Zillah Drive**.

   13.2   Side Trip: Turn right on **East Zillah Drive** to visit a winery on the right in 0.4 mile. Backtrack to Thacker Road, continuing straight ahead with East Zillah Drive to rejoin the main route.

14.6   Right on **Lucy Lane,** just prior to crossing the Sunnyside Canal (unmarked) again. Climb through the orchards. In season, bright foil ribbons flutter and air guns pop to frighten birds from the crops.

16.5   Left on **Highland Drive** at a T intersection.

17.1   Stay on Highland Drive at the intersection with Vintage Road.

   17.1   Side Trip: Turn right on **Vintage Road** to visit a winery in 1.6 miles.

   18.5   Left into the winery. After your visit, backtrack to Vintage Road, turn right, and roll downhill.

   21.1   Right on **Highland Drive** to rejoin the main route, as pavement ends on Vintage Road.

18.1   Right on **Roza Drive** (unmarked).

19.1   Left on **Gilbert Road** (unmarked).

   19.1   Side Trip: Turn left into a gravel driveway for a winery. Umbrella tables and chairs on a broad lawn with expansive mountain and vineyard views, plus availability of soft drinks, juice, wine, and some foods, make this a pleasant stop. Backtrack to Gilbert Road and turn left to rejoin the main route.

20.9   Left on **North Bonair Road**.

21.9   Right on **Highland Drive**, and cross the Sunnyside Canal.

22.4   Left on **Bella Terra Road**.

23.2   Right on **Barbee Road** at a T intersection, and immediately left on **Yakima Valley Highway (Highway 12)** toward Zillah. There is a wide shoulder, but it is very rough.

25.5   Right on **Roza Drive** into Zillah.

26.0   Enter Zillah, where Roza Drive is **Fifth Street**. Zillah is named for the daughter of a Northern Pacific Railroad president.

26.1   Pass the Zillah Community Church (built in 1910) on the right, with its outstanding stained-glass windows. Informal tours are given on request.

26.6   Right on **First Avenue** at a T intersection, and pass the Zillah Cemetery on the left.

27.5   Cross I-82 and the Yakima River; enter the Yakama Indian Reservation.

28.7   Road name changes to **Fraley Cutoff**.

29.6   Right on **East Toppenish Avenue**.

30.3   Enter downtown Toppenish, passing the Old Timer's Plaza and murals.

30.5   Right on **West First Avenue**, location of a visitors information center.

31.0   Left on **Highway 97** at a stop light. Pass Pioneer Park on the left.

31.6   Junction of Highway 97 and Highway 22. End of tour.

Near Bickleton some 1,500 western and mountain bluebirds return to their tiny birdhouses each February. (Photo: Jim Larson)

---

9. PACIFIC OCEAN BEACH EXCURSION

Jean Henderson

Distance: 152 miles
Terrain: rolling or flat, with a few hills
Total cumulative elevation gain: 3,405 feet
Recommended time of year: April–early October
Recommended starting time: 8:30 A.M.
Allow: 3 days; layover days recommended
Points of interest: Light Ship Columbia, Astoria; Fort Columbia Historical State Park, Chinook; Cape Disappointment Lighthouse, circa 1856; North Head Lighthouse, circa 1898; sixteen murals, Long Beach Peninsula; Oysterville National Historic District; Willapa Bay Oyster Interpretative Center, Nahcotta; Cranberry Museum, Long Beach Peninsula; Grays River Covered Bridge, Grays River; Redmen Hall, Skamokawa; Julia Butler Hansen Columbian Whitetail Deer Refuge

◆ ◆ ◆

PUBLIC TRANSPORTATION
Air: commercial service is not available to Cathlamet
Train: Amtrak serves Kelso–Longview; for a bicycle-friendly route to Cathlamet, see *Bicycling the Backroads of Southwest Washington* by Erin and Bill Woods (The Mountaineers, 1994)

PRACTICAL INFORMATION
Key contacts: Greater Astoria Chamber of Commerce, 503-325-6311; Fort Columbia Youth Hostel, 360-777-8755; Long Beach Peninsula Visitors Bureau, 800-451-2542; Skamokawa Vista Park (Wahkiakum Port District), 360-795-8605

STARTING POINT
Cathlamet, Strong Park, Division and River streets: From I-5 take Exit 39 (Kelso/Highway 4) and continue west through Longview and 25 miles along the Columbia River to Cathlamet. Turn left on Greenwood Road and almost immediately right on Butler Avenue, then left on Division Street. Park adjacent to the Strong Museum or behind the Wahkiakum County Court House, 0.1 mile farther.

Washington and Oregon offer many alluring jewels and a legacy of spellbinding history. Take this 3-day tour for a large measure of each, but do not add water: there is an abundance of it here already. Most of the 152 miles are along the shores of the Columbia River, near Pacific Ocean or Willapa Bay beaches, over a wealth of rivers, streams, and sloughs, and in wildlife refuges and estuaries. In short, the water-oriented scenery constantly reels past on a tour so jam-packed with things to do that extra days are definitely advised.

Set out from Cathlamet, the petite seat of Washington's smallest county. Pedal onto Puget Island where farms span the short road to the last remaining ferry on the Columbia River. Operated since 1925, the ferry partnered in earlier days with a Buick and a second boat to carry passengers between Westport, Oregon, and Cathlamet. On the island, passengers rode in the Buick.

Nip in and out of tiny Westport, and shortly abandon the highway bower for the even more shady Clatsop State Forest. Spy on bald eagles, marsh and red-tailed hawks, blue herons, mergansers, and deer and elk in the estuaries and wetlands. In stately Astoria, pass the exact site of the 1811 fort at Fifteenth and Exchange streets, harking back to the elegant era of John Jacob Astor and the Hudson's Bay Company.

Return to Washington on the longest continuous-truss bridge in North America. Pick up the trail of Lewis and Clark again and probe Fort Columbia Historical Park. Then continue to steep in history on a 3-mile side trip above the Pacific Ocean. Hike to lighthouses, contemplate rolling seas, and visit

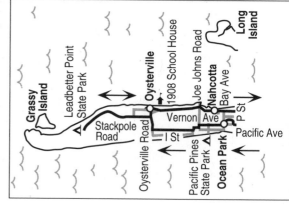

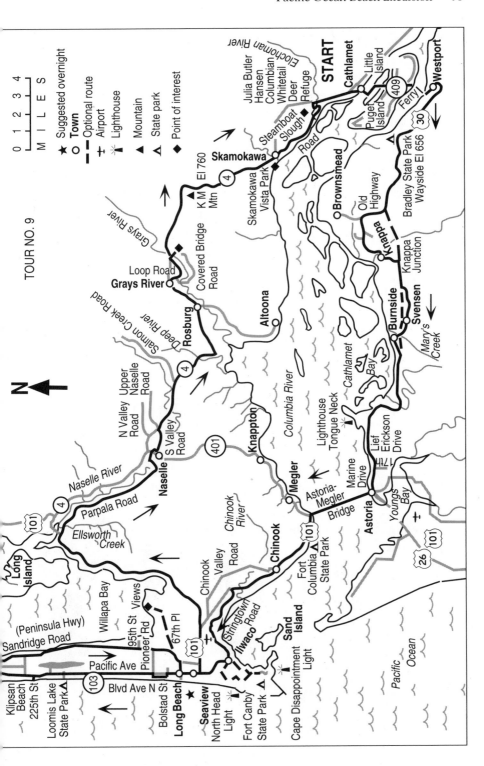

TOUR NO. 9

the Lewis and Clark Interpretative Center in Fort Canby. Lewis and Clark first touched the Pacific Ocean near here in 1805. Here, in the "graveyard of the Pacific," more than 2,000 vessels have been damaged or sunk and approximately 700 lives lost negotiating the Columbia River bar.

Enter the Fort Canby Loop and the Long Beach Peninsula through Ilwaco, the end of the line for the peninsula's famed narrow-gauge Clamshell Railroad. Now a part of history, the fully restored depot is among exhibits in Ilwaco's Heritage Museum, opened in 1983. Continue north to Long Beach, watching for the sixteen murals that chronicle the area's history. The first was completed in 1986, but most were painted for the state's 1989 centennial.

The world's longest beach, Long Beach is a unique mixture of urban amenities, campgrounds, dunes, cranberry bogs, estuaries, and historic sites. End Day One here, and spend Day Two touring the peninsula. Long on activities and views, it stretches north to Leadbetter Point, a Pacific Flyway stopover for nearly 100 species of birds. At its north end, Oysterville whispers of a lively past as the county seat, when, except for San Francisco, it was the richest town in the west. For thirty-eight years it thrived on harvesting and shipping the native oysters that lay thickly in Willapa Bay. The stagecoach brought full loads of passengers to Oysterville along the 28 miles of hard-packed beach, avoiding the incoming tide by traveling up over the dunes. The arduous trip ended in 1893 when the South Bend raiders took the county records home. Oysterville fought back unsuccessfully, the native oysters died in two unusually cold winters, the town withered, and today it is a National Historic Place.

The Pacific Ocean Beach Excursion begins with a ferry trip across the mighty Columbia River. (Photo: Ken Winkenweder)

About 4 miles south, oysters still bankroll about $20 million of the local economy annually. Japanese varieties are cultured in Nahcotta in the pristine Willapa Bay estuary. Watch for mounds of bleached shells that mark the area of the interpretive center, a shellfish laboratory exhibit, and a renowned restaurant. After that, move on to cranberries. They blush in the bogs in the spring and provide a fascinating harvest show for visitors in late fall. Taste samples in the Cranberry Museum on Pioneer Road.

On Day Three reluctantly depart the peninsula to hug the shores of Willapa Bay. Visualize the rare, ancient grove of red cedars on nearby Long Island. While only a 2.5-mile trek, the 274 acres of trees are accessible only by private boat. The ultimate in old-growth, over the last 3,000 to 4,000 years this climax forest has reached a balance of the most enduring plants suited to the site. A short distance further, desert US Highway 101 for the quiet backroad into Naselle, a Finnish town bearing a Chinook name meaning "protected or sheltered." Despite several segments of bisecting highways, Naselle residents hear croaking frogs and bugling elk from their back steps.

Wetlands, trees, quaint communities, and more rivers, streams, and sloughs highlight the remainder of the tour. Between Rosburg and the Columbia River, entire communities literally were "rained in" in winters of yore. Dependent on water routes, residents occasionally risked walking the railroad track used for timber hauls. At regular intervals, anxious ears were pressed to the rails to sense warning vibrations of an oncoming train. Near Grays River, pass Washington's only remaining covered bridge on a public road. Built in 1905, the Grays River Bridge is now on the National Register of Historic Places.

Enter sleepy Skamokawa, "smoke over water," with its back to highway tourists. Established fifteen years prior to Highway 4, it continues to look to interconnecting waterways that funnel drifting fog. Perched on the hillside is Redmen Hall, a Queen Anne-style structure built in 1894 as the Central School. The Order of Redmen, which owned the building at one time, purportedly are descendants of men who played roles of Indians in the American Revolution's Boston Tea Party.

At Skamokawa, begin a restful slide along the Columbia River through the Julia Butler Hansen Columbian Whitetail Deer Refuge. Conclude the tour on a high note, catching one more view of the Lewis and Clark Trail. Then, inspired by the beauty and history of this busy coastal tour, drop back into tranquil Cathlamet.

MILEAGE LOG
DAY ONE: CATHLAMET TO LONG BEACH—57.9 MILES

0.0   Cathlamet, Strong Park at River and Division streets, adjacent to the 1850 home of Judge William Strong, now a museum. The short riverfront walking trail leads to the Elochoman Marina. Bicycle upriver on **River Street**, passing the Wahkiakum County Courthouse on the left. Rest rooms and water are available 24 hours in the Annex Building.

0.1   Bear slightly left on **Broadway** at a stop sign, then jog immediately right on **Main Street**/Highway 409 South, continuing toward the ferry. City Hall is almost straight ahead, with the Pioneer Church immediately behind it. The historic church's upper hall slants toward the speaker's podium, an unusual design.

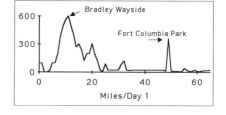

0.4   Cross the Columbia Channel to Little Island. Use the wooden sidewalk on the right side of the bridge. The sign welcoming you to Puget Island is premature.

2.0   Cross Birnie's Slough to Puget Island.

2.3   Pass the Puget Island Grange (store), founded in 1928, on the left.

3.7   Cross West Sunny Sands Road where Highway 409 ends on the ferry dock. Bicyclists ride free on the ferry that departs every 15 minutes daily, 5:00 A.M. to 10:00 P.M.

3.8   Exit the ferry, continuing straight ahead to Oregon Highway 30.

4.0   Cross Plympton Creek and pass through Westport (limited services).

4.2   Right on **Highway 30**.

8.7   Pass **Bradley State Park Wayside** (water, rest rooms) at 656 feet, with views of Puget Island, Cathlamet, and the Columbia River Valley.

13.7   Right on the **Old Highway** (unmarked) toward Brownsmead. Enter the Clatsop State Forest.

14.9   Continue straight ahead toward Knappa at the four-way intersection. The roadway is rough temporarily.

   14.9 Alternative: To save 2.5 miles or to avoid high water (if it has been raining), stay on Highway 30 into Astoria. Rejoin the main route at Mile 33.0.

16.0   Pass the picturesque Knappa Dock with Columbia River views and a network of estuaries. North of this area is a great blue heron rookery on Karlson Island.

16.2   Pass through a three-way intersection.

19.5   Pass the Knappa Cemetery.

19.8   Left at a T intersection on **Old Highway 30** (unmarked).

20.0   Right on **Highway 30**, a marked section of the Lewis and Clark Trail.

21.3   Left on **Old Highway 30** and parallel the new highway. Pavement may be rough.

21.7   Cross Koppiasch Road.

23.7   Enter Svensen. Cross Pearson Road and continue straight through town.

24.4   Continue straight ahead, ignoring the opportunity to return to Highway 30.

25.0   Cross Maki Road.

25.5   Cross Highway 30 at Mary's Creek and enter Burnside (limited services). Cross Labeck Road to a sweeping view of the Columbia River's delta and Washington's shoreline.

26.4   Pass a bird sanctuary on the right.

26.9   Right on **Highway 30** toward Astoria.

33.0   Enter Astoria (all services). Town center and the 4.4-mile-long Astoria–Megler Bridge over the Columbia River are straight ahead. Built in 1966 for $24.5 million, the structure is in the Guinness Book of World Records as the longest continuous-truss bridge in North America.

36.1   Stay right with **Lief Erickson Drive**.

36.4   Pass 17th Street on the left where the road name becomes **Marine Drive**. Outside the Maritime Museum and Park on the right sits the *Lightship Columbia*, the last of its kind on the Pacific Coast, and maintained in fully operational condition.

36.5   **Side Trip:** To visit the Astoria Column, approximately 2 miles round trip, turn left on Sixteenth Street, then right on Lexington Avenue, left on Fifteenth Street, and left immediately at the Pioneer Cemetery on Coxcomb Hill Road. Dedicated in 1926, the Astoria Column is inscribed with all events that led to establishing American claims to the Northwest Territory. From the top of its 164 steps, a sweeping panorama includes the Pacific Ocean, estuaries and the mouth of the Columbia River, and Mount St. Helens. Backtrack to rejoin the main route.

37.1   Stay right to approach the Astoria–Megler Bridge. It is a free ride to Washington. The toll was removed on Christmas 1993.

41.0   Left on **US Highway 101** toward Ilwaco and Long Beach.

41.9   Pass an information signboard on the left noting that the Columbia River and the Pacific Ocean meet near here.

43.2   Pass historic St. Mary's Church on the right. Built nearly a century after Lewis and Clark camped next door, the church is on land donated by Patrick James McGowan, for whom a nearby settlement was named.

43.3   Pass full-size carvings of Lewis and Clark in a park with a picnic table on the right. From here in November 1805, they saw the Pacific Ocean breakers and realized for the first time they had accomplished their mission for President Jefferson. Across the river the Astoria Column juts 125 feet skyward.

43.8   Enter a tunnel. Push the button to warn motorists of cyclists inside. **Caution:** Be aware of the drainage ditch on the far right inside the tunnel. There is an immediate left turn at the exit.

44.0   Left to **Fort Columbia Historical State Park** (water, interpretative walks, youth hostel, picnicking, no camping). The Chinook Indians and Good Chief Comcomly lived here, and in 1792 Captain Robert Gray dropped anchor nearby when discovering the Columbia River. A coastal fort from 1896 to the end of World War I, the area has remains of gun mounts that guarded the river entrance.

44.1   Pass under a stone archway and climb through the park on the one-way loop road.

44.8   Intersect the incoming one-way road. There is rough pavement in places.

44.9   Left on **US Highway 101** at a stop sign.

46.0   Enter Chinook, where in the late 1880s fish traps on posts dotted the waterfront.

46.2   **Side Trip:** Turn right on Houchen Street for 0.5 mile to Washington's first salmon hatchery. See and feed large, jumping salmon and learn how they are raised. Established on this site in 1885, the hatchery was operated by the state from 1895 to 1935. Now a vocational tool for area schools, it is operated by a nonprofit organization that raises about 5 million salmon eggs here annually. Backtrack to rejoin the main route, turn right on US Highway 101.

46.8   Left with **US Highway 101** at a highway junction toward Ilwaco and Long Beach.

48.7   Cross the Chinook River and immediately turn left on **Stringtown Road**. Pedal along the Columbia River with groomed lawns on one side and views into Oregon on the other.

50.7   Pass the Port of Ilwaco Airport on the right.

51.2   Cross a slough and immediately turn left at a T intersection on **US Highway 101** toward Ilwaco.

52.7   Enter Ilwaco (all services). US Highway 101 becomes **Spruce Street** and passes a monument to Captain Gray.

53.1   Left on **Williams Street** and immediately right on **Lake Street**. Pass the Heritage Museum, with the restored Clamshell Railway Depot among its exhibits, on the left.

53.2   Right on **First Avenue Southwest** and immediately left (in one block) at the stop light on **Highway 103** toward Seaview and Long Beach. At the light First Avenue Southwest becomes US Highway 101 North and heads away from the peninsula.

   53.3 Side Trip: Turn left on Highway 100 (North Head Drive) for a 3-mile loop to two historic lighthouses and the Lewis and Clark Interpretative Center in Fort Canby State Park. Hike the jetty between the Pacific Ocean and the Columbia Bar. Carry food. The loop returns to Mile 60.2 on the main route.

53.5   Pass a memorial viewpoint on the right.

54.2   Pass a mural on the right.

56.3   Enter Seaview (services available).

   56.7 Side Trip: Turn left on Thirty-eighth Place for Pacific Ocean beach access. Backtrack to the main route on Highway 103 and continue into Long Beach.

56.8   Pass the Long Beach Peninsula Visitors Center on the right. US Highway 101 heads east from this intersection.

57.1   Seaview. Pass the historic Shelburne Inn (restaurant, lodging) on the left. Established in 1896 as a retreat for visitors from Portland, Oregon, the inn has operated continuously since. Travelers took a sternwheeler up the Columbia River to Astoria, ferried to Megler on the Washington side, then rode the narrow-gauge Clamshell Railroad to the Shelburne Station.

57.8   Pass Gazebo Park on the left. Panels highlight history with photos and information about the peninsula. Murals decorate surrounding buildings.

57.9   Long Beach. Bolstad Street and Pacific Avenue/Highway 103. To the left is the beach. A 2,300-foot-long boardwalk (lighted at night) runs south along the Pacific Ocean to Tenth Street. Bicycles are prohibited on the boardwalk and the fine is stiff.

DAY TWO: LONG BEACH PENINSULA LOOP—38.1 MILES

0.0   Long Beach, Bolstad Street (First Street) and Pacific Avenue. Turn left (west) on **Bolstad Street** and immediately right on **Boulevard Avenue North**.

1.3   Right on **Pioneer Road** (may be labeled 95th Street) and immediately left on **Pacific Avenue**. **Note:** The Cranberry Museum is 0.8 mile ahead on Pioneer Road, but equally accessible from the peninsula's other side.

5.9   Pass the access road to Loomis Lake State Park (water, beach access, rest rooms, small camping area, no views) on the left.

6.2   Pass an unimproved road on the right to Loomis Lake, the peninsula's largest and the only one stocked with fish.

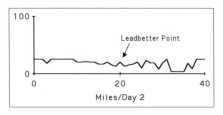

8.1   Left on **225th Street**. The 1891 Klipsan Beach historic lifesaving station is immediately left. Backtrack to Pacific Avenue.

8.5   Left on **Pacific Avenue**.

9.1   Right on **P Street** to enter Ocean Park (all services), established in 1883. I. A. Clark, the partner with R. H. Espy in founding Oysterville, led the movement for a religious community. Today Ocean Park has two religious camps and several churches. Early deeds prohibited saloons and like establishments.

9.8   Right on **Vernon Avenue**/Pacific Avenue.

10.5   Cross Bay Avenue at the blinking light, following the bicycle route on Vernon Avenue.

11.1   Pass access to Pacific Pines State Park (rest rooms, camping, water, beach access, no views) on the left.

12.2   Left briefly on **Joe Johns Road** at a T intersection and immediately right on **N Place**, which becomes **295th Street**.

12.7   Right on **I Street**. Ride through stubby pine trees.

15.0   Right on **Oysterville Road**.

15.8   Left on Stackpole Road/Highway 103 toward Leadbetter Point State Park.

19.5   Pavement ends at Leadbetter Point State Park (pit toilet, hiking trails, information kiosk, pesky insects, no camping). After exploring the park, backtrack to Oysterville Road.

23.2   Left on **Oysterville Road**.

23.4   Pass the Oysterville Store and post office (the oldest in the state) and, just beyond, the historic cemetery, all on the right. Explore the side roads and beaches in this area. California redwood in some homes came as ballast in oyster freighters.

23.5   Cross Highway 103, continuing toward the beach for one block. Turn right on an unmarked road.

23.8   Historic Oysterville's one-room schoolhouse (1908).

24.0   Oysterville's historic church (1892).

24.4   Left on **Highway 103** as the unmarked road merges. Pedal south.

27.3   Enter Nahcotta (rest rooms, water, oyster bed activities, view of Long Island). Pass 275th Place, with boat basin access on the left.

27.4   Left on **273rd Place** toward the Oyster Interpretative Center, oyster-processing businesses, and a restaurant. Backtrack to Highway 103.

27.8   Left on **Highway 103**.

28.0   Pass the state Shellfish Laboratory on the left. While not open to the public, information about oysters is posted and related on a taped message.

28.2   Bear left and cross Bay Avenue, ignoring the opportunity to return to Ocean Park with Highway 103. Continue south on **Sandridge Road**, passing trees, cranberry bogs, and rhododendron nurseries. Watch for deer and birds.

Oysterville on the Long Beach Peninsula whispers of a lively past when, except for San Francisco, it was the richest town in the West. (Photo: Ken Winkenweder)

35.1 Side Trip: Turn left on Sixty-seventh Place and proceed 2.4 miles to the end of the road to the Reikkola Unit of Willapa National Wildlife Refuge (may be a fee at the gate; closed October 1–March 31). The route climbs a couple of hills to look out across Willapa Bay. Backtrack to the main route on Sandridge Road.

36.6   Right on **US Highway 101** toward Seaview. The Long Beach Visitors Information Center sits ahead on the right.
37.2   Right on **Highway 103**.
38.1   Boldstad Street in Long Beach.

DAY THREE: LONG BEACH TO CATHLAMET—57.3 MILES

0.0   Seaview, intersection of Pacific Avenue/Highway 103 and US Highway 101 North. Backtrack on Day One's route from Long Beach to Seaview, then head east on **Highway 101 North** toward Raymond, passing the Long Beach Peninsula Visitors Information Center on the left and cranberry bogs on the right.
1.9   Pass the turnoff for US Highway 101 South toward Astoria on the right.
4.8   Pass the Lewis Unit of Willapa National Wildlife Refuge (rest rooms, water, information) on the left.
10.6   Willapa National Wildlife Refuge. Across the bay is Long Island with its ancient grove of red cedars.
12.7   Right on **Parpala Road** (just before a bridge) toward Naselle, as US Highway 101 North heads to South Bend.

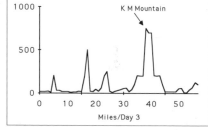
Miles/Day 3

19.9   Cross Highway 401 (unmarked) and continue on **South Valley Road** into Naselle, a Finnish village, and make a sharp right to pass the cemetery on the right at Mile 21.5.
22.7   Right on **Highway 4** (unmarked) toward Rosburg.
24.2   Pass Salmon Creek Park (picnic table, pit toilet, hiking trail, primitive camping) on the left.
24.7   Enter Wahkiakum County at the top of the hill.
26.2   Cross over the Deep River, actually a very deep slough.
29.1   Pass the Rosburg Store (pit toilet, water) on the right. A road goes right, to communities that once were waterbound. Established in 1885, Rosburg now consists of a store, cemetery, and school.
31.0   Enter Grays River. On the right the former creamery building (now Grays River Gallery) hints of dairy beginnings. The covered bridge at Mile 33.0 tells another chapter in the story.
31.3   Right on **Loop Road** in the center of Grays River.
31.8   Left on the **Covered Bridge Road** at a T intersection.
33.0   Grays River Covered Bridge comes into view on the right. This is a photo opportunity of the last covered bridge still in use on a Washington highway. Built in 1905 by a farmer to transport cream to market, the bridge has a 158-foot span and has been altered a couple of times.
33.4   Pass the Grays River Bridge on the right.
33.6   Right on **Highway 4** as Loop Road/Covered Bridge Road ends. **Caution:** Traffic approaching on the left is hard to see.
35.5   Cross bridges spanning the Grays River, sloughs, and wetlands.
38.4   Crest KM Mountain (760 feet).
45.1   Right into **Skamokawa Vista Park** (picnicking, fishing, camping, rest rooms, water) on the Columbia River, passing the office and library on

the left. After visiting the park, backtrack to the park exit and turn right on **Highway 4**.

45.4   Cross Skamokawa Creek, passing Redmen Hall on the left. Built as a school in 1894, the hall's River Life Interpretative Center, meeting facilities, and traveling exhibits are a primary community focus.

50.1   Right on **Steamboat Slough Road** amid mostly vacant Skamokawa buildings. Skamokawa (limited services) maintains its focus on the slough and river.

50.4   Cross the Steamboat Slough, bearing right at the Y intersection to enter the Julia Butler Hansen Columbian Whitetail Deer Refuge. Ride a narrow dike road beside the Columbia River. Watch for oncoming traffic.

55.2   Right on **Highway 4** at a T intersection, leaving the wildlife refuge.

55.3   Cross the Elochoman River.

56.9   Pass a viewpoint of Cathlamet, the Columbia River, and the Lewis and Clark Trail on the right.

57.1   Cathlamet. Turn right on **Greenwood Road**.

57.3   Right on **Butler Avenue** and left on **Division Street** into Strong Park. End of tour.

Cyclists have front-row seats for nature's displays along the byways and backroads of the Great Northwest. (Photo: Behrooz Emam)

OREGON

◆

10. CENTRAL OREGON COAST TO CASCADES LOOP

Allen Throop

Distance: 504 miles
Terrain: hilly, with long climb into Cascade Mountains
Total cumulative elevation gain: 8,300 feet
Recommended time of year: June–September
Recommended starting time: before noon on first day
Allow: 9 days; 5-, 6-, and 7-day shortcut options
Points of interest: Triangle Lake; central Oregon coast; research ship Hero; Umpqua Lighthouse; Smith River; historic Oakland and Albany; Goodpasture, Rochester, Shimanek covered bridges; Belknap Hot Springs; McKenzie River waterfalls; Clear Lake; Sawyer Ice Cave

PUBLIC TRANSPORTATION

Air: commercial airlines serve Eugene's airport; confirm that a bicycle can go as baggage, or ship separately
Train: take Amtrak to Albany; to exit the station, go under the highway overpass on Lyons Street in front of the building; turn left on Third Street toward Corvallis; follow the route described below, beginning on Day Eight, Mile 61.1; at the end of the tour, return to Albany, cross Lyons Street, turn left on Ellsworth, and follow signs to the depot

PRACTICAL INFORMATION

Key contacts: Eugene Visitors Bureau, 503-672-9731; Benton County Fairgrounds (alternate parking), 503-757-1521; Oregon Dunes National Recreation Area, 503-217-3611; Roseburg (Douglas County) Tourist Information, 503-998-6154; Willamette National Forest Supervisor's Office, 503-687-6521; Albany Area Chamber of Commerce, 503-926-1517; Corvallis Area Chamber of Commerce, 503-757-1505

STARTING POINT

Malhon Sweet Airport near Eugene: Southbound on I-5, take Exit 209 and follow Highways 99E and 99 south to the airport. Northbound on I-5, take Exit 195 and head west on Belt Line Highway, then north on Highway 99. Follow the signs to the airport from Highway 99. There is a parking fee.

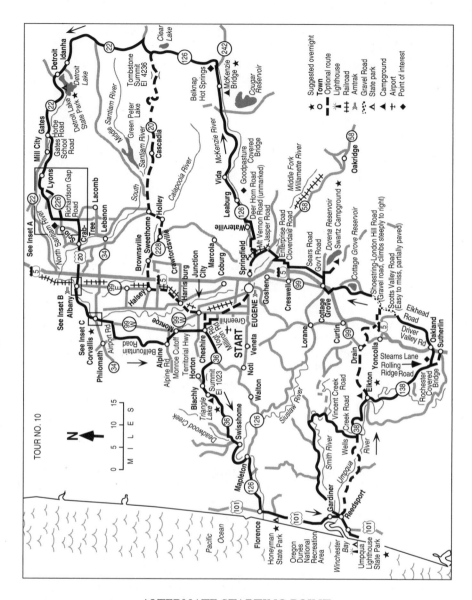

TOUR NO. 10

ALTERNATE STARTING POINT

Benton County Fairgrounds, Corvallis: You can eliminate about 20 miles from the route by beginning in Corvallis. To reach the fairgrounds from I-5 Exit 228, head west on Highway 34 into Corvallis. After crossing the Willamette River and entering Corvallis, continue straight ahead on Harrison Boulevard where Highway 34 goes left. Turn left again on Fifty-third Street, passing fairground buildings on the right. In 0.25 mile, turn right into the South Lot. Park in the South Lot of Benton County Fairgrounds. Call the fairgrounds office in advance at 503-757-1521 regarding parking availability. No liability is assumed for vehicles or their contents. To join the main route from the fairgrounds, ride south on Fifty-third Street for 2.8 miles, turn right on Plymouth Drive for 2 miles, then left on Bellfountain Road at the stop sign, continuing south for 2.5 miles. This intersects with the main route at Day 9, Mile 6.0. Refer to Day Nine, Mile 6.0, for directions to Highway 36 (Day One, Mile 7.0).

SHORTCUTS

To shorten this tour, use Eugene as a hub and follow a choice of spokes. Possibilities include ending the tour on Day Six by riding from Springfield to the Eugene airport for about 270 miles total, or turning west on Highway 20 on Day Seven and riding through Sweet Home and Brownsville back to Eugene for a total of 430 miles.

This tour is a delightful sample of western Oregon. Roll on two wheels across the fertile Willamette Valley and the Coast Range, down the spectacular central Oregon coast, and into Douglas County. Swing back inland and then south through the historic community of Oakland, cross the foothills for a while before turning in to the western Cascade Mountains along the McKenzie River. As the river dwindles, the route steepens and Douglas fir trees give way to hemlocks and finally lodgepole pines.

The challenge of the uphill climb is rewarded with views of the higher Cascade peaks and a long, almost straight downhill run out of the mountains. Leave the mountains behind to spend the last days passing through the rich agricultural land sought 150 years ago by the Oregon Trail pioneers. Although the tour covers the most distance of this book's Oregon routes, the 504 miles are not the most difficult, and shortcuts are offered. The tour is planned for camping on most overnights, but other lodging options are described, when available.

Junction City and Eugene offer all the amenities of home and plenty of options for overnight lodging before or after the tour. Eugene has more of everything, including heavy traffic, but is farther off the main route than is Junction City. The nine-day loop heads north from Eugene's airport, quickly turning west to begin a gradual, but steady, climb along the Long Tom River. The river's name is a corruption of an Indian word. As the route climbs from the Willamette Valley into the Coast Range, roadside scenery changes from grass-seed fields to Christmas tree farms to forests. End Day One in Triangle Lake Park, with overnight alternatives at either Junction City or Florence.

On Day Two, the almost total downhill ride from Triangle Lake to Florence starts with a drop over the ancient landslide that dams Triangle Lake, then winds gradually lower into Mapleton. Towns along the way are small, but bear names significant of their roots. Deadwood refers to trees found in the vicinity and Swisshome reflects the nationality of the town's first residents. The route from Mapleton to Florence is flat, but may seem like a 10 percent uphill slog once the afternoon sea breezes start. Florence, a bustling, picturesque coastal community with all amenities can be the overnight destination for Day Two, but nearby Honeyman State Park is a better choice. Sand dunes and a lake highlight this campground. The cafe building and some of the shelters were constructed by the Civilian Conservation Corps during the Great Depression of the 1930s.

Day Three features a short day and short hills. The ocean is hidden behind the dunes and trees of the Oregon Dunes National Recreational Area. Find

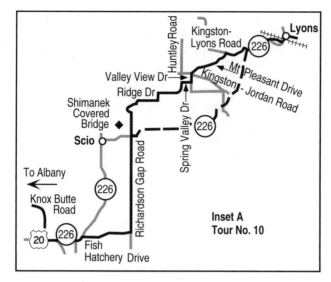

Inset A
Tour No. 10

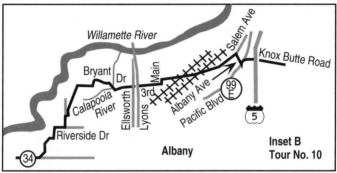

Inset B
Albany   Tour No. 10

trailheads to the dunes or the beach at Honeyman, Oregon Dunes Overlook, and Tahkenitch Lake campground in Siuslaw National Forest. Numerous freshwater lakes behind the dunes are populated with fishermen, and fish, if anglers' stories are true.

To enter Reedsport, cross a narrow-shouldered bridge with a narrow sidewalk. Fortunately, the roadway is flat. Upstream from the bridge, a sail is always unfurled on the *Hero*, a permanently docked Antarctic exploration vessel open for inspection. The Umpqua Lighthouse, the next major landmark, is not open. An overlook in front of it offers a panorama of the coast, sand dunes, the mouth of the Umpqua River, and, at times, whales. Camp in Umpqua Lighthouse State Park for the night.

Begin Day Four with a trip back over that blasted bridge north of Reedsport. Frustration will be short-lived because the Smith River run back into the Coast Range is what bike touring is all about: a good road, a very easy grade, and generally not much traffic. Do not make a wrong turn along here because it is a long ride to any settlements on the side routes. There is a solitary store between Reedsport and Wells Creek. Toward the day's end, drop down from the Vincent Creek saddle on a steep road with sharp curves, then follow the Umpqua River for a gentle 10-mile ride into Elkton. This community offers a good opportunity to dine out, but no motel—plan to camp in the recreational-vehicle (RV) park. The stores are not large, but the restaurants are above average.

Day Five starts with 23 miles of scenery, a challenging hill, and road-hogging log trucks. After a third of the day's cycling is over, stop for cinnamon rolls or cake in the well-preserved town of Oakland, explore the antique shops, fill the water bottles, and then pump up the steep and long Shoestring Road toward Cottage Grove. Test your attention by watching for turnoffs in unexpected places. End the day camping at Dorena Lake in the foothills of the Cascades.

Six days into the tour, reach into the very southern tip of the Willamette Valley where hills are rollers. The ride up the McKenzie River offers numerous restaurants and small stores as you head into the Cascades. Stop to watch boaters and rafters navigating the rapids or fishermen trying to land the big one. Weekend traffic along this stretch of road thunders as heavily as rapids in the river.

On Day Seven Belknap Hot Springs marks the beginning of the steady climb north to Santiam Pass. The springs are open to the public and the resort has food and lodging. Balance the soothing nature of the waters against demands of pedaling uphill after the stop. Campgrounds are frequent between McKenzie Bridge and Mill City. Enjoy the unusual geographic features caused by geologically young lava flows: Sahalie Falls, a forest submerged under Clear Lake, and Sawyer Ice Cave. A brief pedal or a short walk from the main route suffices for each diversion. For any cyclist not pulling a rowboat on a trailer, boat rentals are available for viewing the submerged forest at Clear Lake. End the day at Detroit Lake.

The Day Eight route continues the descent out of the Cascades and crosses the North Santiam River to find quieter surroundings than Highway 20. Pedal a flat road from Mill City to Lyons, then start climbing where the route joins Highway 226. The Shimanek Covered Bridge marks the return to the Willamette Valley. Oregon is the western state with the most surviving covered bridges.

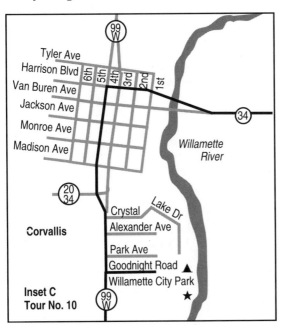

The red Shimanek Covered Bridge has had an especially tumultuous past. Due primarily to erratic high winds and flooding on Thomas Creek, it is the fifth covered bridge on this site.

Fragrant strawberries, other fruits, vegetables, grains, and grasses cover the flat fields on the way west to Albany. Stop to see the Monteith House, built in 1894, in Albany. The wealth generated in this community's heyday as an area commerce center is also displayed in other elegant mansions. Continue southwest, and switch to art in Corvallis. Enjoy the artwork in one Corvallis gallery, the architecture of the old church in which it is located, the statuary in Central Park that it faces, and the generally friendly nature of the city that was given a name from Latin words meaning "heart of the valley."

On Day Nine ride above the Willamette Valley floor in the eastern foothills of the Coast Range. From this elevated viewpoint, the grassy fields and Christmas tree farms of the valley brush the foreground green for the distant blue Cascades and your return to Eugene's airport.

MILEAGE LOG

DAY ONE: EUGENE'S MALHON SWEET AIRPORT
TO TRIANGLE LAKE PARK—32.1 MILES

0.0   Eugene's Malhon Sweet Airport terminal. From the terminal, follow the one-way traffic out of the parking area. Turn left where the first sign reads "TO TERMINAL." This is **Greenhill Road**. Continue on Greenhill past the airport.

4.2   Left on **Milliron Road** at a T intersection.

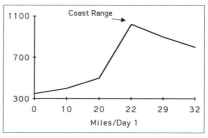

    4.2 Alternative: For supplies or lodging—and about 3 additional miles of flat cycling—go right at this intersection, then left on Highway 99 to Junction City (restaurants, supermarkets, last motel until Florence). When leaving Junction City, return south on Highway 99 toward the airport, then turn right on Highway 36. Rejoin the main route at Mile 7.0.

5.5   Right on **Vogt Road**.

7.0   Left at the T intersection on **Highway 36**.

10.0   Cheshire (small store). As the Willamette Valley gives way to the Coast Range, the crops change from grass seed to Christmas trees.

19.4   Alderwood Wayside (rest rooms, no potable water).

22.4   Summit of the Coast Range (1,023 feet). The climb is steep but short. The Christmas tree farms give way to Douglas fir forests.

30.5   Blachley (small store).

31.2   Community of Triangle Lake (small store).

32.1   Enter Triangle Lake Park (fee, no showers, not elaborate), operated by the Blachley Grange, on the left.

DAY TWO: TRIANGLE LAKE PARK TO
HONEYMAN STATE PARK—43.3 MILES

0.0   Triangle Lake Park. Turn left on **Highway 36**. The steep downhill is part of the ancient landslide that holds back Triangle Lake.

12.4   Deadwood (small store, cafe).

17.5   Swisshome (small store).

25.5   Continue straight ahead in Mapleton as Highway 36 merges into **Highway 126**. From Mapleton to Florence, RV parks are scattered along the

Siuslaw River, which is tidal here.

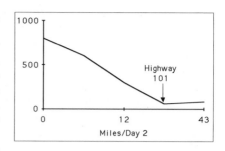

40.0 Left (south) on **US Highway 101** in Florence (supermarkets, motels, restaurants). Visit the old town area adjacent to the harbor for a variety of cafes and shops. On the way out of Florence, the route crosses the Siuslaw River Bridge, a monument to aesthetic bridge architecture, but not a bicycle-friendly design. **Caution:** Both the roadway and the sidewalk are narrow and traffic is heavy. Crosswinds can be strong. Ride carefully on the roadway or walk your bike on the sidewalk.

43.3 Right into Honeyman State Park (cafe, picnic area, camping, showers, swimming, rest rooms, water). Follow the signs to the campground and ask for the location of the biker-hiker area.

DAY THREE: HONEYMAN STATE PARK TO
UMPQUA LIGHTHOUSE STATE PARK—25.2 MILES

0.0 Honeyman State Park. Leave the campground and turn south (right) on **US Highway 101**. Between Honeyman and Gardiner, the numerous access points and campgrounds are part of the Oregon Dunes National Recreation Area.

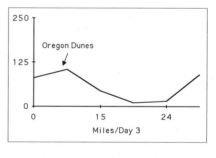

14.9 Gardiner (market, cafe).

17.8 Cross a narrow bridge across the Umpqua River.

18.3 Reedsport (supermarkets, restaurants, motels, RV parks).

22.7 Right on **Salmon Harbor Drive** in the town of Winchester Bay (restaurants, market, lodging, county RV park).

24.0 Left on **Lighthouse Road** at the Y intersection, then ride up a steep hill to the Umpqua Lighthouse and a grand view of the Pacific Ocean.

25.2 Right and down a steep hill into the Umpqua Lighthouse State Park campground (camping, picnic area, water, rest rooms, showers).

DAY FOUR: UMPQUA LIGHTHOUSE
STATE PARK TO ELKTON—72.5 MILES

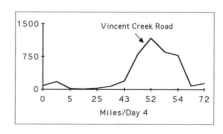

0.0 Umpqua Lighthouse State Park. Following Day Three's mileage log for about 7 miles, backtrack to Reedsport on US Highway 101 past the lighthouse and Winchester Bay. Reedsport has the last supermarket until Cottage Grove. Cross the Umpqua River again.

A trail through the dunes on the central Oregon coast (Photo: Allen Throop)

9.8 **Alternative:** Taking Highway 38 out of Reedsport saves 26 miles, but the route is along a busy highway rather than a bucolic, winding backroad. There is an elk viewing area just east of Reedsport on Highway 38. Rejoin the main route at Mile 54.9.

10.5   Right on the **Smith River Road**. Keep the Smith River on your right for the next 30 miles. The pavement is good, the grade easy, the scenery pleasant, but occasionally the truck traffic is heavy. (Avoid the South Side and North Fork roads.)

29.9   Smith River Store, the only service available between Reedsport and Highway 38.

36.0   Smith River Falls (picnic area, rest rooms, no potable water).

43.0   Right on **Vincent Creek Road**/BLM Road 20-9-33.0, just before a picnic area (rest rooms).

45.0   Stay left on Vincent Creek Road at a Y intersection.

51.3   At the unnamed summit, the road becomes **Wells Creek Road** and a long downhill starts.

52.8   Ferntop Road comes in from the right and Wells Creek Road steepens. **Caution:** There are cattle guards at the bottom of the hill.

54.9   Left on **Highway 38**.

55.3   Wells Creek (store, cafe, RV park).

72.5   Elkton (small store, restaurants, RV park with showers). Camp in the Elkton RV park. The nearest motel is in Sutherlin (see Day Five, Mile 22.0).

DAY FIVE: ELKTON TO DORENA LAKE—67.9 MILES

0.0 Elkton. Continue east on **Highway 38**.

0.3 Right on **Highway 138** toward Sutherlin, immediately after crossing the Elk Creek Bridge. This road of rolling hills can have heavy truck traffic heading for the lumber mills in Sutherlin and Roseburg.

> **0.3 Shortcut:** At the turnoff to Highway 138, continue east on **Highway 38** toward Drain and Eugene. This shortcut from Elkton to Shoestring Road is 15 miles shorter than the main route. It bypasses historic Oakland and some hills.

3.2 Tunnel.

13.4 Drain (market, cafes). Named for Charles Drain, an early settler.

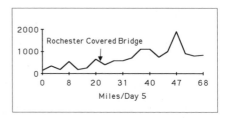

13.7 Right at a blinking light on **Cedar Street** toward Yoncolla. A sign indicates this road is the Douglas County Bike Route 7.

15.9 Left on **Boswell Road** (County Road 54).

22.5 Right on **Anlauf–Boswell Road**.

24.4 Left toward **Elkhead** and **Scotts Valley** (County Road 7). Pass under I-5. (It is legal, but not recommended, to ride on I-5 to Cottage Grove.)

29.5 Left on **Shoestring Road** to rejoin the main route at Mile 45.5.

22.0 Left on **Rolling Ridge Road** (County Route 10) toward Green Valley.

> **22.0 Alternative:** For lodging in a motel rather than camping at the end of Day Four, stay on Highway 138 into Sutherlin, about 4 miles past Rolling Ridge Road. (From Reedsport to Sutherlin is 72 miles.) To rejoin the main route from Sutherlin, return via Highway 138. Turn right on Stearns Lane, then rejoin the main route at Mile 23.3.

22.9 Right on **Old Highway 225** (Rochester Bridge Road). Cross the Rochester Covered Bridge built in 1933.

23.3 Left on **Stearns Lane** toward Oakland.

25.5 Cross under I-5, staying on Stearns Lane.

27.2 Left at a T intersection on **Front Street** in Oakland, a town established in 1852. Turn right immediately on **Locust Street** for a choice of restaurants, a small store or two, antique shops, and a historical museum along the well-preserved main street of Oakland (last water for 25 miles). When leaving town, go left on **Fourth Street**, then right on **Oak Street**, which becomes **Driver Valley Road** east of Oakland.

31.4 Left on **Elkhead Road**.

42.5 Right on **Scotts Valley Road** at an easy-to-miss, poorly marked intersection. The pavement is intermittent for the next 4 miles. The road is paved in front of houses only.

45.5 Right on **Shoestring–London Hill Road**, another obscure unmarked turn. This gravel road climbs steeply to the right.

46.7 Pavement begins again.

47.9 The climb ends and a downhill run starts.

50.5   Left on **London Road** toward Cottage Grove at a stop sign.

51.7   London (small store).

53.6   Pass a road on the right that loops around the east side of Cottage Grove Reservoir and leads to two Army Corps of Engineers' campgrounds on the lake.

60.3   Bear right on **Sixth Street**. (Lathim Road goes left to I-5 southbound.)

61.5   Cross I-5.

62.3   Right on **Highway 99** in Cottage Grove (motels, restaurants, small bike shop).

62.8   Right on **Main Street** at the light.

63.4   The last supermarket before the day's destination at Swarz Campground is on the left just before the I-5 underpass.

64.0   Left on **Currin Road**, following signs to the Forest Service Ranger Station.

64.1   Right on **Row River Road**, then almost immediately left again to stay on **Row River Road**. (The Row River Connector No. 1 goes right here.)

67.5   Continue straight on **Government Road**. Cross the river, climb a short hill, and turn left into the Corps of Engineers' Swarz Campground.

67.9   Dorena Lake, Swarz Campground (camping, picnic area, water, rest rooms, showers).

DAY SIX: DORENA LAKE TO MCKENZIE BRIDGE CAMPGROUND—73 MILES

0.0   Dorena Lake, Swarz Campground. Following the mileage log for Day Five, backtrack about 3 miles toward Cottage Grove on **Government Road**.

0.5   Continue backtracking by going straight on **Row River Road** at the end of Government Road.

3.1   Right on **Sears Road**.

11.1   Look behind and right for the castle on the hill. It is a private home.

12.7   Right on **Cloverdale Road** toward Pleasant Hill at the T intersection.

14.0   Right at the Milepost 12 marker, then immediately right again on **Rodgers Road**.

14.8   Left on **Enterprise Road**.

19.7   Right on the frontage road between Pleasant Hill School and Highway 58.

20.2   The frontage road ends. Turn left across **Highway 58** and ride north on **Jasper Road**.

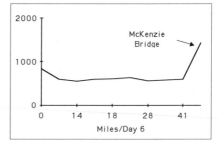

22.5   Pass Jasper Park (water, rest rooms, picnic tables) on the right. The park has access to the Middle Fork of the Willamette River. An entrance fee is charged at times.

22.9   Cross the Middle Fork of the Willamette River.

23.1   Left at the stop sign toward Springfield, to remain on Jasper Road.

26.7   Right on **Mount Vernon Road** (unmarked). The sole indication of this turn is a blinking light over an intersection sign a few hundred yards before the intersection. Beware of the railroad tracks just after the turn.

   26.7   Alternative: If you miss the intersection, turn right on 42nd Street, then right again on Main Street (Highway 126) and rejoin the main route at Mile 27.9.

Cyclists explore one of the numerous viewpoints and beach access areas along the Oregon coast. (Photo: Richard Burgess)

26.8   The route (Mount Vernon Road) turns left and becomes **Fifty-seventh Street** in Springfield.

27.9   Right on **Main Street** (Highway 126). Pass a supermarket on the left. The center of Springfield (all services) is about a mile to your left. The Springfield Museum at 590 Main Street is in an old power transformer station.

    27.9 Alternative: To shorten the tour to six days, cycle from Springfield to Malhon Sweet Airport. Turn left on Highway 126 and ride through Springfield to Eugene. The route joins Highway 99 in Eugene. Follow Highway 99 north to the airport, about 15 miles from Fifty-seventh Street.

32.8   Right on **Deer Horn Road**, just before Highway 126 crosses the McKenzie River.

40.1   Left on **Bridge Street**.

40.3   Pass a small county park (water, tables, rest rooms) on the shore of the McKenzie River on the right.

40.4   Right on **Holden Creek Lane** at the end of the bridge.

40.7   Bear right on **Highway 126**. Stores, motels, and restaurants are along the highway from here to McKenzie Bridge.

48.0   Pass the Goodpasture Covered Bridge on the right. It is the longest covered bridge still in daily use in Oregon.

66.0   Delta Campground (camping, picnic area, water) is 0.7 mile to the right. All Forest Service campgrounds on the rest of this route are in the Willamette National Forest.

73.0   Right into McKenzie Bridge Campground (reserved campsites, picnic area, water).

DAY SEVEN: MCKENZIE BRIDGE CAMPGROUND TO DETROIT LAKE STATE PARK—61.6 MILES

0.0   McKenzie Bridge Campground. Exit right to continue east on **Highway 126**.

0.3   Enter the town of McKenzie Bridge (store, restaurants). The route passes J. B. Harris State Park (rest rooms, water) on the left.

4.5   Pass Paradise Campground (fee camping, picnic area, water, rest rooms) on the left.

4.9   Pass the Highway 242 turnoff to McKenzie Pass, a steep, winding but spectacular side trip to recent lava flows, glacier-covered mountains, and grand views. The McKenzie Bridge Ranger Station personnel can advise whether the road is free of snow and open.

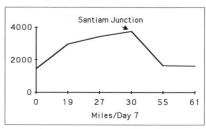

5.9   Pass the turnoff to Belknap Hot Springs on the left. Feel the climb on Highway 126 steepen here.

13.9   Pass Olallie Campground (fee camping, picnic area, water, rest rooms) on the left.

16.0   Pass Trail Campground (no-fee camping, picnic area, rest rooms).

18.0   Pass Ice Cap Campground (fee camping, picnic area, water, rest rooms) on the left.

19.6   Pass the Sahallie Falls parking lot (rest rooms) on the left. The upper McKenzie River cascades here over a relatively recent lava flow similar to the one that dammed the valley to form Clear Lake and its submerged forest.

20.0   Coldwater Cove Campground (fee camping, picnic area, water, rest rooms) on Clear Lake is a mile to your right.

21.3   Pass the road to the small resort on Clear Lake on the right. The access road is 0.3 mile long and is steep. Boat rentals are available here.

22.0   Pass Fish Lake Forest Service Campground (fee camping, picnic area, water, rest rooms) on the left.

24.8   Right on **Highway 20** toward Bend.

24.8   **Shortcut:** To shorten the tour to 7 days, turn left on Highway 20 to Sweet Home in 43 miles. Then ride west on Route 228 about 20 miles through Brownsville to Highway 99E in Halsey. Ride south about 20 miles on Highway 99E through Junction City to Malhon Sweet Airport near Eugene. Forest Service campgrounds are available along Highway 20. Motels are available in Sweet Home, near Brownsville, and in Junction City.

25.1   Pass Sawyer Ice Cave on the right. Ice can be found any time of the year in these volcanic lava tubes. Take your flashlight for exploring.

28.1   Left on **Highway 22** toward Salem at Santiam Junction. From here to Detroit, the route is mostly downhill and the shoulders are wide.

33.5   Pass Maxwell Butte Sno-Park (rest rooms) on the left.

43.4   Marion Forks (cafe on the left, two campgrounds on the right; upper campground has water and a fee, lower one has neither).

45.5   Pass Riverside Campground (camping, picnic area, water, rest rooms) on the left.
51.3   Pass Whispering Falls Campground (camping, picnic area, water, rest rooms) on the left.
55.3   Enter the small community of Idanha (small store).
58.0   Hoover Campground (camping, picnic area, water, rest rooms) is about a mile to the left.
59.7   Detroit (supermarket, restaurants, motel, RV parks).
61.6   Detroit Lake State Park campground (camping, picnic area, water, rest rooms) is on the left. Reservations are recommended because this campground is often full in the summer when boaters flock to Detroit Lake.

DAY EIGHT: DETROIT LAKE STATE PARK TO CORVALLIS—75.4 MILES

0.0   Detroit Lake State Park. Exit left out of the campground on **Highway 22** toward Salem.

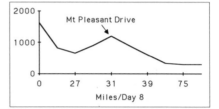

10.9   Pass Niagara County picnic area (water, rest rooms) on the left.
15.1   Left on **Horbe Road** in Gates (small store, motel).
15.5   Right on **Gates School Road**, after crossing the North Santiam River.
19.4   Right at the Mill City Post Office on **First Street**.
19.8   Left on **Broadway Avenue** (markets, restaurants). Fishermen's Bend, a Bureau of Land Management campground with showers, is across the river and then left on Highway 22 in about 2 miles. On the way to Lyons, stay with Broadway as it becomes **Linn Boulevard**, then **Lyons–Mill City Drive**, and finally **Main Street** in Lyons.
27.2   Left on **Highway 226** in Lyons (store, cafe).
29.7   Continue almost straight ahead on **Kingston–Lyons Road**.
   29.7   Alternative: Stay on Highway 226 to avoid the steep, uphill climb. This route also misses a downhill run through rolling farmland. At **Richardson Gap Road**, turn left to rejoin the main route at Mile 40.7.
31.5   Left on **Mount Pleasant Drive**.
34.0   Cross Kingston–Jordan Road and begin riding on **Valley View Drive**.
34.5   Right on **Spring Valley Drive**.
35.0   Left on **Huntley Road**, which becomes **Ridge Drive**.
39.0   Left on **Richardson Gap Road**. Cole School Road is on the right. Start a steep downhill to the Shimanek Covered Bridge at Mile 39.8.
40.7   Cross Highway 226. Scio (small store, cafe) is 2.3 miles to the right.
45.3   Right on **Fish Hatchery Drive**.
48.5   Left on **Highway 226**.
51.4   Cross the South Santiam River.
52.8   Right at the T intersection on **Highway 20**, then almost immediately right on **Knox Butte Road** toward Timber Linn Park.
58.8   Ride under I-5 to enter Albany (all services, no campground).
59.2   Right at the light on **Albany Avenue** toward East Albany. Turn left in one block on **Salem Avenue**. Avery Park (rest rooms, water) is on the left.

59.7   Cross two sets of bicycle-eating railroad tracks.

60.5   Left on **Main Street**, then right immediately on **Third Avenue**.

61.1   Cross Lyons and Ellsworth streets, which connect to the Amtrak and Greyhound stations.

61.3   Pass a choice of restaurants in Two Rivers Market on the right.

61.6   Follow Third Avenue as it becomes **Bryant Drive** and heads downhill, crosses a bridge, and makes a sharp left turn. Bryant Park (water, rest rooms) is on the right at the bottom of the hill.

64.2   Right on **Riverside Drive** as Bryant Drive ends.

69.5   Right on **Highway 34** at the end of Riverside Drive. (There is a commercial campground about 2 miles to the left.)

72.3   Left at the light toward Eugene on **Highway 20/34**.

 72.3   **Alternative:** Ride straight ahead to the Corvallis city center (all services, including bike shops). Rejoin the main route by turning left on Fourth Street, then following Highway 99W south through Corvallis. **Note:** To end the tour at the alternate starting point, Benton County Fairgrounds in Corvallis, ride straight at the end of the bridge onto Harrington Street. Turn left on Fourteenth, then take the first right onto Campus Way, which becomes a bike path. The path ends in about 3 miles at Fifty-third Street across from the fairgrounds and parking lot.

73.4   Take the Eugene exit after crossing the Willamette River. The exit merges into **Highway 99W South**/Fourth Street.

74.9   Left on **Goodnight Road**.

75.4   Corvallis; turn left into Willamette City Park campground (no showers).

Day Nine: Corvallis to Eugene's Malhon Sweet Airport—52.6 miles

0.0   Corvallis, Willamette City Park campground. Following the mileage log for Day Eight, backtrack less than a mile on **Goodnight Road**.

0.7   Left on **Highway 99W**. **Note:** If the campground was bypassed on Day Eight, continue south on Highway 99W.

2.1   Right on **Airport Road**.

6.0   Left on **Bellfountain Road**.

16.2   Enter Bellfountain (small store).

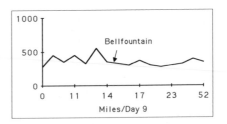

18.6   Left on **Alpine Road** at the stop sign in Alpine (small store).

21.0   Right on the **Monroe Cutoff**.

21.9   Right on **Highway 99W**.

22.3   Enter Monroe (stores, restaurants, winery).

22.8   At the south end of town, continue straight on **Territorial Highway** toward Cheshire. At this point Highway 99W goes left across the Long Tom River.

29.5   Cross High Pass Road. (Junction City, near the start of the tour, is 4 miles to the left.)

43.5   Left on **Highway 36** in Cheshire. The route now becomes the reverse of Day One's mileage log. **Note:** To return to the Benton County Fairgrounds and the alternate starting point, turn right on Highway 36.

45.7   Right on **Vogt Road**.
47.2   Left on **Milliron Road**.
48.5   Right on **Greenhill Road**.
52.3   Right into Eugene's Malhon Sweet Airport.
52.6   Malhon Sweet Airport terminal building. End of tour.

---

11. SOUTH COAST AND REDWOODS LOOP

Allen Throop

Distance: 440 miles
Terrain: mostly short hills with a few long climbs and descents
Total cumulative elevation gain: 10,600 feet
Recommended time of year: June–September
Recommended starting time: before 2:00 P.M. on the first day
Allow: 9 days; 6-day shortcut option
Points of interest: agricultural fields and packing facilities, Medford; Oregon's south coast; California Redwood forests; historic Jacksonville

PUBLIC TRANSPORTATION
Air: commercial airlines serve the Medford area
Train: the nearest Amtrak station is Eugene, approximately 80 miles north of Dillard (Day Three, Mile 22.6)

PRACTICAL INFORMATION
Key contacts: Medford—Jackson County Chamber of Commerce, 503-779-4847; Roseburg (Douglas County) Tourist Information, 503-672-9731; Umpqua National Forest Supervisor's Office, 503-672-6601; Brookings—Harbor Chamber of Commerce, 800-535-9469; Jedediah Smith Campground Reservations (Mistix Service), 800-444-7275; Illinois Valley Tourist Information (Cave Junction), 503-592-2631; Siskiyou National Forest Supervisor's Office, 503-471-6509; Six River National Forest/Gasquet Ranger Station, 707-457-3131

STARTING POINT
Medford Airport terminal: Take I-5 to Exit 32 (Central Point) north of Medford and follow the airport signs approximately 2 miles. Choose from pay and free parking lots near the terminal.

SHORTCUT
A Day Six alternate route from Gold Beach to Grants Pass trims the tour to 6 days and 396 miles. (While bicycling on I-5 is legal in Oregon, and could be used for some alternatives, it is not recommended.)

Oregon's southern coast is spectacular, creating a setting for a memorable bicycle tour. Explore 440 miles that combine the ocean's rugged, rocky coastline,

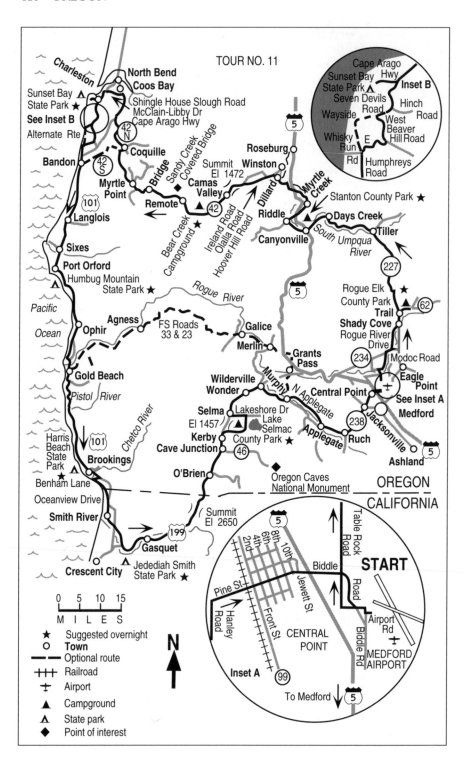

TOUR NO. 11

Inset B

Cape Arago Hwy
Sunset Bay State Park ▲
Seven Devils Road
Wayside
Hinch Road
West Beaver Hill Road
Whisky Run
Rd
E
Humphreys Road

Charleston

North Bend
Coos Bay
Shingle House Slough Road
McClain-Libby Dr
Cape Arago Hwy

Sunset Bay State Park ★
See Inset B
Alternate Rte

42 N

Coquille
Bridge
Sandy Creek Covered Bridge

Bandon
42 S

Myrtle Point
Remote
Camas Valley
Summit El 1472
Winston
Roseburg
Myrtle Creek

Stanton County Park ★

Langlois
Bear Creek Campground ★
Ireland Road
Olalla Road
Hoover Hill Road
Riddle
Days Creek
Tiller

Sixes
Canyonville
South Umpqua River

Port Orford
Humbug Mountain State Park ★
227

Pacific

Rogue River
Rogue Elk County Park ★
Trail
62

Ocean
Agness
FS Roads 33 & 23
Galice
Merlin
Shady Cove
Rogue River Drive
234

Ophir
Grants Pass
Modoc Road

Gold Beach
Wilderville
Wonder
Murphy
N Applegate
Central Point
Eagle Point
See Inset A
Medford

Pistol River
Selma
El 1457
Lakeshore Dr
Lake Selmac
Applegate
238
Jacksonville

Harris Beach State Park
101
Chetco River
Kerby
Cave Junction
46
County Park ★
Ruch
Ashland
5

Brookings
O'Brien

Benham Lane
Oceanview Drive
Oregon Caves National Monument

OREGON
CALIFORNIA

Smith River
Summit El 2650
199
Gasquet

Crescent City
Jedediah Smith State Park ★

0 5 10 15
M I L E S

★ Suggested overnight
○ Town
— Optional route
+++ Railroad
+ Airport
▲ Campground
Λ State park
◆ Point of interest

N

5
Table Rock Road
8th
4th
6th
2nd
10th
Biddle
START
Pine St
Jewett St
Front St
Hanley Road
Biddle Rd
Airport Rd
CENTRAL POINT
MEDFORD AIRPORT
Inset A
99
To Medford 5

fruit orchards of the Medford area, Douglas fir forests, dairy land along the Coquille River, and the massive redwoods of northern California.

On Day One leave the Medford area's extensive apple and pear orchards for a more thirsty landscape of dry pastures dotted with scrub oak and brush above the valley's irrigation systems. End the day along the Rogue River where glimpses of the rapids, drift boats, and rafts make it easy to understand why tourism and fishing are a significant portion of Jackson County's economy.

Start Day Two with a challenging 11-mile climb up the side of Threehorn Mountain through a second-growth Douglas fir forest. Roll downhill the remainder of the day, slipping quickly at first, more gently later, along the South Umpqua River to Canyonville.

On Day Three, leave Canyonville, watching for the nation's only nickel mine, visible for a short time on a hilltop. Then welcome a pleasant, almost level ride to Riddle, Myrtle Creek, Dillard, and Winston. Although Myrtle Creek's namesake, the myrtle tree, grows to a limited extent in the area, it is far more prevalent along the south Oregon coast, where shops feature products turned from the beautiful wood.

Wood is again the theme in Dillard. A huge plant producing plywood and lumber hugs the highway for more than a mile. Winston's claim to tourists is the Wildlife Safari. Because bicycle helmets are inadequate deterrence to hungry lions, car rentals are available. Then leave the South Umpqua River and rise up, and eventually over, the Coast Range. Unless a strong afternoon sea wind is blowing, the downhill ride to Bear Creek Campground is a breeze.

Overnight in the route's most primitive campground, then on Day Four continue down to sea level and through communities with unusual names like Bridge and Remote. Follow the Coquille River valley as it widens out and dairy cattle pastures replace the forests. The Coos County Logging Museum at Myrtle Point details the timber story of the south coast. If the boat ramp parking lots along the Coquille River are full, the annual migration of salmon or steelhead and fishermen is under way.

Pass Coaledo, a locality reminiscent of the coal mining here a century ago, then wind along the tidal backwaters and sloughs of Coos Bay, and climb over a low rise. To branch into Coos Bay, take the alternate route past giant stacks of logs and mountains of wood chips being loaded on ships headed for Japan. Both routes drop to Charleston, a fishing harbor at the mouth of the Coos River. Explore the variety of commercial and sports fishing docks in Charleston. South of town, investigate the short picturesque beaches, separated by rocky headlands. Sea lions, harbor seals, and, occasionally, sea otters cover the reefs near Cape Arago, and talk unabashedly. Nearby Sunset Bay State Park is the day's destination.

As you cycle south on US Highway 101, the first section of the Day Five route features hills. The road name, Seven Devils, reflects the frustration of the early road builders, and modern cyclists' fight to top the steep hills. Visit the South Slough Sanctuary Visitors Center for natural history exhibits, trails, and views over the South Slough of Coos Bay.

In Bandon, a town of cheese, cranberries, and tourists, try the curds at the factory, get a latte fix, find a perfect myrtle wood bowl, or send a postcard home. Near harvest time in the fall, plan on the Bandon Cranberry Festival. At any time, the Coquille River Museum in the former Coast Guard Station features

A spectacular stretch of coast near Gold Beach on the South Coast and Redwoods Loop (Photo: Andrew Herstrom)

the maritime, lifeguard, and Coast Guard history of this harbor community. Beach Loop Road can take forever for those who succumb to the numerous overlooks and beach access points along this spectacular section of coastline. At the end of Beach Loop Road, return to US Highway 101, leaving the ocean until Port Orford. Enter a major cranberry-growing area where in the late fall bogs are flooded and floating harvesters rake in the bobbing cranberries.

In Port Orford all boats are pulled from the water when the seas get rough. South of Port Orford, look for Humbug Mountain, the prominent headland interrupting the coastline. Under some weather conditions the wind is extremely strong where the highway turns inland at the foot of the mountain. Spend the night at Humbug Mountain State Park.

On Day Six, alternate between stretches along the coast and hilly inland climbs over the headlands. Gold Beach, the only city encountered, is named for the precious metal carried by the Rogue River from original outcrops far upstream. You can almost visualize the miners who swarmed over the area in the 1850s. Visit the Coos–Curry Historical Museum at the fairgrounds toward the south end of town. Enter Boardman State Park and take a break for walks to overlooks or windswept headlands. The most frequently asked question on the ride into Brookings is, "Is this the last hill?" The answer is no. Recuperate at Harris Beach State Park, the overnight stop.

The Day Seven route can be summarized as short and flat. That should prompt smiles after the ups and downs of the previous few days. Enjoy diversions like walking along Harris Beach, looking at the lily fields (the area boasts it is the lily-growing capital of the world), and exploring the magnificent red-

122

wood forests near your campsite in Jedediah Smith State Park in northern California.

On Day Eight bid farewell to the coast and swing northeast to tackle the Siskiyou Mountains. Start on a cut into the side of very steep hills and adjacent to the picturesque Smith River. Unfortunately, the narrow, winding road is usually shared with cars, log trucks, and numerous recreational vehicles. The day's final steep climb to the Collier tunnel is only 2 miles long, but can feel much farther on a hot afternoon.

From Highway 199 the years of gold mining in the Illinois Valley are not evident, but as early as the 1850s rivers ran red with mud from placer mines. To recover the precious metal, the miners who rushed to the area washed away massive quantities of earth with water streaming from giant nozzles. The few small, active gold mines in this area and in other tributaries of the Rogue River are tucked away in the hills. After one last steep hill between Kerby and the day's destination, camp at Lake Selmac County Park.

The tour's final 60 miles back to Medford include a combination of busy and quiet roads, small and large communities, forgotten towns and tourist-packed Jacksonville, gentle and steep hills, plus pine forests and apple orchards. With the exception of ocean views, the ride on Day Eight replays all elements of the entire loop, a fitting end to a magnificent tour.

MILEAGE LOG
DAY ONE: MEDFORD AIRPORT TO
ROGUE ELK COUNTY PARK—26.1 MILES

0.0   Medford Airport terminal. Follow the one-way traffic flow from the terminal, turning right toward Central Point at the stop sign.

    0.0 Alternative: Turn left to go into Medford (all services). Motels are about 1.5 miles south on Biddle Road, as well as tours of orchards and fruit packing facilities. Return to the airport to begin the tour.

0.3   Cross Biddle Road.

0.6   Right on **Table Rock Road**.

5.5   Pass the Tou Velle State Park picnic area (water, rest rooms) on the right. Like all parks on Day One's route, Tou Velle offers good access to the Rogue River, may have an entrance fee, and is day-use only.

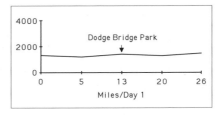

6.4   Right on **Modoc Road**.

7.9   Pass the trailhead to Upper Table Rock (rest room in parking area), a 1.25-mile walk to a panoramic view, on the left.

11.6   Right on **Highway 234** toward Shady Cove.

13.0   Left on **Rogue River Drive**. Dodge Bridge County Park (rest rooms, picnicking, day-use fee) is on the right, just past the intersection.

17.5   Pass Takelma County Park (picnicking, rest rooms) on the right.

20.3   Left on **Highway 62** in Shady Cove (supermarket, restaurants, motel). A county picnic area (rest rooms, water) is on the right, just before the intersection.

22.8   The community of Trail (small store).

22.8   **Alternative:** To bypass Rogue Elk County Park, turn left toward Tiller, where motels are available in about 26 miles. Rejoin the main route at Mile 29.7 of Day Two

26.1   Right into Rogue Elk County Park campground (fee, showers).

DAY TWO: ROGUE ELK COUNTY PARK TO STANTON COUNTY PARK—54.7 MILES

0.0   Rogue Elk County Park. Turn left on **Highway 62** and retrace the Day One route 3.3 miles back to Trail.

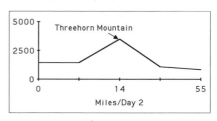

3.3   Trail (small store). Turn right on **Highway 227** toward Tiller. Start an 11-mile climb that gets gradually steeper.

14.5   Threehorn Mountain summit (3,306 feet).

16.8   Pass a campground (no water, no fee) in the Umpqua National Forest on the right. As you pedal, you can admire the beautiful, large sugar pines.

29.7   Tiller (store, restaurant, ranger station, motels).

45.5   Days Creek (small store).

53.1   Canyonville (motels, restaurants, supermarket). Turn right on **Main Street** at the T intersection toward I-5 northbound. Keep right and off the freeway in about a mile.

54.7   Right into Stanton County Park (hot showers, fee). The lower campground is more secluded than the upper, more obvious one.

DAY THREE: STANTON COUNTY PARK TO BEAR CREEK CAMPGROUND—46 MILES

0.0   Stanton County Park. Turn right at the park exit toward "FREEWAY NORTH." In about a mile go under I-5. Do not get on the freeway.

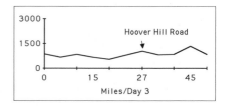

4.1   Riddle (cafes, markets). Turn right on **Main Street** at the stop sign.

4.7   Right on **Fifth Street**, before the railroad tracks. Road name changes to **Pruner Road**.

6.5   Right on the **Riddle Bypass Road** at the stop sign. Cross the South Umpqua River and I-5, then follow the main road as it turns left on **Old Pacific Highway**. Restaurants and markets are scattered along the 5 miles from here to the city of Myrtle Creek.

11.6   Pass a covered bridge on the left.

11.7   Stay on the main road as it turns left, crosses a creek, and enters the city center of Myrtle Creek. Delightful old Mill Park (picnic area, rest rooms, water, fee camping) is one block to the left.

12.1   At the north end of town, follow the straight road fork to go up a steep hill on **Dole Road** (unmarked at this intersection). The left fork (the main road) joins I-5 in 0.2 mile. There are nasty railroad crossings along the next 5 miles.

17.9   Straight ahead toward Dillard at a stop sign. To the right are I-5 and a motel.
18.6   Right on **Dillard Highway** toward Dillard, after crossing the South Umpqua River.
22.6   Left on **Brockway Highway** toward Brockway in Dillard (store, cafe straight ahead).
   22.6 Alternative: More services are 1.5 miles straight ahead in Winston (supermarket, restaurants, motel, RV park). Return to the main route at Mile 24.0 by riding west on Highway 42 in Winston.
24.0   Left on **Highway 42.**
25.9   Left on **Hoover Hill Road.** This road starts with a short, steep hill, but is quiet and actually shorter than staying on Highway 42.
28.2   Left on **Olalla Road.**
30.8   Right on **Ireland Road.**
31.7   *Sharp* left to stay on Ireland Road.
33.2   Bear left to rejoin **Highway 42.** Start a 3-mile climb.
38.0   Camas Valley (cafe, store).
45.2   Right toward Bear Creek Recreation Area on a winding, poorly maintained, and now-bypassed section of Highway 42.
46.0   Bear Creek Campground (rest rooms, stream water only, hiking trails), operated by the Bureau of Land Management. The campground is just off the highway, but the site feels secluded.

DAY FOUR: BEAR CREEK CAMPGROUND TO
SUNSET BAY STATE PARK—63.5 MILES

0.0   Bear Creek Campground. Turn left out of the campground toward Coos Bay.
0.3   Right to rejoin **Highway 42.**
7.8   Pass Coquille River Ranch on the left (campground, cabins).
8.8   Community of Remote (no services). Sandy Creek Covered Bridge, built in 1921, and a picnic area (rest rooms, picnic tables) are on the right.

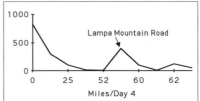

15.9   Enter the community of Bridge (store, RV campground).
24.8   Enter Myrtle Point (motel, logging museum at Seventh and Maple, restaurants, supermarket).
26.1   Left on **Spruce Street**, the main business thoroughfare of Myrtle Point. Road name changes to **Lampa Mountain Road** after crossing the Coquille River.
30.5   Right toward Coquille. Three Coos County parks (rest rooms, boat ramps) are on the right in the next 12 miles.
33.4   Right at an unmarked intersection.
34.6   Right again at another unmarked intersection.
38.6   Left on **Highway 42 South** toward Coquille.
   38.6 Alternative: To shorten the tour by 25 miles by riding directly into Bandon (16 miles), turn right on Highway 42 South, a narrow and winding but flat road. To rejoin the main route on Day Four,

Sandy Creek Covered Bridge near Remote (Oregon has the most covered bridges of any western state.) (Photo: Allen Throop)

turn right on Filmore Avenue, then left on First Street and rejoin the main route at Mile 34.2.

38.9   Pass a picnic area (rest rooms, water, intriguing playground) on the left.

39.0   Left on **Highway 42 North** toward Coos Bay. Coquille (motels, supermarkets, restaurants) is to the right.

50.0   Highway 42 merges into US Highway 101 North.

52.5   Left on **Shingle House Slough Road**, a winding road with no shoulder.

   52.5 Side Trip: To ride into Coos Bay to see the port or for services including a bike shop, stay on US Highway 101. This alternate adds about 3 miles on very busy, but slightly less hilly, roads. After visiting Coos Bay, continue into Charleston and rejoin the main route at Mile 60.5.

54.5   Left on **McClain–Libby Drive**.

60.0   Left on **Cape Arago Highway**.

60.5   Charleston (motels, restaurants, fresh fish, markets, shops, RV parks). Continue south on Cape Arago Highway toward Sunset Bay State Park. Pass the turnoff for Bastendorf Beach County Park (camping, beach access) on the right. **Note:** The Day Five route returns to Seven Devils Road, which you pass on the climb out of Charleston.

63.5   Sunset Bay State Park campground (camping, water, rest rooms, showers, beach access) is on the left. This is the main state park campground and the end of this day's route.

    63.5   Alternative: For the less-expensive biker-hiker campground, continue south on Cape Arago Highway 2.5 miles.

64.6   Pass Shore Acres State Park (formal gardens, ocean views). The overlooks between Shore Acres and Cape Arago are great spots for listening to a cacophony of sea lions and harbor seals.

66.0   Ride on to Cape Arago State Park at the end of the road. Follow signs to a primitive campground. Showers at Sunset Bay State Park campground are available to biker-hiker campers staying at the primitive campground.

DAY FIVE: SUNSET BAY STATE PARK TO
HUMBUG MOUNTAIN STATE PARK—58.1 MILES

0.0   Sunset Bay State Park exit. Turn right on **Cape Arago Highway** toward Charleston.

2.3   Right toward Seven Devils Road and Bandon.

2.5   Right on **Seven Devils Road**.

6.8   South Slough Sanctuary Interpretative Center (free) is 0.2 mile to the left.

8.9   Bear left on **West Beaver Hill Road** (continue on the paved road).

    8.9   Alternative: For mountain biking on a hilly road that also has beach access, continue straight on the gravel road toward Seven Devils Wayside. Rejoin the main route at Mile 15.9.

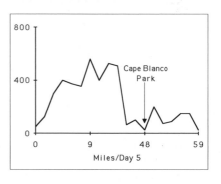

12.6   Right on East Humphreys Road (unmarked) toward Whisky Run Beach and Seven Devils Wayside.

15.9   Left on **Seven Devils Road**.

18.8   Right on **US Highway 101**.

20.2   Pass Bullards Beach State Park (picnicking, camping, beach access, picturesque old lighthouse) on the right.

20.5   Cross the Coquille River.

21.4   Right on **Riverside Drive**.

23.0   Right on **First Street** in Bandon (motels, restaurants, gift shops). Supermarkets are a short distance south on US Highway 101. Follow the designated Oregon Coast Bike Route and Discovery Drive signs through Bandon.

23.5   Pass the Coquille River Museum on the right.

24.0   Left up a steep hill on **Edison Street**, then make a very *sharp* right at the top of the hill on **Fourth Street**. Stay with the obvious route as the name changes to **Seventh Street,** then to **Beach Loop Road**. Numerous parks and other access sites in the next 4 miles lead to rocky headlands or sandy beaches with views of an ever-changing arrangement of shoreline, cliffs, and sea stacks.

28.6 Right on **US Highway 101** as Beach Loop Road ends.

38.9 Langlois (market, cafe). RV campgrounds are scattered from here to Port Orford.

46.7 Sixes (small store, post office).

47.7 Cape Blanco State Park (camping, wind, views), the most westerly point in Oregon, is 5 miles to the right.

51.4 Port Orford (supermarkets, motels, restaurants). Battle Rock Park (water, picnic tables, rest rooms) is on the right at the south end of town. Signs point to the harbor, which is worth the extra 0.5-mile ride. From here to California, the road surface is often rough, due to landslides of the weak, unstable rocks.

57.4 Pass Humbug Mountain Trail on the right.

58.1 Left into the Humbug Mountain State Park campground (camping, picnicking, water, rest rooms). **Note:** A picnic area is 0.7 mile further along US Highway 101; a motel and cafe are located on US Highway 101 another 1.5 miles farther south.

DAY SIX: HUMBUG MOUNTAIN STATE PARK TO HARRIS BEACH STATE PARK—49.9 MILES

0.0 Humbug Mountain State Park. Turn left at the campground exit on **US Highway 101** toward Gold Beach. The road for the next mile is narrow and winding.

6.3 Pass Prehistoric Gardens (Oregon's Triassic Park) on the right. If dinosaurs scattered through the thick coastal vegetation are of interest, stop here.

13.1 Pass Ophir Rest Area (beach access) on the right.

14.0 Right toward **Nesika Beach** (market, RV park), a small community spread over the next mile.

15.3 Right on **US Highway 101**, continuing toward Gold Beach.

15.5 Pass Geisel Monument Wayside (picnic tables, water, rest rooms) on the right. Graves of the Geisel family men who were killed in 1856 near here in Rogue River Indian Wars share this site with a small picnic area.

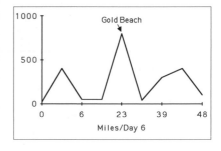

16.2 Right on the **Old Coast Road**, a great piece of Oregon history. This narrow road rolls up and down over sand dunes. Few motorists notice it, so enjoy an almost private route.

17.8 Pass Otter Point State Park trailhead (no facilities) on the right. Beach access is at the second sign.

19.2 Pass Miner's Fort site, another relic of the Rogue River Indian wars, on the left.

19.9 Follow Old Coast Road as it swings left next to the Rogue River, passing a US Highway 101 access road on the left.

21.3   Right on **US Highway 101** and cross the Rogue River on one of the historic concrete coastal bridges. The bridge is narrow, but level.

  21.5   **Shortcut:** At the south end of the bridge, an optional 90-mile 2- or 3-day shortcut route to Murphy via Grants Pass can be taken, which cuts 1 or 2 days from the tour but bypasses great coastal scenery and the redwoods. This shortcut, 149 miles from this mileage point, has one mountain pass plus Siskiyou National Forest and Josephine County campgrounds, and totals 396 miles. To begin the shortcut, turn left on Jerry Flat Road, which becomes Forest Service Road 33.

  35.3   Pass **Quosatana** Forest Service campground (tables, camping, water, rest rooms).

  49.2   Resort and RV park; for a 3-day shortcut, this is an overnight stop for Day Six.

  50.1   Right on **USFS Road 23**, and begin the climb.

  64.9   Climb ends.

  87.9   Right in Galice (store, restaurant) toward Merlin and Grants Pass.

  94.5   Pass Indian Mary county campground (picnicking, camping, water, rest rooms) on the left. This is an overnight stop for Day Six for a 2-day shortcut, or an overnight stop for Day Seven for a 3-day shortcut.

102.8   Cross under I-5 in Merlin (restaurant, stores).

102.9   Right on the frontage road (Highland Drive) to stay on the main route into Grants Pass (all services), a possible overnight stop for Day Seven for a 3-day shortcut.

106.2   Merge into Sixth Street (Highway 199).

108.6   Straight onto Highway 230.

113.4   Left on North Applegate Road (just before a long bridge), to rejoin the main route at Day Nine, Mile 24.0, for the remaining 36 miles to the end of the tour.

22.3   Gold Beach (restaurants, motels, supermarkets, shops, county museum).

33.1   Pass the Cape Sebastian State Park (no facilities) entrance. Great views and hiking trails await if you are willing to pedal up a steep, 0.5-mile hill. The name stems from Spanish exploration in 1603. Details are given on the nearby historical marker.

39.1   Enter Samuel H. Boardman State Park. For the next 11 miles, numerous day-use areas offer hiking trails and views around the spectacular cliffs, sea stacks, and natural bridges.

41.9   Cross the Thomas Creek Bridge. At 345 feet, it is the highest in Oregon.

49.9   Right into Harris Beach State Park (camping, picnicking, easy beach access). A tourist information center is on US Highway 101 opposite the park entrance.

DAY SEVEN: HARRIS BEACH STATE PARK TO
JEDEDIAH SMITH STATE PARK, CALIFORNIA—27.9 MILES

0.0   Harris Beach State Park. Turn right on **US Highway 101**, at the park exit.

1.0   Enter Brookings (supermarket, motels, restaurants, bike shop).

2.1   Cross the Chetco River.

3.5   Right on **Benham Lane**.

4.0   Follow Benham Lane left as it becomes **Ocean View Drive**/County Road 872.

8.4   Bear right on **US Highway 101**.

9.2   Enter California.

9.4   Stop at the California Fruit Inspection Station. Most non-California fruit must be discarded.

9.9   Left on **Ocean View Drive**.

15.5   Cross US Highway 101.

16.0   Left on **First Street**.

17.1   Right on **Fred Haight Drive** at the main intersection in Smith River (store, restaurant to the left).

20.3   Right on **US Highway 101**.

20.5   Left on **North Bank Road**.

23.1   Pass Ruby Van Deventer County Park (picnicking, camping, water, rest rooms) on the right.

27.3   Left on **Highway 199** toward Grants Pass.

27.9   Right into Jedediah Smith State Park (picnicking, camping, rest rooms, showers). This is redwood country. The Stout Redwood Grove is a beautiful spot for quiet contemplation, especially on a misty morning. **Note:** A cafe and market are 0.7 mile down the road. In late summer, you can use a trail and bridge from the campground to reach them. See Day Eight, Mile 2.3, for road access.

Day Eight: Jedediah Smith State Park, California to Lake Selmac County Park—53.6 miles

0.0   Jedediah Smith State Park. Turn right on **Highway 199** toward Grants Pass.

0.1   Pass the Redwood National Park Ranger Station (small visitors center) on the left.

0.7   Hiouchi Cafe, market, motel, and RV park. **Caution:** The highway is narrow and winding with poor visibility, no shoulder, and no guardrail for many sections over the next 20 miles. Stay alert! The traffic can be heavy. The scenery along the Smith River is great, but enjoying it while riding safely is a challenge.

2.3   Pass South Fork Road on the right.

2.3 Side Trip: To visit the Stout Redwood Grove, follow this road 3 miles. Some of the road to this impressive stand of redwoods is gravel. Backtrack to rejoin the main route.

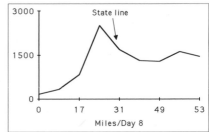

9.6   Gasquet (motel, cafe, store, Six Rivers National Forest Ranger Station); services are scattered along a few miles of highway.

11.9   Pass Panther Flat Forest Service Campground (picnicking, camping, water, rest rooms) on the left.

14.0   Pass Grassy Flat Forest Service Campground (picnicking, camping, water, rest rooms) on the right.

17.1   Pass Patrick Creek Forest Service Campground (picnicking, camping, water, rest rooms) on the right. A lodge and restaurant are on the left. **Caution:** The next 5 miles are the most dangerous section of highway. Take the road when necessary, giving way in the frequent pullouts when possible.

28.6   Pass Oregon Mountain Rest Area (rest rooms) on the left. **Caution:** tunnel. There are blinking lights to warn motorists of bicycles inside. You can activate the lights by pushing the button near the tunnel entrance. To ride through without contending with vehicles, start out when you can hear no approaching traffic from either direction.

31.1   Pass the California Agricultural Inspection Station. No stop required for northbound traffic into Oregon.

31.6   Enter Oregon. Cafes, stores, and RV parks are scattered from the state line to Selma.

43.8   Pass a road to Illinois River State Park. A picnic area (rest rooms, water) is about 0.5 mile to the left.

44.4   Cave Junction (motels, restaurants, supermarket, RV parks).

    44.4   Side Trip: The Oregon Caves National Monument is about 19 miles to the right. The hill to the caves is long and steep. The Illinois Valley Tourist Information Center is 200 yards east on the Caves Highway. After your visit, backtrack to rejoin the main route.

46.7   Kerby (store). Pass the Josephine County Historical Museum on the right.

48.9   Right on **Reeves Creek Road. Caution:** Beware of the cattle guard just after the intersection.

    48.9   Alternative: If you are not planning to camp in Lake Selmac County Park campground, continue straight (north) on Highway 199. Another campground is about 40 miles down the road, and motels are 9 miles farther in Jacksonville.

53.6   Left into Josephine County's Lake Selmac County Park campground, across from the swimming area (showers, camping, picnicking, swimming).

DAY NINE: LAKE SELMAC COUNTY PARK TO MEDFORD AIRPORT—60 MILES

0.0   Lake Selmac County Park campground. Turn left on **Reeves Creek Road** at the campground exit.

0.5   Left on **Lakeshore Drive.** On Lakeshore Drive to the right are the Lake Selmac store and resort.

2.5   Right on **Highway 199** toward Grants Pass. Cross a bridge and enter Selma (supermarket, cafe).

11.2   The locality known as Wonder (store).

14.3   Bear right toward **Wilderville** (store).

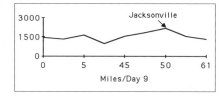

15.0   Right on **Fish Hatchery Road** at the Wilderville store.

19.6   Continue straight on **South Side Road** where Fish Hatchery Road turns left to cross the Applegate River.

23.5   Left on **Murphy Lane**, an obscure turn just before a market in the town of Murphy, or turn left on Murphy Creek Road past the market.

23.6   Left on **Highway 238**. Cross the Applegate River.

24.0   Right on **North Applegate Road**.

32.4   Pass Missouri Flat Cemetery (water, tables, rest rooms) on the right.

36.1   Left on **Highway 238**. To the right is Applegate (picnic area on the river, store).

42.1   Pass the turnoff to Jackson County's Cantrall Buckley Park and Campground (picnic tables, camping, water, rest rooms), about a mile to the right. The day-use area is closed on some weekdays.

43.8   Ruch (market, cafe). About a mile east of Ruch, tailings piles left behind by gold dredges many years ago are now pine-covered boulder piles 0.5 mile north of the highway.

51.3   Jacksonville (restaurants, shops, motel, hotel, historical museum, supermarket). As early as 1851, Jacksonville was a center for gold mining, but it now relies on tourists and the Britt Music Festival audience for its support.

51.5   Left on **Fifth Street** in Jacksonville. Apple, pear, and other orchards mark the return to the Bear Creek Valley near Medford.

52.9   Left on **Hanley Road**.

57.0   Continue on the main road as Hanley Road becomes **Pine Street** in the town of Central Point, then **Biddle Road**.

59.4   Left toward the Medford Airport.

60.0   Medford Airport terminal. End of tour.

◆

12. THE GREAT BASIN AND CASCADES LOOP

Allen Throop

Distance: 492 miles
Terrain: flat ancient lakebeds to high mountain passes
Total cumulative elevation gain: 9,000 feet
Recommended time of year: June–September
Recommended starting time: before 10:00 A.M. on the first day
Allow: 9 days
Points of interest: Fort Rock; wide vistas of the Great Basin; Summer Lake Hot Springs; Crater Lake National Park; Mount Bachelor; Cascade Mountains and Cascades Lakes area

◆ ◆ ◆

PUBLIC TRANSPORTATION

Air: scheduled airlines serve Redmond; from the airport pedal west to Redmond and the turn south on US Highway 97, then stay on US Highway 97 for 31 miles; the flat route goes through Bend (all services) and US Highway 97 generally has wide shoulders and heavy traffic

Train: Amtrak serves Klamath Falls, providing access to the route at Chiloquin, reached by riding north about 30 miles on US Highway 97; return to Klamath Falls by staying on Highway 140 west of Beatty, Day Five, Mile 39.8 (Amtrak also serves Chemult, but bicycles cannot be checked to this stop)

PRACTICAL INFORMATION
Key contacts: Bend–Deschutes County Chamber of Commerce, 503-382-3221; Deschutes National Forest Supervisor's Office (Bend), 503-382-6922; Lake County Chamber of Commerce, 503-947-6040; Fremont National Forest (Lakeview), 503-947-2151; Klamath County Department of Tourism, 800-445-6728 or 503-884-5193; Rogue River National Forest (Prospect Ridge Station), 503-560-3623

STARTING POINT
Sunriver, Abbot Drive between the church and the Country Mall: From US Highway 97, turn on South Century Drive (near milepost 153) toward Sunriver. At the bottom of the hill, turn right at the first street (Beaver Drive). Continue down Beaver Drive past the Country Store and the post office (both on the left), and turn left into a parking lot. Turn right in the next parking lot and proceed to the unpaved section at the rear of the lot. Before leaving your vehicle, contact American Property Management Company, 503-593-8704. The company offers parking, but does not assume liability for vehicles or their contents.

SHORTCUTS
To shorten the tour, look to its middle and US Highway 97. Design shorter loops to Lakeview, Crater Lake National Park, or the Cascades Lakes area by using this busy highway as the connector. US Highway 97 is generally straight with wide shoulders. Interesting attractions are limited to Lava Lands Forest Service Visitor Center and the High Desert Museum between Bend and Sunriver. To create a shortcut, choose the section in which you are interested, then figure the intervening distances using this US Highway 97 milepost list: Redmond, 121; Bend, 136; Sunriver, 153; junction with Highway 31, 170; Gilchrist, 182; Crescent, 185; Chemult, 203; Collier Memorial State Park campground, 244; junction to Chiloquin and Crater Lake, 248.

Ready to trade people and services for 9 days along a spectacular route with awe-inspiring scenery? This memorable tour in south-central Oregon covers 492 miles of wide-open spaces, long distances with long views, sparsely populated landscapes, and Oregon's only national park, Crater Lake. Look elsewhere for fast-food franchises, bike shops, bakeries, or espresso at every corner. Lakeview, population 2,500, is the largest city visited. The sole bike shop along the route is in the resort community of Sunriver, where the tour starts and ends.

Sunriver occupies the site of Camp Abbot, a World War II military base. While Camp Abbot lasted only a year, Sunriver is a thriving community with a much better track record. Leave town on a flat backroad near the Little Deschutes River, and head south. After LaPine, you will begin a gradual, but continuous, climb into vegetation that alternates between small lodgepole pines and enormous, wonderful ponderosa pines. The break from the pine forests to

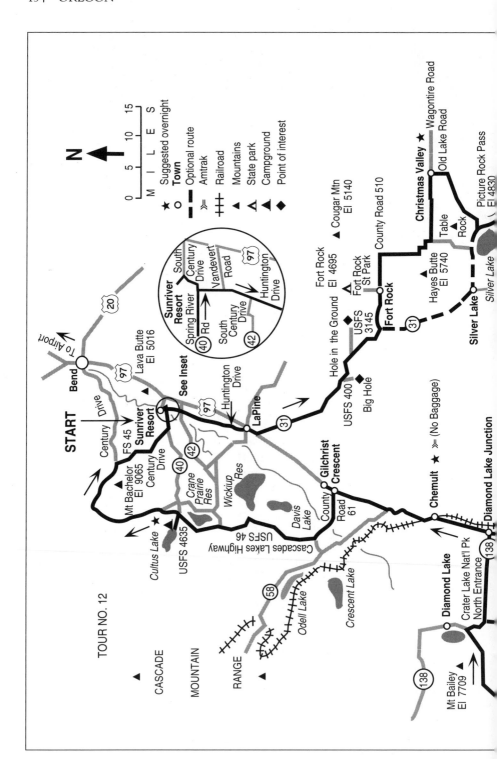

TOUR NO. 12

CASCADE

MOUNTAIN

RANGE

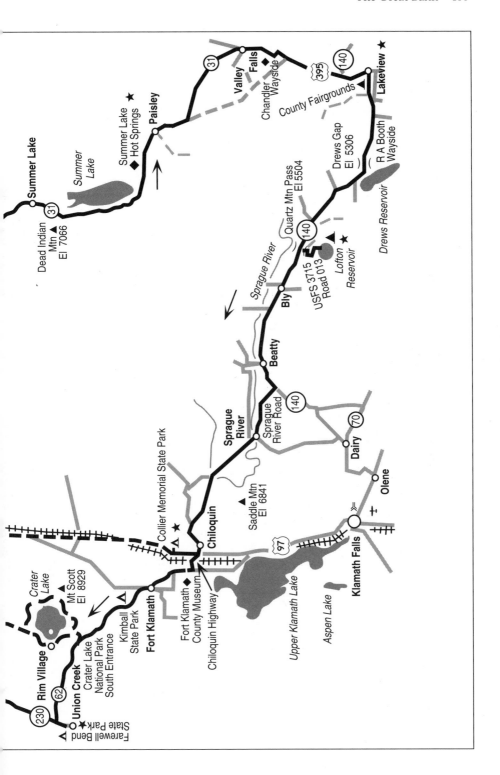

the sagebrush of the high desert comes very sharply before the turnoff from Highway 31 toward Fort Rock. The change in vegetation marks the start of the Great Basin. The basin, covering most of Nevada, plus parts of Oregon, California, Utah, and Arizona, is a huge geographic area. Here, due to topography and the climate, rivers flow into Summer Lake, Utah's Great Salt Lake, and others where the evaporation rate is high and no water flows out.

The small community of Fort Rock is nestled at the base of its namesake, a fascinating volcanic formation that dominates the area. A collection of historic buildings forms a growing museum on the western edge of town. Fort Rock State Park, with its interpretive displays, is about 1.5 miles off the main route. The prominent rock was important to Native Americans and pioneer settlers in the area.

For flat cycling, few places beat the road from Fort Rock to Christmas Valley. Once the area was covered by an ancient lake, its bottom thick with accumulations of microscopic animal skeletons. The resulting sediment, known as diatomaceous earth, is now mined near Christmas Valley, screened to correct size, and sold as kitty litter and for other uses throughout the Northwest. Alfalfa is the mainstay of the area's agricultural industry. Using water pumped from under the old lakebed, farmers dot an otherwise-arid landscape with green alfalfa circles. Spend the night in the small community of Christmas Valley.

Leave the lakebed on Day Two and climb to 4,830-foot Picture Rock Pass. Motorists seldom even slow here, but a few minutes of exploration yield prehistoric pictographs and the ruts of a wagon trail worn into the pass. Getting a wagon up the trail looks like much more work than pedaling up the present road.

With your one and only significant climb for the day behind, relish the downhill run with its grand view of the Summer Lake basin and surrounding ranges. Off in the haze at the south end of the lake, you can see the day's destination. Read the historical marker at the picnic area in the Summer Lake community to learn about Captain John Fremont's 1843 expedition and the naming of Summer Lake and Winter Rim. At day's end, the warm pool of Summer Lake Hot Springs campground makes a nice change of pace from riding. On a good day, the wind in the area blows swim suits dry in a few minutes. On a bad day, the wind can topple semitrailer trucks.

Start Day Three the delicious way with breakfast in Paisley, approximately 6 miles farther along the route. Covered boardwalks in front of the store and restaurant give Paisley its Western feel. Cattle, timber, and a ranger station keep it going. Carry insect repellent. Paisley has good reason for holding an annual Mosquito Festival.

As you continue south to Valley Falls, the eastern skyline is dominated by the 2,000-foot Abert Rim, one of Oregon's highest and longest geologic fault scarps. Abert Lake, a few miles northeast of Valley Falls, sits at the bottom of a large basin and has no outlet. Fortunately, the route to the south climbs gradually out of the basin, then rolls over sagebrush-covered hills into Lakeview. The geyser steam from Hunter Hot Springs welcomes cyclists with a spout of steam every few minutes.

Lakeview, despite its setting at the base of the Warner Mountains, is at approximately 4,800 feet, making it the highest city in Oregon. The Schminck Memorial Museum on E Street is an early settler's home featuring period furniture, glassware, tack, tools, and the like. Visit the rodeo museum at the fairgrounds for that sport's story. While the name Lakeview seems like a promoter's hyperbole, the reference is to Goose Lake, south of town. Although not in sight from town, Goose Lake may have been larger and thus actually visible when the city was established in 1876.

Day Four features relatively low mileage, a short climb, and a longer climb as you leave the western edge of the Great Basin and head west. After a short pump up to Drews Gap, the route drops, skirts Drews Reservoir, and then climbs to Quartz Mountain summit (5,504 feet). At the high point, the route forsakes Highway 140 to wind along Fremont National Forest roads into the Lofton Reservoir Campground.

Although the route for Day Five is along the often-visible Sprague River, one of the few places you can actually reach the water is a picnic area early in the day. From Bly to the town of Sprague River, the route parallels one of the last logging railroads in Oregon. The Oregon California Eastern (OCE) route is now owned by the state. Eventually Bly should be connected to Klamath Falls via a paved bike route on the old rail line. Chiloquin offers cafes, a motel, a market, and recreational-vehicle (RV) parks. Collier Memorial State Park, only a few miles north of the direct route to Crater Lake National Park, has an outdoor logging museum as well as camping.

On Day Six, you will not see, only skirt, Agency Lake and its and surrounding wetlands on the north end of the Klamath Basin. Soak up local history at

A beautiful rural scene along the Great Basin and Cascades Loop (Photo: Andrew Herstrom)

Mile 13.8. Fort Klamath, occupied by soldiers for about twenty-five years from 1863, displays the fort's history during various wars between settlers and Indians, providing both perspectives. The skyline to the northwest is dominated by remnants of Mount Mazama. This ancient volcano, which erupted about 7,000 years ago, left a huge depression that eventually filled to become Crater Lake. A roadside sign west of the town of Fort Klamath identifies the skyline features and explains the geologic history. The climb into Crater Lake National Park is long and steady.

At the south entrance to Crater Lake National Park, you have a choice. When the north entrance is snow-free and open (generally from July through September), you can detour to spend the night in a park campground, ride up to the rim, circle the west side of the lake, and exit through the north entrance to connect with the main route. If the weather is good but the north entrance is closed, you can look at the spectacular lake and the extinct volcano in which it sits by opting for the 14-mile side trip to Rim Village. The lake, at 1,932 feet, is the second deepest in North America. With or without the side trip, a 17-mile downhill ends the cycling day at Farewell Bend Campground near the community of Union Creek.

On Day Seven, prepare to ascend, drop some, then climb again as you head north, then east, in the Cascades. Pass the north entrance to Crater Lake National Park, then enjoy a 14-mile downhill to US Highway 97, one of the longest straight sections of highway in Oregon. Pedaling down in a head wind is a bummer. On US Highway 97, the route flattens out, the traffic is heavy, but the shoulder is wide. Spend the night in Chemult.

Traffic buzzes past for only 5 miles on Day Eight. Turn off the highway north of Chemult to the Cascades Lakes area about a mile south of what was the last company town in Oregon. Although the Gilchrist family sold their namesake town, mill, and the timber lands in 1991, a very well-kept settlement with a store larger than the one in Crescent remains.

At Mile 24.3 the Cascades Lakes Highway begins. The smooth pavement winds its way up and down hills, around lakes, and past lava flows. Views of snow-covered Mount Bachelor, South Sister, and other peaks of the Cascades to the north are enough to elicit smiles from cyclists on this lightly traveled road. Stop for the night at Cultus Lake Campground.

On Day Nine, the tour's uphill struggles end with a strenuous climb toward the base of Bachelor Butte. The glacier that reshaped the older Cascades peaks did not sculpt this relatively young, classic volcanic cone. To really get to the top of Oregon, take a chair lift to Bachelor Butte's 9,060-foot summit for a last look before descending into Sunriver. The sensational panorama includes much of the country covered on this wide-ranging tour of the Great Basin and Cascades.

MILEAGE LOG

DAY ONE: SUNRIVER TO CHRISTMAS VALLEY—78.8 MILES

0.0	Sunriver. From the parking area on Abbott Drive, return to the large Sunriver sign on South Century Drive.
0.7	Right on **South Century Drive** toward Mount Bachelor.
1.4	Left to continue on South Century Drive.
4.5	Cross LaPine Recreation Area Road (a state park campground is to the right) and Burgess Road. Proceed straight on **Huntington Drive**.

16.8   Right on **US Highway 97** in LaPine (stores, restaurant, motels).

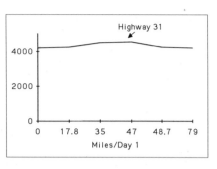

18.5   Left on **Highway 31** toward Silver Lake and Lakeview.

  39.2   Side Trip: U.S. Forest Service (USFS) Road 400 on the right leads 0.5 mile to Big Hole. The dusty, unsurfaced road heads to a 300-foot depression created by a volcanic explosion. Backtrack to rejoin the main route.

  44.5   Side Trip: USFS Road 3145 on the left leads 2 miles to Hole-in-the-Ground, a volcanic feature similar to Big Hole, but deeper and more impressive. The unpaved road is suitable for mountain bikes. Backtrack to rejoin the main route.

47.7   Left on **Fort Rock Road**.

  47.7   Shortcut: To save about 19 miles, stay on less-scenic Highway 31 and ride to Silver Lake (cafe, small store, small RV park) for the night. From Silver Lake, continue southeast on Highway 31. Rejoin the main route on Highway 31 at about 10 miles east of town (Day Two, Mile 12.9).

53.7   Pass the Fort Rock Valley Homestead Village Museum on the right.

53.8   Enter the settlement of Fort Rock (small store). Proceed straight through Fort Rock on **County Route 510** toward Christmas Valley. The flat route crosses an old lakebed and makes numerous right-angle turns.

  53.8   Side Trip: To visit Fort Rock State Park (picnic area, water), take the paved road 3 miles roundtrip to the left. Displays explain the geology and history of the starkly beautiful rock that dominates the skyline on this part of the tour.

78.8   Intersection of Wagontire Road and Old Lake Road. Enter Christmas Valley (store, cafes, motels, RV park).

DAY TWO: CHRISTMAS VALLEY TO
SUMMER LAKE HOT SPRINGS—46.7 MILES

0.0   Christmas Valley, intersection of Wagontire Road and Old Lake Road. Ride south on **Old Lake Road** toward Silver Lake and Lakeview.

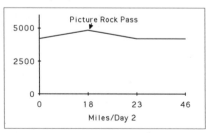

12.9   Left on **Highway 31**.

18.7   Picture Rock Pass (4,830 feet). It is named for the petroglyphs on large rocks a short way south of the highway on an unmarked trail near the pass sign.

25.2   Community of Summer Lake (store, restaurant, pleasant picnic area, bed and breakfast).

26.5   Pass the Summer Lake Wildlife Refuge. A campground (no water) is about a mile down the unpaved entry road on the left.

46.7   Summer Lake Hot Springs and RV and tent campground (private, fee, showers). The indoor pool is about 100° Fahrenheit.

DAY THREE: SUMMER LAKE HOT SPRINGS TO LAKEVIEW—51.2 MILES

0.0   Summer Lake Hot Springs. Continue left (south) on **Highway 31**.

5.8   Paisley (restaurant, small store, motel, ranger station), suggested breakfast stop.

28.5   Continue south on Highway 31 through Valley Falls (store, cafe, RV park, motel, all wrapped up into one building).

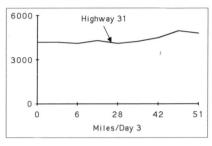

30.3   Pass Chandler Wayside (picnic tables, water, rest rooms) on the right.

49.3   Hunter Lake Hot Springs (restaurant, motel) on the right. Watch for the geyser erupting from the pond.

51.2   Junction of Highway 140 and US Highway 395. Continue into Lakeview (Hunter Lake Hot Spring, motels, RV parks, supermarkets, restaurant). Camping is available at the county fairgrounds.

DAY FOUR: LAKEVIEW TO LOFTON RESERVOIR CAMPGROUND—38.6 MILES

0.0   Lakeview, junction of Highway 140 and US Highway 395. Head west on **Highway 140** toward Klamath Falls. The next store and restaurant are in Bly on Day Five, Mile 21.9. The next motel is in Chiloquin on Day Five, Mile 74.0.

13.3   Pass the R. A. Booth Wayside (water, rest rooms) on the right.

15.2   Crest Drews Gap and drop to Drews Reservoir.

29.6   Quartz Mountain Pass (5,504 feet). Turn left on **USFS Road 3715** toward Lofton Reservoir.

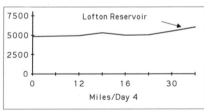

29.6 Alternative: If you are not camping at Lofton Reservoir, continue straight on Highway 140 for another 47 miles or more for alternative camping and lodging options.

36.6   Pass the road to Holbrook Reservoir.

38.0   Left on **Road 013** toward Lofton Reservoir.

38.6   Lofton Reservoir Campground (water, rest rooms) in Fremont National Forest.

DAY FIVE: LOFTON RESERVOIR CAMPGROUND TO COLLIER MEMORIAL STATE PARK—79.4 MILES

0.0   Lofton Reservoir Campground. Backtrack 9 miles to Quartz Mountain Pass via USFS Roads 013 and 3715, following the mileage log for Day Four.

9.0   Left on **Highway 140** and ride downhill toward Bly.

17.7   Access to the Sprague River picnic area (steep hill, water, rest
rooms) is about 0.2 mile to the
right.

Quartz Mountain

Miles/Day 5

21.9   Bly (small store, cafe).
32.0   Enter Beatty, which sometimes
has a store/cafe.
39.8   Right on **Sprague River Road**
toward Sprague River.
49.8   Enter Sprague River (cafe, small store).
55.8   Pass a small store, cafe, and RV park on the left.
74.0   Chiloquin (market, cafes, motels, RV parks). Turn right at the first stop
sign (unmarked) toward US Highway 97. Cross the Williamson River,
then bear right at the Y intersection on the **Chiloquin Highway** toward Crater Lake.
75.7   Right on **US Highway 97** and ride north to Collier Memorial State
Park.
   75.7   **Alternative:** If you are not visiting Collier Memorial State Park,
continue straight toward Crater Lake at the US Highway 97
junction.
79.1   Pass the first entrances to Collier Memorial State Park. Picnic grounds
(right) and a logging museum (left). Much of the equipment on display
was used by the Collier family businesses in this area.
79.4   Right into Collier Memorial State Park campground (picnicking, rest
rooms, water, showers, logging museum).

DAY SIX: COLLIER MEMORIAL STATE PARK TO
FAREWELL BEND STATE PARK—49.4 MILES

0.0   Collier Memorial State Park.
Exit left on **US Highway 97** to
return to the Crater Lake and
Chiloquin junction.

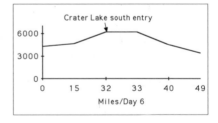

Crater Lake south entry

Miles/Day 6

3.8   Right on **Chiloquin Highway**
toward Crater Lake.
6.8   Right on **Highway 62**.
13.8   Pass Fort Klamath Frontier
Military Post County Museum
(rest rooms, water) on the left.
14.8   Enter the town of Fort Klamath (small cafe, stores, motels, RV parks).
Camping is available at the nearby Kimball State Park.
19.8   Begin a steady climb to Crater Lake. Although Highway 62 is in the park,
no fees are charged cyclists who stay on the highway. Picnic areas and
viewpoints of the Annie Creek Canyon are spread out along the climb.
32.2   Pass the south entrance of Crater Lake National Park (entrance fee) on
the left.
   32.2   **Side Trip/Alternative:** Bicycle touring is the best way to see
Oregon's only national park, although the hills may be challenging with loaded bikes. The road to the rim and Rim Village is open
year-round and makes a great side trip (7 miles to Rim Village) or

an alternative route that takes you through the park to rejoin the main route farther north. From the turnoff, the road is level for 4 miles to the park headquarters. A motel and other services a few miles from Highway 62 are open from mid-May to November. The road then rises steeply for 3 miles to Rim Village (camping in summer, meals year-round), where Crater Lake can first be seen. There is no road access to the lake itself. Alternative routes that shorten this tour by 14 or 23 miles pass beyond Rim Village through the park to the north entrance, where you connect to the main route again. The north entrance should be open from July Fourth until the snow closes it again. The north entrance is 21 miles from the south entrance via the west rim (park headquarters, Crater Lake Lodge, restaurants, stores) and 30 miles via the east rim (no services, no water past the park headquarters). The east rim alternative passes the trail to Cleator Cove where boat tours of the lake start. At the north entrance, rejoin the main route at Mile 26.5 of Day Seven.

45.3   Bear left on **Highway 62** as Highway 230, the road to Diamond Lake, joins from the right.

49.4   Right into Farewell Bend State Park campground (water, rest rooms) in Rogue River National Forest.

49.4   Alternative: Continue 0.5 mile farther south on Highway 62 to Union Creek (small store, restaurant, cabins, trail with viewpoints on the Rogue River Gorge).

DAY SEVEN: FAREWELL BEND STATE PARK TO CHEMULT—50.8 MILES

0.0   Farewell Bend State Park campground. Exit left on **Highway 62** for 0.5 mile, then go straight on **Highway 230** toward Diamond Lake. The road climbs steadily for most of the next 26 miles.

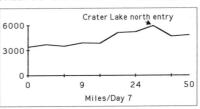

23.6   Right on **Highway 138** at a T intersection. Diamond Lake (campgrounds, pizza parlor, motel, store) starts about a mile to the left on Highway 138.

26.5   Pass the north entrance to Crater Lake National Park on the right.

41.0   Left on **US Highway 97** toward Bend at Diamond Lake Junction.

47.0   Rest area (picnic tables, rest rooms, water).

50.8   Chemult (restaurants, motels, RV parks, small store, ranger station).

DAY EIGHT: CHEMULT TO CULTUS LAKE CAMPGROUND—52.3 MILES

0.0   Chemult. Head north on **US Highway 97** toward Bend. Most traffic turns west on Highway 58 at Mile 8.0. Ignore the turn.

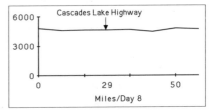

15.3   Left on **County Road 61** toward Crescent and Davis lakes.

One of the Three Sisters mountains rises over Elk Lake. (Photo: Andrew Herstrom)

        The turnoff is at the south end of the town of Crescent (restaurant, store). Gilchrist (larger store) is a mile farther north on US Highway 97.

24.3   Right on the **Cascades Lakes Highway** (USFS Road 46). Deschutes National Forest campgrounds abound on this route.

39.3   Pass North Davis Lake Campground (picnicking, camping, water, rest rooms).

46.3   Pass Quinn River Campground (picnicking, camping, water, rest rooms).

50.3   Left on **USFS Route 4635** toward Cultus Lake.

52.3   Cultus Lake Campground (picnicking, camping, water, rest rooms). **Note:** A nearby resort has cabins, a restaurant, and a small store.

DAY NINE: CULTUS LAKE CAMPGROUND TO SUNRIVER—45.1 MILES

0.0   Cultus Lake Campground. Backtrack 2 miles to Cascades Lakes Highway (USFS Route 46), following the mileage log for Day Eight.

2.0   Left on **Cascades Lakes Highway** (USFS Route 46). Campgrounds are also at Lava Lake, Elk Lake, and Sparks Lake.

26.0   Pass the Mount Bachelor Ski Resort on the right. A chair lift and snack bar operate all year. The highway becomes **Century Drive**/Highway 242 at Mount Bachelor.

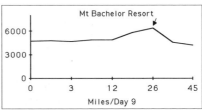

143

28.5   Right on **USFS Route 45** toward Sunriver.
39.8   Left on **Route 40**, which becomes Spring River Road, then **South Century Drive.**
44.4   Left on **Abbot Drive** in Sunriver to return to the parking area.
45.1   Sunriver, parking area. End of tour.

◆

13. WALLOWAS AND BLUE MOUNTAINS LOOP

Allen Throop

Distance: 428 miles
Terrain: mountainous
Total cumulative elevation gain: 15,700 feet
Recommended time of year: June–September
Recommended starting time: before noon the first day
Allow: 8 days; layover days recommended; 4- and 5-day shortcuts
Points of interest: Umatilla County Historical Museum, Pendleton; Pendleton Woolen Mills; the Wallowa Mountains; Hells Canyon Viewpoint; Oregon Trail Interpretative Center, Baker City; Sumpter and Granite; Lehman Hot Springs

◆ ◆ ◆

PUBLIC TRANSPORTATION
Air: commuter service is available to Pendleton from Portland; bikes must be shipped ahead by a delivery service
Train: Amtrak stops three times a week in Pendleton, LaGrande, and Baker City as it connects Portland with Denver; baggage service is not available, so bikes must be shipped ahead

PRACTICAL INFORMATION
Key contacts: Umatilla County Historical Museum, Pendleton, 503-276-0012; Umatilla National Forest Supervisor's Office, 503-276-4978; Wallowa National Forest and Hells Canyon Recreation Area, 503-426-4978

STARTING POINT
Umatilla County Historical Museum (108 Southwest Frazer Avenue) in Pendleton: From I-84 take Exit 209 and head north into Pendleton on US Highway 395, which becomes Frazer Avenue. Free parking is available in the lot serving both the museum and Amtrak. Check with museum staff before leaving your car there. The museum assumes no liability for cars or their contents.

SHORTCUTS
LaGrande is a hub around which shortcuts to this tour can pivot. To cycle only a portion of this trip, start in LaGrande. For a 4-day, 209-mile option, cycle from LaGrande to Baker City on Highway 203 (72 miles) or Highways 30 and 237

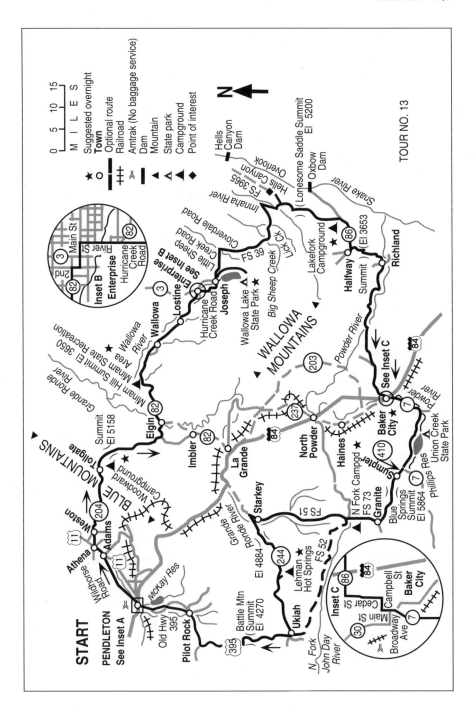

TOUR NO. 13

(about 65 miles) and pick up the main route there on Day Six, continuing to Lehman Hot Springs at the end of Day Seven, and return about 38 miles to LaGrande on Highway 244 (via I-84). For a 5-day, 290-mile option, cycle 20 miles to Elgin on Highway 82, and pick up the main route on Day Two, Mile 20.2, then ride the main route to Baker City, Day Five, Mile 66.9, and from Baker City return 72 miles to LaGrande via Highway 203 or Highways 30 and 237.

Rate the scenery on this tour with a capital P for phenomenal, but prepare to earn it. This is the toughest of the Oregon routes, with several high passes and long days, punctuated with slow, peaceful riding through historic towns. The 428 miles feature fantastic views, long hills, and a soak in Lehman Hot Springs. Options are described for shortcuts and a side trip to a Hells Canyon Overlook.

Before or after your cycling tour, visit the historic underground of Pendleton, the Pendleton Woolen Mills, and Umatilla County Historical Museum. The streets of Pendleton may be the busiest of the entire trip, but they quickly give way to a bucolic ride along Wildhorse Creek. Once, this road was Highway 11, the main route from Pendleton to Milton-Freewater and southeastern Washington. With the relocation of Highway 11 to the east, this road became a cyclist's dream: little traffic, a low grade, small communities, and pastoral scenes along the creek and across the rolling wheat fields of the Columbia River Plateau. Finish Day One with a moderately steep climb off the plateau and east into the Blue Mountains. The effort of the climb is rewarded with views. Camp in the Umatilla National Forest near a 5,158-foot pass.

Day Two is one of the easiest sections of the tour. First, head south and drop into Elgin, then climb to the east up through wheat country again before a quick downhill to the Wallowa River. A slight detour leads to the overnight campsite in primitive Minam State Recreation Area.

On Day Three, wind east through the Wallowa River Gorge until the topography breaks out into a wide valley patchworked with irrigated pasture and hay fields lying under the snow-covered Wallowa Mountains. Stop at the Forest Service Information Center in Enterprise for mountain views and literature about the area. Notice a massive ponderosa pine, the species that is the mainstay of the local timber industry, in the lobby. Continue south to visit Joseph, a town quickly becoming an artists' community. Finally, negotiate a steep climb over the glacial moraine that forms Wallowa Lake, probably the most photogenic lake in the state. This gives way to a level ride south into Wallowa Lake State Park campground, nestled under the mountains at the edge of the Eagle Cap Wilderness.

Consider a layover day in the Wallowa Lake area. Spend the hours on diversions such as exploring Joseph's museums, artists' shops and factories, and cafes; riding the aerial tram up Mount Howard; hiking into the wilderness area; fishing along a stream or from a rented boat; or simply relaxing in a charming setting.

Before continuing your cycling on Day Four, prepare with adequate food and water. No services exist between Joseph and Halfway, a small community on the other side of the Wallowas. Uphill slogs are rewarded with a few good downhill runs, but beware of sharp curves and short unpaved sections. Peer into the deepest canyon in the country on the optional 6-mile round trip to the overlook of the Hells Canyon of the Snake River. End the day at Lakefork Campground in Hells Canyon National Recreation Area.

On Day Five, shortly after leaving the campground, the topography once again breaks out into a wide valley with irrigated pastures. The pleasure of riding along Pine Creek is lessened somewhat when you realize you are heading for the prominent ridge on the southwestern skyline near Halfway. Eventually, the view to both the north and south from the ridge, and the downhill ride into Richland, make the climb worth the effort. From Richland rise steadily along the Powder River west toward Baker City on a route that can be hot, dry, and windy. (Tail winds are rarely remembered. Head winds get stronger as the years go by.)

After finally leaving the river, keep an eagle eye on the sagebrush country. Golden eagles soar overhead and sometimes perch on poles near the highway. East of Baker City, the Oregon Trail Interpretative Center tells of the pioneers who moved their wagon trains through this country and of the miners and ranchers who followed. Ruts adjacent to the highway near here are remnants made by trail pioneers who could not imagine the luxury of twenty-one gears, paved highways, or lightweight rain gear. Arrive in Baker City for a wide choice of lodging options for the night.

Supermarkets and services are a 3-day pedal from Baker City, so check your gear and supplies and shop accordingly. On Day Six, follow the Powder River south and then west on another steady climb through farmland and forest. Note the gold dredge tailings beginning to dominate the landscape at the upper end of Phillips Reservoir. Sumpter Valley's historic railroad huffs and puffs through the tailings, but on weekends only. On other days, a short side trip to the Railroad Park yields rest rooms, an unguided tour of the railroad rolling stock, and a playground.

From the end of the reservoir to Granite, look for the obvious signs of the area's gold dredging history. Cafes and shops in Sumpter emphasize that history. A state park featuring the floating gold dredge in Sumpter is scheduled to open in 1996. Granite, another former mining camp, perches on a hillside. Unfortunately, there is no treated water at the night's campground above here. You must treat water from the North Fork of the John Day River or carry it from an earlier stop.

On Day Seven climb, drop, climb, and drop again through a mixture of forests and meadows as you head north, then west. If early morning starts appeal, ride at sunup to catch a large herd of elk gracing hills near the Grande Ronde River. You can balance the appeal of the shortcut into Ukiah with that of Lehman Hot Springs, a strong incentive to finish the day on the main route. Water flows through three pools. The hot spring water is scalding, but reaches the third pool at a pleasant swimming temperature. Give yourself a deserved treat for seven days on the road: take a long soak.

Take pleasure, too, in the last day's ride, which is mostly downhill, with grand views once more of the Columbia River Basin's wheat fields. Then prepare yourself for encountering traffic near Pendleton. It may be a jolting contrast to the quiet roads that have been home for the last few days.

Cyclists rest before tackling the Wallowas and Blue Mountains Loop, the toughest of the Oregon tours. (Photo: Allen Throop)

MILEAGE LOG

DAY ONE: PENDLETON TO WOODWARD CAMPGROUND—42.8 MILES

0.0   Pendleton, Umatilla County Historical Museum. Follow the one-way traffic flow on **Frazer Avenue**. Pass under the Highway 11 Bridge and follow the main traffic as it turns left. Turn right immediately (in one block) on **Emigrant Avenue**. Ride under Court Avenue Bridge, then turn right on **Court Place** at the stop sign, and follow it past the Pendleton Woolen Mills and a hospital.

1.0   Right on **Southeast Twentieth**, and immediately left on **Highway 11/30**.

1.2   Left to stay with **Highway 11**. Cross the railroad tracks.

2.7   Left on **Wildhorse Road** where a sign points to Mount Hebron. Pavement is old and rough.

14.3   Left on **Main Street** in Adams (small store, park, rest rooms).

14.5   Right on **Commercial Street**.

14.8   Left on **Highway 11**.

19.1   Left on **Third Street**. Enter Athena (shops, restaurant).

19.3   Pass Athena City Park (water, rest rooms, swimming pool) on the right.

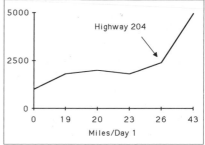

19.5   Right on **Main Street**.

20.4   Cross Highway 11.

22.7   Left on **Water Street** to enter Weston (cafe).

23.1   Right on **Main Street** at the blinking light in the center of Weston.

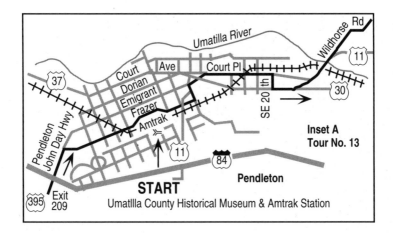

Inset A
Tour No. 13

START
Umatilla County Historical Museum & Amtrak Station

Pendleton

Start climbing into the Blue Mountains.

26.0 Right on **Highway 204** at a T intersection. Continue climbing.

38.7 The tiny settlement of Tollgate (cafe, store) has only its name to recall days when a toll was charged to use the then-private road.

41.6 Pass the E. J. Haney Viewpoint on the right. Look out onto the rolling volcanic plateaus of northeastern Oregon. A store is not far down the road.

42.8 Right into Woodward Campground (picnic tables, camping, rest rooms, water) in the Umatilla National Forest.

42.8 **Alternative:** For indoor lodging options, continue into Elgin (Day Two, Mile 20.2) for the first night for 63 miles on Day One, and to Enterprise (Day Three, Mile 31.9) for the second night for 47.8 miles on Day Two. Day Three is only 14.6 miles, allowing for extra time to explore the Wallowa Lake area.

DAY TWO: WOODWARD CAMPGROUND TO
MINAM STATE RECREATION AREA—36.1 MILES

0.0 Woodward Campground. Turn right on **Highway 204** toward Elgin.

4.5 Pass Woodland Campground (no water), on the left.

20.2 Enter Elgin (cafes, supermarket, motel) on **Division Street**.

21.3 Left on **Eighth Avenue**/Highway 82, and then right to stay on **Highway 82**.

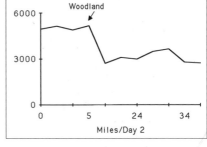

29.7 Minam Hill summit (3,650 feet).
Begin a 5-mile downhill section with a steep drop-off on the right.

34.5 Left toward **Minam State Recreation Area** at the bottom of the hill and just before the Minam store, motel, and bridge. **Caution:** The last section is a gravel road with cattle guards.

36.1 Minam State Recreation Area (camping, picnicking). Unlike most Oregon state parks, this site has no showers or flush toilets.

DAY THREE: MINAM STATE RECREATION AREA TO WALLOWA LAKE STATE PARK—46.5 MILES

0.0   Minam State Recreation Area. Retrace the Day Two route 1.6 miles back to Minam.

1.6   Left on **Highway 82**. Cross the river and head up the beautiful Wallowa River Canyon.

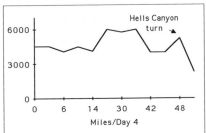

4.4   Pass a rest area (picnic tables, rest rooms, water).

7.4   Pass a rest area (picnic tables, rest rooms, water).

14.2   Wallowa (market, cafes).

22.2   Lostine (small store).

31.2   Pass the Wallowa–Whitman National Forest and Hells Canyon National Recreation Area Forest Service Visitors Center and Ranger Station on the left.

31.9   Enterprise (supermarket, cafes, restaurants, motels). Stay on Highway 82 through the main section of town.

32.7   Straight on **Hurricane Creek Road**. The intersection is not well marked, but Highway 82 forks to the left here. **Note:** Staying on Highway 82 to Joseph is 3 miles shorter, but less scenic.

40.5   Right on **Highway 82** in Joseph (museum, stores, galleries, cafes, accommodations). The small town is named for Chief Joseph of the Nez Perce who once lived in and fought for this valley. South of Joseph, the road climbs up and over a glacial moraine that forms the spectacular Wallowa Lake. The grave of Old Chief Joseph (Chief Joseph's father) is on the moraine at a marked turnout on the right.

46.5   Wallowa Lake State Park campground (rest rooms, showers). Nearby are a small store, restaurants, lodging, Mount Howard tram, and other tourist facilities.

DAY FOUR: WALLOWA LAKE STATE PARK TO LAKEFORK CAMPGROUND—58.6 MILES

0.0   Wallowa Lake State Park. Retrace Day Three's route 6 miles on **Highway 82** to Joseph.

6.0   Joseph. Turn right on **Little Sheep Creek Road** (toward Imnaha). There are no services for the next 75 miles, from Joseph to Halfway, at Mile 22.8 of Day Five.

14.0   Right on **Cloverdale Road**, which becomes Wallowa–Whitman Forest USFS Route 39.

32.5   Pass Lick Creek Campground (picnic tables, rest rooms, water) on the left.

41.8   Right toward Halfway to stay on **USFS Route 39** along the Imnaha River.

43.5   Pass Blackhorse Campground (picnic tables, rest rooms, water) on the left.

44.0   Pass Ollokot Campground (picnic tables, rest rooms, water) on the left. A long climb up to Lonesome Saddle follows.

48.0 Side Trip: For a view into the deepest canyon in the country, turn left on USFS Route 3965. A paved road leads to the Hells Canyon Overlook making a 6-mile round trip.

49.2   Lonesome Saddle (5,200 feet). Enjoy the downhill ride, but beware of sharp corners and unpaved sections.

58.6   Right into Lakefork Campground (picnic tables, rest rooms, water).

Day Five: Lakefork Campground to Baker City—76.9 miles

0.0   Lakefork Campground. Turn right on **USFS Route 39** toward Halfway.

8.2   Pass a picnic area (picnic tables, rest rooms) on the left.

13.8   Right on **Highway 86** as USFS Route 39 ends, to continue toward Halfway and Baker City.

22.8   Left, staying on Highway 86. **Note:** Halfway (stores, cafes, motel) is 1.5 miles straight ahead.

23.7   Pass Pine Ranger Station on the left.

29.2   Summit (3,653 feet). After a long, steady climb from Halfway, an exhilarating downhill leads to Richland.

36.0   Richland (stores, cafes). Most of the next 20 miles are along the Powder River.

69.3   The route here follows the Oregon Trail for about a mile.

69.3 Side Trip: Oregon Trail Interpretative Center (no admission fee) is an uphill mile to the right. Backtrack to rejoin the main route.

74.6   Cross I-84. The road then bends left and becomes **Cedar Street** in Baker City.

76.3   Right on **Campbell Street**.

76.7   Left on **Main Street**.

76.9   Corner of Main Street and Broadway Avenue in Baker City (all services, Wallowa–Whitman National Forest Supervisor's Office, motels, bicycle-friendly RV parks).

Day Six: Baker City to North Fork John Day Campground—53 miles

0.0   Baker City, Main Street and Broadway Avenue. Pedal south on **Main Street**, which becomes **Highway 7** as it heads toward John Day and Sumpter. Baker City has the last supermarket and major services until the end of the tour.

18.2   Pass Union Creek State Park Campground (picnicking, camping, rest rooms, showers, water) on Phillips Reservoir on the left.

22.9   Pass the Sumpter Valley Railroad Park on the left (0.25 mile). A steam train runs from the park to Sumpter on weekends.

25.2   Right on **Highway 410** toward Sumpter.

28.1   Sumpter State Park, with its floating gold dredge, is scheduled to open in 1996.

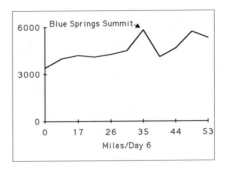

28.3   Sumpter (small stores, cafes, museum, motel). Leaving town (last lodging until Lehman Hot Springs or Ukiah), bear left toward Granite.

30.7   Pass McCully Forks Wallowa–Whitman National Forest campground (stream water only) on the right. The climb to Blue Springs Summit starts here.

35.0   Blue Springs Summit (5,864 feet).

44.2   Continue straight as the road name changes to **USFS Road 73**. Pass the turnoff to the colorful former mining town of Granite (small store) on the right.

47.0   Pass neatly stacked rocks along the creek on the right. They were piled here by industrious Chinese laborers who reworked the claims after the first gold miners rushed through the area.

52.3   Straight on USFS Route 51.

53.0   Enter the North Fork John Day Umatilla National Forest campground (stream water only) on the left.

DAY SEVEN: NORTH FORK JOHN DAY CAMPGROUND TO LEHMAN HOT SPRINGS—47.9 MILES

0.0   North Fork John Day Campground. Turn left on **USFS Route 51** toward LaGrande at the campground exit.

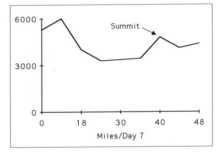

1.7   Right on **USFS Route 51** toward LaGrande.

     1.7 Alternative: To trim approximately 10 miles from the route, stay to the left and ride directly to Ukiah, approximately 38 miles from this point on USFS Route 52. This alternative trades a visit to Lehman Hot Springs for sweeping views of the John Day River drainage and wilderness. Rejoin the main route on Day Eight, Mile 16.7.

5.3   Crocker Hill Summit (5,943 feet). Start down into the Grande Ronde River Valley. Watch for a large herd of elk often in the fields along this section. Numerous small picnic areas are along the river between Miles 18 and 24.

27.9   Starkey (store). This is the only store on today's route, and it has a limited selection.

28.5   Left on **Highway 244**. The climb from this point gets gradually steeper.

Whether traveling on two wheels or more, be prepared for a delightful adventure. (Photo: Allen Throop)

39.1   Summit (4,884 feet).
46.7   Left on an unnamed road signed to **Lehman Hot Springs**.
47.9   Lehman Hot Springs (camping, cabins, snack bar). Soaking in the pool
       is a fantastic end to a hard day of riding.

DAY EIGHT: LEHMAN HOT SPRINGS TO PENDLETON—66 MILES

0.0   Lehman Hot Springs. Back-
       track on Day Seven's route 1.2
       miles to Highway 244.
1.2   Left on **Highway 244** toward
       Ukiah.
6.6   Pass Bear Wallow Creek Uma-
       tilla National Forest camp-
       ground (no water) on the right.

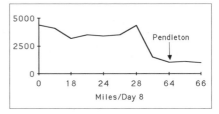

7.2   Pass Lane Creek Umatilla National Forest campground (water) on the
       right.
16.7   Ukiah (stores, cafe, motel, ranger station, RV park).

The rewards of a tough uphill climb are often sweeping panoramas and exhilarating downhill slides. (Photo: Adventure Cycling Assn. [Greg Siple])

18.1	Right on **US Highway 395** toward Pendleton.
29.0	Pass Battle Mountain State Park (water, rest rooms, tables, very steep access road downhill) on the left. The park commemorates the last battle in Oregon (in 1878) between European settlers and Native Americans.
44.1	Bear right to stay on US Highway 395 toward Pendleton.
51.5	Community of Pilot Rock (supermarket, cafes).
53.0	Left on an **Old US Highway 395** that parallels the present highway.
55.0	Cross US Highway 395 to continue on Old US Highway 395.
60.0	Merge with **US Highway 395** to continue toward Pendleton.
64.5	Pendleton (all services).
65.7	Pass under I-84, then bear right on **Frazer Avenue** at the light.
66.0	Umatilla County Historical Museum. End of tour.

IDAHO

◆

14. THE IDAHO PANHANDLE

Gayle Newman

Distance: 450 miles
Terrain: flat to hilly to mountainous
Total cumulative elevation gain: 16,007 feet
Recommended time of year: May–October
Recommended starting time: 8:00 A.M.
Allow: 9 days; 3- and 6-day shortcuts
Points of interest: Spokane Falls; Fort Sherman historical buildings, Coeur d'Alene; Lake Coeur d'Alene; Cataldo Mission; Railroad Museum, Wallace; Mining Museum, Wallace; Miners Cemetery, Wallace; Sprag Pole Museum, Murray; Cabinet Gorge; Lake Pend Oreille; Treaty Rock Park, Post Falls; Falls Park, Post Falls

◆ ◆ ◆

PUBLIC TRANSPORTATION

Air: most major airlines serve Spokane; verify that a bicycle can be carried as baggage
Train: the Amtrak station is located at West 221 First Avenue in Spokane; pick up the main route in downtown Spokane

PRACTICAL INFORMATION

Key contacts: Spokane Chamber of Commerce, Washington, 509-624-1393; Riverside State Park, Spokane, Washington, 509-456-2729; St. Maries Chamber of Commerce, 208-245-3563; Coeur d'Alene Central Reservations, 800-876-8921; Kellogg Visitor Center, 208-784-0821; Wallace Chamber of Commerce, 208-753-7151; Sandpoint Visitor Center, 800-800-2106; Priest River Chamber of Commerce, 208-448-2721; Friends of the Centennial Trail, Washington, 509-324-1756
Notes: This spectacular tour includes a critical link that lacks paving until the summer of 1996. No viable detour exists. Therefore, before embarking on your tour, please phone the Shoshone County Public Works Department in Idaho at 208-753-5475 or 208-682-3957 for information on the Enaville–Thompson Pass Highway in Idaho. This 7.7 miles of gravel road begins at Mile 25.6 of Day Four. Because it is a steep, uphill grade, touring bicycles are not recommended on this section of road.

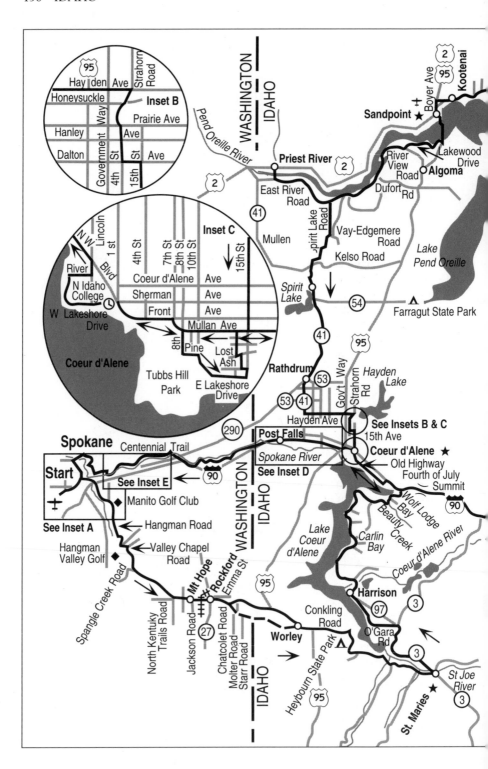

Inset B

95 Hayden Ave · Strahorn Road
Honeysuckle
Way · Prairie Ave
Hanley · Ave
Dalton · 4th St · 15th St · Ave
Government St

Inset C
N W · Lincoln · 1 st · Blvd · 4th St · 7th St · 8th St · 10th St · 15th St
River · N Idaho College
Coeur d'Alene · Ave
Sherman · Ave
Front · Ave
Mullan Ave
W Lakeshore Drive · 8th · Pine · Lost Ash
Coeur d'Alene
Tubbs Hill Park · E Lakeshore Drive

WASHINGTON · IDAHO
Pend Oreille River
Priest River · 2
East River Road
41
Mullen
Spirit Lake Road
Sandpoint ★ · Boyer Ave · 2 · 95 · **Kootenai**
River View Road · Algoma · Lakewood Drive
Dufort Rd
Vay-Edgemere Road
Kelso Road
Lake Pend Oreille
Spirit Lake · 54 · **Farragut State Park**
41 · 95
Hayden Lake
Gov't Way · Strahorn Rd
Rathdrum · 53
53 · 41
Hayden Ave · **See Insets B & C**
15th Ave
290 · **Post Falls**
Spokane · Centennial Trail · Spokane River · **See Inset D** · **Coeur d'Alene** ★
Start · **See Inset E** · 90 · Old Highway Fourth of July Summit
Manito Golf Club · 90
See Inset A · Hangman Road · Wolf Lodge Bay · Beauty Creek
Hangman Valley Golf · Valley Chapel Road
WASHINGTON · IDAHO
Lake Coeur d'Alene · Carlin Bay · Coeur d'Alene River
Spangle Creek Road · **Mt Hope** · **Rockford** · Emma St · 95
Harrison · 97 · 3
North Kentuky Trails Road · Jackson Road · 27 · Chatcolet Road · Molter Road · Starr Road · **Worley** · Conkling Road · O'Gara Rd
Heyburn State Park · 95 · 3
IDAHO · St Joe River · 3
St. Maries ★

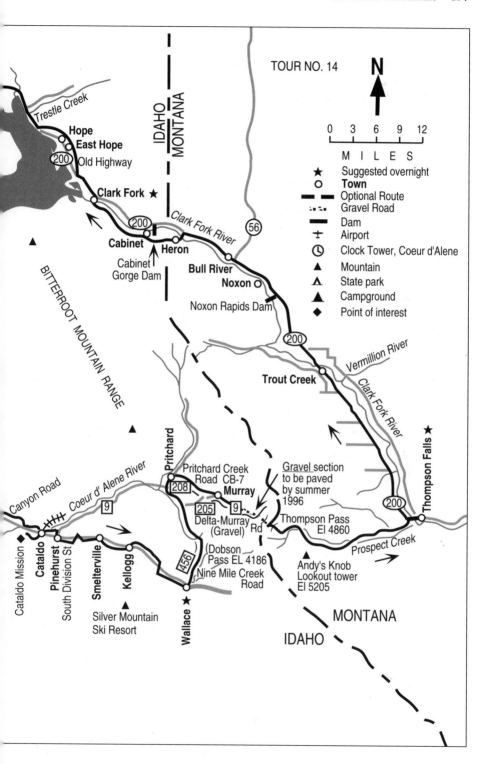

TOUR NO. 14

N

MILES

| 0 | 3 | 6 | 9 | 12 |

★ Suggested overnight
○ **Town**
▬ Optional Route
▬ Gravel Road
▬ Dam
╆ Airport
🕓 Clock Tower, Coeur d'Alene
▲ Mountain
⏶ State park
▲ Campground
◆ Point of interest

Trestle Creek

Hope
East Hope
Old Highway
200

IDAHO | MONTANA

Clark Fork ★

Clark Fork River
200
56

Cabinet   **Heron**
Cabinet
Gorge Dam
Bull River
Noxon ○
Noxon Rapids Dam

200

Vermillion River

Trout Creek

Clark Fork River

BITTERROOT MOUNTAIN RANGE

Pritchard

Pritchard Creek
Road CB-7
Murray
208
205 9
Delta-Murray
(Gravel) Rd

Gravel section
to be paved
by summer
1996

Thompson Pass
El 4860

Thompson Falls ★

200

Canyon Road

Coeur d' Alene River
9

(Dobson
Pass EL 4186
Nine Mile Creek
Road

Prospect Creek

Andy's Knob
Lookout tower
El 5205

MONTANA

Cataldo ◆
Pinehurst
South Division St
Smelterville
Kellogg
456

Cataldo Mission

Silver Mountain
Ski Resort
▲

Wallace ★

IDAHO

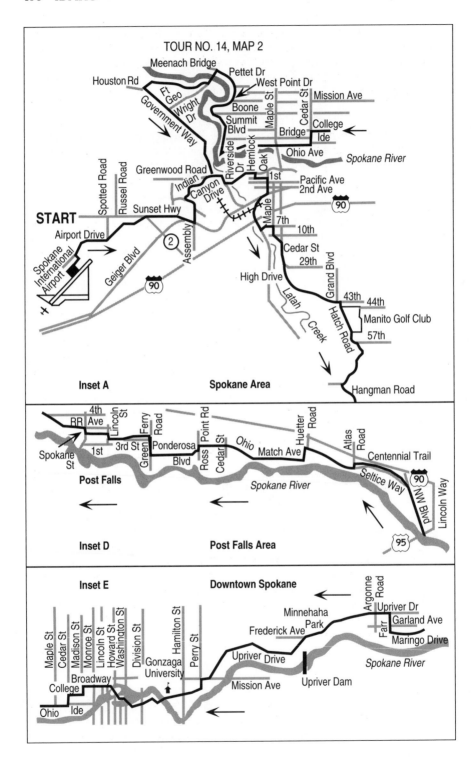

TOUR NO. 14, MAP 2

Inset A — Spokane Area

Inset D — Post Falls Area

Inset E — Downtown Spokane

Also note that, at this writing, portions of the Centennial Trail from Coeur d'Alene to Post Falls, and from Gonzaga University to the T. J. Meenach Bridge in Spokane, are not totally complete. The main route closely follows the intended pathway of the trail system. Check in Riverside State Park in Spokane or with the visitors center in Coeur d'Alene for Centennial Trail updates.

STARTING POINT

Spokane International Airport, Spokane, Washington: From I-90 take Exit 277 and follow the signs to the airport. Park and secure your car in the parking garage, then follow the one-way route out of the airport.

SHORTCUTS

To shorten this 9-day adventure into a 3-day loop from Spokane to St. Maries and Coeur d'Alene and back, combine Days One, Two, and Nine for 179 miles. For a 6-day loop beginning and ending in Coeur d'Alene, combine Days Three through Eight for 271 miles. To reach Coeur d'Alene from the main route's starting point, continue east from Spokane toward Idaho on I-90 for about 30 miles. Make parking arrangements with a local motel or bicycle shop in Coeur d'Alene.

Explore mines and waterways of Idaho's Panhandle on a 9-day figure-eight tour. The Spokane, Coeur d'Alene, Clark Fork, and Pend Oreille rivers connect Lake Coeur d'Alene, Lake Pend Oreille, and Spokane to furnish 60 percent of the route. Over the entire 450 miles, fascinating examples of early road construction, mining, Indian encounters, and logging testify to the massive effort expended in the last 150 years toward taming the land and its people.

Begin in Spokane, Washington, pedaling along a segment of the annual Bloomsday Marathon course and through the Brownes Addition, an elegant historic neighborhood. Cross into the Hangman Creek area to descend through the Hangman Valley where Colonel George Wright hung seven Indians in 1858 to avenge an earlier attack on Colonel E. J. Steptoe. Enjoy a roller-coaster ride from here to Lake Coeur d'Alene, sliding up and over the Palouse hills, a fertile farming district that spans Washington and Idaho. Enter Heybourn State Park where a maze of lakes and marshes mark the St. Joe River's flow north into Lake Coeur d'Alene, then continue into tiny St. Maries for the night.

On Day Two, ride north from St. Maries, squiggling around the points and bays of Lake Coeur d'Alene's eastern shore. Poor mining practices have turned the Coeur d'Alene River and Lake Coeur d'Alene into a reservoir of mining wastes. Although the pollution has been reduced, heavy-metal concentrations still exist in both. At Wolf Lodge Bay, round the lake's northern shore, then scoot into the resort town of Coeur d'Alene. Coeur d'Alene grew around Fort Sherman, constructed in 1879 to "control" the Coeur d'Alene Indians. Pioneers settled around it, but when gold was discovered in 1883, hordes of people flocked to the Coeur d'Alene Valley, precipitating the town's incorporation in 1887. Some of Fort Sherman's original buildings are still standing on the site of the current city park and North Idaho College. Stay the night in Coeur d'Alene.

Start Day Three in a historic Coeur d'Alene neighborhood near Tubbs Hill, then return to Wolf Lodge Bay to continue over the Fourth of July Summit along the original Mullan Road. In 1854 John Mullan, a military captain and topographical engineer, searched for a northern wagon trail and railroad route from Fort Benton to Fort Walla Walla. In the fall of 1861, Mullan's party constructed a trail as far as the Cataldo Mission, only to see their work washed away by heavy rains and flooding. Fallen trees and sixty crossings of the Coeur d'Alene River made the road soggy and difficult, if not impossible, to maintain. Abandoned for about 100 years, the Mullan Road became northern Idaho's interstate highway route in the 1960s.

Read a silver story in the mine tailings, sluices, smelters, dredges, pioneer cemeteries, and abandoned and working mines that litter the route from Cataldo to Wallace and Murray. The unofficial gateway to the Silver Valley is the Cataldo Mission, sitting on a knoll on Mission Flats above the Coeur d'Alene River. The Cataldo Mission is the oldest standing building in Idaho. The Coeur d'Alene Indians sent for the "Black Robes" and in 1842 Jesuit missionaries came to work with them. Father Ravalli designed the mission and began construction in 1850. Idaho's largest silver-producing district, Silver Valley is the source of approximately half of the nation's newly mined silver. At day's end in Wallace, explore its rich mining history, museums, and cemetery.

Begin Day Four with an invigorating climb up Dobson Pass. Catch your breath on the descent to Beaver Creek Bottoms and the North Fork of the Coeur d'Alene River. After Murray, a living ghost town, continue on up Thompson Pass (4,860 feet). (**Note:** This includes the 7.7-mile section to be paved by the summer of 1996.) On the other side of this pass, Montana spreads a welcome mat, a 22-mile downhill to the Clark Fork River. This western edge of Montana is just a teaser, enough to germinate plans for a return to "Big Sky Country." End the day in Thompson Falls, Montana.

On Day Five, tag along with the Clark Fork River past the Cabinet Mountains and Cabinet Gorge. Cross back into Idaho and the town of Clark Fork on the southern tip of Lake Pend Oreille. Stretching for 143 miles, Lake Pend Oreille earns its title as the largest lake in Idaho. Enjoy great wildlife viewing, fishing, and scenery in and around the lake, and spend the night in Clark Fork.

Pay close attention to its northeastern shoreline. It shapes your ride on Day Six into Sandpoint. Along the way, view the site of what once was Lake Missoula. During the last Ice Age, the lake was as deep as 2,000 feet and its waters played a significant role in shaping the landscape of several states. Sandpoint, the day's destination, offers a thriving artists' community and many festivals throughout the year.

On Day Seven cross the "long bridge" out of Sandpoint and begin a relaxing backroad tour along the Pend Oreille River, flowing west out of Lake Pend Oreille. The shores of the pristine, glacial Priest Lake, only 22 miles to the north, may tempt you into a layover day. End the day in Priest River.

Pass Spirit Lake on Day Eight. Started in 1902 as a Panhandle Lumber community, the town survives on agriculture, logging, and tourism. Fifteen buildings in the town square date to 1907. Learn more from the display of historical photographs in a local hardware store. Return to Coeur d'Alene for another night on the shores of Lake Coeur d'Alene.

Follow the many twists and turns of the Centennial Trail on Day Nine. A cooperative effort between the states of Idaho and Washington, the Centennial Trail links 63 miles of recreational trails. Stop in at Falls Park in Post Falls where Frederick Post's sawmill once stood. He built it in 1880 as Post Falls's first business. Cross under a covered bridge on the trail and revel in the wildflowers. Stick with the Centennial Trail most of the way back to Spokane, Washington, flowing along with the Spokane River. Along the way, you can enjoy sights such as the Walk on the Wildside Zoo, Gonzaga University, downtown Spokane, Spokane Falls, the 1974 World's Fair site, and Riverside State Park.

MILEAGE LOG

DAY ONE: SPOKANE AIRPORT, WASHINGTON TO ST. MARIES—69.6 MILES

0.0   Spokane Airport, T intersection with airport exit road and Airport Drive. Turn right (east) toward Spokane on **Airport Drive**.

1.3   Ride straight through an intersection with Spotted Road, then angle right on **Sunset Highway**, following signs for Business Loop I-90 and West Spokane.

3.3   Left on **Assembly Street**, passing Deska Drive on the right.

3.8   Assembly Street becomes **Indian Canyon Drive**.

4.8   Angle right as Indian Canyon Drive merges with **Greenwood Road**.

5.1   Right on **Government Way** at a T intersection, and immediately left on **Riverside Drive**. This section of the ride follows the annual Bloomsday Marathon route.

6.2   Right on **Hemlock Street** and pedal uphill.

6.3   Left on **First Avenue**, one block up the hill. This is the historic Brownes Addition of Spokane.

6.5   Right on **Oak Avenue** and cross Pacific Avenue.

6.7   Cross Second Avenue and turn right on **Sunset Boulevard**.

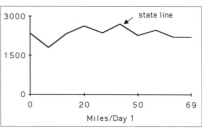

6.8   Bear left at the fork, riding under the train trestle and I-90. Begin a sweeping downhill, being careful not to miss your next turn shortly beyond the overhead freeway bridges.

7.2   Left on **Seventh Avenue**.

7.7   Right on **Maple Street** at the stop sign.

7.9   Pass Tenth Avenue on the right, as the main arterial turns left and uphill. Follow the bike-route signs. Maple Street becomes **Walnut Street** at this point, continuing uphill, then turning right to become **Cedar Street**.

8.7   Along the ridge above Latah Creek, Cedar Street becomes **High Drive**.

11.0   Stay with High Drive at the stop sign, after passing Grand Boulevard on the left.

11.2   Right on **Hatch Road** (sometimes referred to as Boundary Road) at the stop sign. Turn right again with the arterial, passing Manito Golf Club on the left.

12.1   Bear right at the fork, continuing on Hatch Road, ignoring Fifty-seventh Avenue straight ahead. This is a great, winding downhill. **Caution:** no shoulder.

13.4   Midway down Hatch Road, turn left on **Hangman Road**. Hangman Creek was originally called Sin Too Too Olley, meaning "river of small fish."

17.7   Pass a golf course on the right.

17.9 Right and downhill at the fork to continue along the golf course.

18.5 The road turns to gravel for the next 0.4 mile.

18.9 At the top of a short incline, follow the road left, turning right at the stop sign on **Valley Chapel Road**.

22.2 Follow the road left, passing Spangle Creek Road on the right.

29.0 Pass an intersection with North Kentucky Trails Road.

29.9 Pass through Mount Hope (no services).

31.7 Bear left at the fork. Jackson Road is to the right.

34.1 Left on **Highway 27** at the stop sign at a T intersection.

34.2 Right on **Emma Street**, heading into Rockford.

34.7 Right on **First Street** at the main intersection in Rockford (store, motel, rest rooms, water).

36.4 Pass Chatcolet Road on the right.

36.4 **Alternative:** Turn right on **Chatcolet Road**, a hard-packed, relatively flat gravel road. **Note:** This alternative route, 0.7 mile longer, is recommended because, though it has a 4.1-mile section of relatively flat, hard-packed gravel, US Highway 95 north of Worley is extremely narrow and heavily used.

38.0 Bear left at the fork, crossing a narrow bridge. Molter Road is off to the right.

38.1 Pass Molter Road on the left.

39.1 Cross another bridge, staying left at the end of it. Pass Starr Road on the right.

40.5 Return to pavement. Pass Idaho Road on the left. Continuing on Chatcolet Road, cross the Idaho state line.

46.9 Right on **US Highway 95 South** at the stop sign in Worley (store, water). Rejoin the main route at Mile 46.2 below.

39.4 Enter Idaho.

42.5 Right on **US Highway 95 South** at the stop sign.

46.2 Enter Worley (store, water).

48.1 Left on **Conkling Park Road**.

53.8 Enter Heybourn State Park (water, rest rooms). Created in 1908, this is Idaho's oldest state park. Descend to Lake Coeur d'Alene on a rough, narrow road.

55.3 Right at the stop sign, passing a road on the left to Chatcolet picnic and boat ramp area.

56.2 Pass the day-use picnic area (water, rest rooms) on the left.

57.3 Left on **Route 5 East** at the stop sign at a T intersection.

58.1 Pass Rocky Point Marina turnoff on the left.

68.6 Enter St. Maries (all services), established in 1889 when its first sawmill began operating.

69.6 Intersection of Main and Ninth streets, the town center.

DAY TWO: ST. MARIES TO COEUR D'ALENE—56.4 MILES

0.0 St. Maries, intersection of Ninth and Main streets. Ride south on **Main Street**.

0.3 Follow the road as it swings right to become **Fourth Street**.

0.4 Left on **College Avenue** and immediately left again on **Third Street** at the four-way stop.

0.5 Cross the railroad tracks, then the St. Joe River. This is **Route 3**, the White Pine Scenic Route.

0.9 Pass the St. Joe River Road on the right.

8.2 Pass a historical marker on the left. Due to flooding from the St. Joe River, the St. Joseph Indian Mission, established here in 1842, moved north in 1846 to become the Cataldo Mission.

8.8 Enter Kootenai County, the first county formed in Idaho Territory.

11.3 Continue straight toward Coeur d'Alene on **US Highway 97** as Route 3 turns right toward Kellogg and Wallace.

11.9 Left on **O'Gara Road** toward Kootenai High School.

19.1 Left on **US Highway 97** at a T intersection.

19.2 Enter Harrison (store, water, rest rooms). Harrison was formed in 1889 when settlers convinced President Harrison to wrangle a strip of reservation from the Coeur d'Alene Indians for a sawmill.

19.3 Pass a geological marker noting that Lake Coeur d'Alene is really a submerged valley. The St. Joe River flooded and formed Lake Coeur d'Alene after deposits created a large glacial moraine that dammed the river.

21.3 Cross the Coeur d'Alene River. A sportsman's access is on the right just before the bridge. Continue on the dike road to connect to the other bank.

30.3 Pass Carlin Bay on the left at a public dock (cafe).

40.5 Pass Squaw Bay (store, resort, marina).

40.6 Pass a campground (rest rooms, water) on the left.

45.4 Cross Beauty Creek. A campground is to the right on an unpaved road.

46.9 Pass Wolf Lodge Bay (fishing area, pit toilets, wildlife viewing area) on the left.

47.4 Pass a Lake Coeur d'Alene Scenic Byway map and pullout on the left.

47.7 Cross a bridge, bearing left at the fork.

47.9 Left on **I-90** westbound toward Coeur d'Alene. Wolf Lodge Campground (private facility with camping, restaurant, water, rest rooms) is straight ahead and to the right at the T intersection.

49.6 At **milepost 20** on I-90, just before the third bridge, go around the eastern end of the barricade. Walk your bike down the embankment to the old highway, then turn left and pass underneath I-90.

49.7 Follow the **Old Highway** around to the right through the parking lot along the shores of Lake Coeur d'Alene on the left.

53.1 Pass a historical marker on the left that describes the *Amelia Wheaton* steamer, built in 1880 by the Army. It originally carried hay and supplies for Fort Coeur d'Alene.

54.9 Left on **Mullan Avenue**. The center of Mullan Avenue still has old trolley car tracks.

55.5 Pass Fifteenth Street.

55.8 Continue straight past the Centennial Trail marker. Head into Coeur d'Alene (all services).

The Idaho Panhandle Tour offers mines, waterways, and in-city explorations.
(Photo: Ken Newman)

56.0   Follow Mullan Avenue as it passes city hall on the left and turns right to become **Seventh Street.** Take an immediate left on **Front Avenue**, then skirt the city park that leads up to the Coeur d'Alene Hotel complex.

56.4   Pass the Coeur d'Alene Hotel entrance. Straight ahead is the clocktower and the city park. The visitor center is one block to the right on First Street.

DAY THREE: COEUR D'ALENE TO WALLACE—51.5 MILES

0.0   Coeur d'Alene, clocktower in the city park next to the Coeur d'Alene Hotel. Backtrack on Day Two's route for 0.4 mile along **Front Avenue**, with the lake on the right.

0.4   Follow the sidewalk/bike path right on **Seventh Street** and left on **Mullan Avenue** in 0.05 mile (about 100 yards), following bike-path signs.

0.5   Right on **Eighth Street**, following the bike-path signs.

0.7   Left on **Pine Avenue.** Stay on Pine Avenue, crossing Ninth Street.

0.8   Right on **Tenth Street.** In about 50 feet, the road forces a left on **Mountain Avenue**, then immediately jogs right to follow the lakeshore past Tubbs Hill Park on the right. At this point, the route is on **East Lakeshore Drive.** Tubbs Hill was part of the homestead of Tony Tubbs, which

164

he subdivided in 1883. The park provides a great view of the lake and the city.

1.3 Left on **Fifteenth Street** as East Lakeshore Drive ends at the Jewitt House entrance. Today a senior center, the house was built by Edward Rutledge Timber Company in 1917.

1.4 Left on **Ash Avenue**.

1.5 Take the first right on **Fourteenth Street** (unmarked), then left immediately on **Lost Avenue** at the T intersection, and again take the first right in just a few feet on **Fourteenth Street**.

1.6 Cross Young Avenue and then Bancroft Avenue.

1.7 Right on **Mullan Avenue** at the stop sign.

2.3 Right on **Coeur d'Alene Lake Drive**, which will become the **Old Highway**. I-90 is visible off to the left.

2.9 Go straight through an unmarked intersection, passing a road on the right.

3.0 Pass under Potlatch Hill Road, keeping Lake Coeur d'Alene on your right.

7.6 Enter a parking lot at the end of the Old Highway. Ride through the lot.

7.7 Walk your bike up the I-90 embankment, repeating Day Two's Mile 49.6 maneuver in reverse. Squeeze through the barricade to head east on I-90. From here to the Cataldo Mission, the route closely follows the Mullan Road constructed in 1859 to 1861. **Note:** The bike path heading into the trees ends at a picnic area (rest rooms) just beyond the edge of the woods.

9.7 Pass Exit 22 to Wolf Lodge Road, continuing east on I-90.

15.7 Cross the Fourth of July Summit (3,081 feet). In 1861 John Mullan's road crew spent the Fourth of July here. Just off the exit, "Mullan's Tree" bears an inscription used to mark the roadway at regular intervals. The tree has been a stump since 1962 when it was blown over in a wind storm. From here the route drops down to Mission Flats.

21.7 Take **Exit 34** at the junction with Route 3. Turn left at the end of the exit to cross over I-90.

21.8 Right on **Canyon Road** at the T intersection.

26.2 **Side Trip:** To visit Cataldo Mission (3 miles round trip), turn right on this unmarked gravel road. In 0.6 mile the road takes a sharp turn to the left to parallel I-90, before it bends right and crosses over I-90. At this point the road is paved. After crossing I-90, follow the road right and enter Old Mission State Park (rest rooms, water) at 1.5 miles. At the park's interpretative center, an informative movie recounts the mission's history. Backtrack to rejoin the main route.

28.4 Enter Cataldo (store). Cross the railroad tracks and turn left at the intersection on **Riverview Drive**.

30.1 Pass an unmarked road on the right, and turn right on **Coeur d'Alene River Road** at the stop sign.

31.5 Cross I-90.

31.6 Left on **Silver Valley Road** at the T intersection.

32.9 Enter Pinehurst (store, water, rest rooms).

33.6 Left on **South Division Street** at the stop sign, toward I-90. Pass under I-90 and loop back around to pass under I-90 again, returning to the south side of the highway.

36.5   Enter Smelterville (store, restaurant, water, rest rooms) where the road becomes **Main Street**.

36.9   Continue straight ahead, passing First Avenue on the right.

37.0   Go straight across Airport Road (unmarked).

37.4   The road is closed at this point, forcing a turn. Turn left, following the bike path signs.

37.6   Right at the end of the fence to ride east on the bike path parallel to I-90.

39.2   Enter Kellogg (all services). The bike path comes to a T intersection with Bunker Road. Turn left to continue to Wallace.

39.2   **Side Trip:** Turn right for the Kellogg Visitor Information Center, 0.4 mile on the left in the Gondola Station. A "Trail of the Arts" brochure is available at the visitor center. Watch for chainsaw carvings, murals, and "junque sculptures" along the route.

39.4   Right on **Jacob Boltz Road** at the stop sign.

39.8   Jacob Boltz Road becomes **Cameron Avenue**.

40.0   Go straight through a four-way stop. From here to Division Street the route passes six sculptures and paintings listed on the "Trail of the Arts" tour.

40.3   Cross Division Street, staying with Cameron Avenue.

41.7   Pass a road to the right going under I-90.

43.9   Pass a historical marker on the 1972 Sunshine Mine Disaster that took the lives of ninety-one men. Cross Big Creek Road, staying north of I-90.

45.4   Follow the **Silver Valley Road** to the right under I-90.

45.6   The road curves left, passing Yellowstone Avenue on the right.

46.2   The road curves left, and then immediately right, to become **Mullan Avenue**.

46.8   Pass a turnoff on the left for I-90 and Mullan Creek. This part of the route is the **East I-90 Business Loop**.

50.6   Enter Wallace (all services), named for Colonel W. R. Wallace. Wallace was founded in 1884 when rich mineral ores were discovered here.

50.7   Pass an intersection on the left, crossing over I-90. The tourist information center is to the left before I-90.

51.3   Enter the city center.

51.4   Left on **Pine Street**.

51.5   T intersection with Sixth Street. The Railroad Museum is straight ahead, and downtown Wallace is to the right.

DAY FOUR: WALLACE TO THOMPSON FALLS, MONTANA—56.4 MILES

0.0   Wallace, Railroad Museum at Sixth and Pine streets. Turn right out of the parking lot on **Sixth Street**. Ride under I-90, where the street is renamed **Nine Mile Creek Road**.

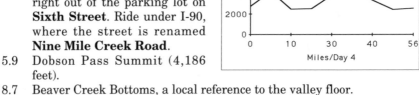

5.9   Dobson Pass Summit (4,186 feet).

8.7   Beaver Creek Bottoms, a local reference to the valley floor.

12.7 Pass Forest Route 205 on the right, a turnoff to Murray that turns to gravel.

16.0 Right on **Forest Route 208** toward Murray.

16.3 Stay left.

16.7 Continue straight ahead, crossing Pritchard Creek and passing through an intersection.

17.6 Cross Pritchard Creek.

17.7 Right on **Pritchard Creek Road** (also known as CB-7 and Forest Road 9).

23.6 Enter Murray (all services).

24.2 Continue straight out of town on **CB-7** toward Thompson Pass.

25.6 Note: Until the summer of 1996, expect a gravel section from here to the summit of Thompson Pass. **Caution:** The steep grade dictates wide and/or knobby bicycle tires for this section.

33.3 Thompson Pass (4,860 feet). Enter Montana.

55.4 Right on **Route 200** toward Thompson Falls at a stop sign.

55.5 Cross the Clark Fork River.

56.4 Enter Thompson Falls (all services). Continue straight 0.4 mile to the town center.

Day Five: Thompson Falls, Montana to Clark Fork—60.5 Miles

0.0 Thompson Falls, Montana, intersection of Galatin and Main streets. Head north out of town on **Main Street**/Route 200.

1.3 Cross the Clark Fork.

1.4 Pass the junction with Prospect Creek Road (Road 471) on the left.

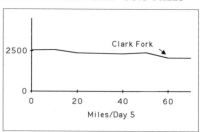

20.5 Enter Trout Creek (store, water).

34.9 Pass the turnoff to Noxon (restaurant) on the left.

40.0 Pass the junction with Route 56 on the right.

40.1 Enter Bull River (store, rest rooms, water).

42.5 Enter Idaho.

46.5 Left on an unmarked road at the turnoff, following the signs for Heron.

47.4 Cross the Clark Fork River on a one-lane bridge.

47.9 Cross the railroad tracks, and then, at the T intersection, turn left on the unmarked paved road (may be referred to locally as Heron Road).

48.2 *Sharp* right on an **unmarked road**, following the signs for Clark Fork.

53.0 Pass the turnoff on the right for Cabinet Gorge.

59.5 Cross a one-lane wooden bridge over the Clark Fork River to enter the town of Clark Fork (motel, restaurant).

60.2 Follow the road right (passing the road entering from the left) where it becomes **Stephen Street**.

60.4 Left on **Fourth Avenue**/Route 200 at a stop sign.

60.5 Left on **Main Street** toward the center of town.

Day Six: Clark Fork to Sandpoint—27 miles

0.0   Clark Fork, intersection of Main Street and Fourth Avenue/Route 200. Ride north out of town on **Main Street**/Route 200.

3.5   Cross a bridge. Turn right immediately on the **Old Highway** (unmarked). The first views of Lake Pend Oreille are to the left. Lake Pend Oreille is 143 miles long and is 1,225 feet deep at one point on its south end.

9.1   Continue straight into East Hope (store). The road to the left goes out to Route 200. Pass a memorial to David Thompson, who began a fur trading post near here in 1809. A geographer and surveyor, Thompson mapped the route the highway follows along Lake Pend Oreille.

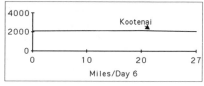

9.9   Enter the old section of town. Hope was formed in 1882 when the Northern Pacific Railway was under construction.

10.6   Right on **Route 200 North** at the stop sign.

10.9   Pass a geological site noting Lake Missoula, formed during the last Ice Age, was massive, reaching more than 200 miles into Montana. Eastern and central Washington were ravaged by repeated floods when the Lake Missoula ice dam broke. Lake Pend Oreille is a small remnant of Lake Missoula.

22.7   Enter Kootenai (store, restaurant).

23.7   Go straight on **Kootenai Cutoff Road** at the stop sign. Route 200 continues to the left.

24.4   Continue straight at the stop sign, crossing US Highway 2.

24.7   Cross a bridge, then immediately turn left on **Boyer Avenue**, passing the airport runways on the right.

25.8   Pass the airport entrance on the right.

26.3   Enter Sandpoint (all services).

26.4   Cross railroad tracks.

27.0   Cross Main Street. To reach the town center, turn left on Oak Street at the four-way stop.

Day Seven: Sandpoint to Priest River—27.2 miles

0.0   Sandpoint, old marina parking lot where the bike path across Long Bridge over Lake Pend Oreille begins. Proceed south on the bike path, crossing the lake.

2.4   Right across US Highway 95 on **Lakewood Drive**, immediately after crossing the lake.

2.9   Bear right at the fork.

5.5   Pass Swingy Point Park (restaurant) on the right.

7.5   Bear left at the fork where the route becomes **River View Road** (unmarked).

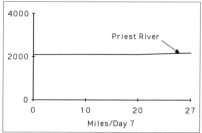

10.5   Follow the road as it turns sharply left, passing a road on the right.

10.8   Stay on River View Road as it jogs right and then left.

11.0   Cross the railroad tracks at the stop sign.

11.5   Pass a road on the right and continue following River View Road.

12.5   Cross the railroad tracks at the stop sign and pass through the Morton Slough Game Management Area.

14.5   Right on **Dufort Road** at the stop sign.

15.6   Cross railroad tracks and follow Dufort as it turns sharply left.

18.5   Follow Dufort Road, renamed **East River Road**, as it passes Vay Edgemere Road on the left.

21.5   Pass the Spirit Lake Road turnoff on the left.

26.8   Right on **Wisconsin Street** at the stop sign, cross the Priest River, and pedal into the town of Priest River (all services).

27.2   Left at the stop sign on the **US Highway 2 Business Loop** toward the town center.

The backroads of the Idaho Panhandle provide an introduction to the state's varied history. (Photo: Jeanne McHale)

DAY EIGHT: PRIEST RIVER TO COEUR D'ALENE—48.4 MILES

0.0 Priest River, intersection of Wisconsin Street and US Highway 2. Ride south on **Wisconsin Street**, again crossing the bridge over the Priest River.

0.4 Left on **East River Road**. Backtrack 5.3 miles on the Day Seven route.

5.7 Right on **Spirit Lake Road**.

14.2 Follow Spirit Lake Road as it turns sharply left.

17.5 Left on **Route 41** at the stop sign.

19.4 Enter the town of Spirit Lake (all services).

20.2 Pass a turnoff on the left for Route 54 and Farragut State Park.

30.3 Left to ride east on **Route 53**, following the signs for Coeur d'Alene.

30.6 Right on **Route 41** at the stop sign. A bike lane begins here.

31.5 The bike lane continues on the opposite side of the road.

34.8 Left on **Hayden Avenue**.

39.6 Cross US Highway 95 at a major intersection in Hayden Lake (all services).

39.8 Cross Government Avenue.

40.7 Right on **Strahorn Road**.

41.3 Right on **Fourth Street** (unmarked) at the stop sign.

41.5 Follow Fourth Street left, passing Honeysuckle Avenue on the right.

42.0 Cross straight through the intersection, passing Prairie Avenue.

43.5 Left on **Dalton Avenue** at the four-way stop.

44.0 Right on **Fifteenth Street** at the four-way stop.

45.2 Enter Coeur d'Alene (all services).

46.4 Ride under I-90.

47.4 Cross Sherman Avenue.

47.5 Right on **Mullan Avenue**. Continue straight past the Centennial Trail.

48.0 Passing city hall on the left, the road turns right and becomes **Seventh Street**. Before crossing Front Street, take an immediate left on the **Centennial Trail** (bikepath/sidewalk). Ride directly toward the Coeur d'Alene Hotel complex.

48.4 Pass the Coeur d'Alene Hotel entrance on the left. The city park and clocktower are straight ahead.

DAY NINE: COEUR D'ALENE TO SPOKANE AIRPORT, WASHINGTON—53.3 MILES

0.0 Coeur d'Alene, clocktower in the city park on the lake, immediately south of the Coeur d'Alene Hotel. Proceed south along the lake, away from the hotel, using the pathway closest to the shore.

0.1 Proceed straight on the bike lane along **West Lakeshore Drive**. Do not turn right on Park Drive.

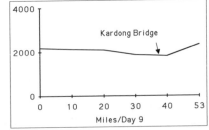

West Lakeshore Drive becomes **Rosenberry Drive**. North Idaho College is on the right. Several of Fort Sherman's original buildings remain standing on the campus.

0.7 Follow the road around to the right where Rosenberry Drive becomes **River Avenue**.

1.1 Left on **Lincoln Way** at the stop sign. Until the Centennial Trail is complete, do not follow signs for it at this point. Continue straight instead.

1.2 Cross the railroad tracks and turn left on **Northwest Boulevard** at the stop sign. This is a busy intersection.

1.6 Pass the on-ramp to US Highway 95 on the right.

1.7 Pass under US Highway 95.

2.5 Left on **Seltice Way** at an intersection with Northwest Boulevard. Right immediately on the **Centennial Trail**. This turn comes at the intersection crossing just prior to Seltice Way.

3.6 Left on **Atlas Road**, as the bike path drops down to it. Pathway ends here.

3.7 Right on **Seltice Way** at the stop sign.

4.8 Left on **Huetter Road** (not well marked).

5.1 Cross the railroad tracks and immediately turn right on **Ohio Match Avenue**.

6.6 Straight at a stop sign, crossing Cedar Street.

7.1 Left on **Ross Point Road** at a stop sign.

7.3 Right on **Ponderosa Boulevard**.

8.3 Right on **Green Ferry Road** at a stop sign.

8.8 Pass Third Street on the left.

8.9 Left on the **Centennial Trail**, just before the railroad tracks.

9.6 Right on **Third Street**, as the trail bends left and ends.

10.0 Right on **Lincoln Street**.

10.1 Left on the **Centennial Trail** again, just before crossing the railroad tracks.

10.3 Enter Post Falls (all services).

10.4 Right on **Spokane Street** at the T intersection. The Centennial Trail continues on the sidewalk. Cross the railroad tracks, come to an intersection, and turn left on **Railroad Avenue**. Use the crosswalk to continue on the Centennial Trail directly across the street.

 10.4 Side trip: To visit Treaty Rock Park (rest rooms, water), which contains a rock with Indian carvings that allegedly depict a contract between Frederick Post and Coeur d'Alene Chief Andrew Seltice, continue straight across Railroad Avenue and ride under I-90. Turn left on Seltice Way. The park is on the left side in 1 mile. Backtrack to rejoin the main route.

10.5 Pick up the Centennial Trail across the street.

10.6 Jog left, then right across Fourth Street to stay with the Centennial Trail. To the left on Fourth Street is Post Falls Park (rest rooms, water).

13.1 Wind down to an intersection with Railroad Avenue and Pleasant View Road. Pick up the Centennial Trail on the northwest corner of the intersection, using the crosswalks to do so. On the trail, go behind a factory outlet mall next to I-90, passing an access road on the left.

15.1 Cross the Spokane River and enter Washington State.

15.3 *Sharp* right with a hairpin curve in the trail.

15.6 Pass under the freeway and continue west on the north side of I-90.

15.9   Continue straight across Spokane Road and pick up the trail again. Keep I-90 on your left.

16.1   Pass a rest area on the left. To continue on the Centennial Trail, consisting of old cement blocks for the next mile, go straight.

26.0   Pass rest rooms and water on the left.

26.9   Pass under I-90 on the trail.

27.9   Swing right and cross the Spokane River. Turn left at the end of the bridge, riding west with the Spokane River on your left.

29.1   Ride on **Maringo Drive** as the separated pathway ends and the Centennial Trail shoots out on a residential street.

29.2   Right on **Farr Road**, the first right.

29.7   Left on **Upriver Drive** at the stop sign.

30.0   Straight through the intersection with a light, crossing Argonne Road.

31.3   Pick up the separated pathway on the left side of the road or stay in the designated bike lane.

31.6   Enter Spokane (services 6 miles ahead).

32.3   Pass Minnehaha Park (pit toilets) on the right.

32.5   Pass Upriver Dam on the Spokane River on the left.

32.7   Left with **Upriver Drive**. Frederick Avenue continues straight ahead.

33.1   The separated pathway ends, but is replaced by wide bike lanes on either side of the road.

35.8   Pick up the separated bike path on the river side of the road.

35.9   Right at the stop sign on the **Mission Avenue** sidewalk.

36.0   Left on **Perry Street**. Use the crosswalk for direct access to the Centennial Trail across the intersection.

36.5   Skirt the edge of Gonzaga University, founded by Father J. M. Cataldo, on the right.

36.6   Ride straight across maintenance roads and onto an overpass across Hamilton Street.

37.0   Cross the blue Don Kardong Bridge over the Spokane River, and turn right with the pathway. Take either fork in the path. They reunite in a mile.

37.8   Just before the Spokane Coliseum, turn right and cross a wooden bridge back over the Spokane River. Turn left at the end of the bridge.

38.0   Pass under Washington and Stevens streets.

38.1   Left at an intersection of trails and then continue straight. Do not turn left across the bridge. Staying right, pass the YWCA on the left. Turn left at the T intersection and cross the Blue Bridge over the river, keeping the YWCA on your left. (When the Centennial Trail is complete, the route will continue straight through downtown Spokane along the banks of the Spokane River.)

38.2   Cross another section of the Blue Bridge.

38.3   Left as the Blue Bridge ends. Continue straight past the totem pole, ignoring a path to the left and crossing another branch of the river on a foot/bike path. Come out to the corner of Post North and Broadway West. Turn left on **Broadway West**.

38.6   Ride straight across Lincoln Street at the intersection.

38.7   Cross Monroe Street and turn left on **Madison Street**. Turn right immediately on **College Avenue** at the T intersection.

38.9   Left on **Cedar Street**.

39.0   Pass Bridge Avenue on the right, and Ide Avenue on the left, going under a railroad trestle where Cedar Street curves right.

40.9   Cross Maple Street, a major thoroughfare.

41.1   The road becomes **Ohio Avenue**.

42.0   Follow a ridge above the Spokane River where Ohio Avenue is renamed **Summit Boulevard**.

42.5   Cross Boone Avenue, continuing on Summit Boulevard.

43.1   Bear left on **West Point Drive**.

43.2   Stay left on **West Point Drive**, passing Milford Place on the right.

43.3   Left on **Pettet Drive**, dropping back down along the river.

44.0   Left on **Fort George Wright Drive** at a T intersection. Cross the T.J. Meenach Bridge.

44.2   Right as the bridge ends, following the pathway across the highway and continuing west along the south side of the Spokane River.

45.6   Left on **Houston Road** (unmarked) at the military cemetery, leaving the Centennial Trail. Turn left again on **Government Way** at the T intersection. (The Centennial Trail continues straight to end at Nine Mile Falls on the Spokane River.)

48.3   Right on **Greenwood Road**.

48.6   Left on **Indian Canyon Drive**, which shortly becomes **Assembly Street**.

50.1   Right on **Sunset Highway**.

50.3   Stay right at the fork, following signs for the airport.

50.6   Bear right at the fork, remaining on Sunset Highway/US Highway 2 West.

51.2   Bear left at the fork, following airport signs. Follow the road right as it merges with **Airport Drive**.

52.2   Pass **Spotted Road** on the right.

53.3   Enter Spokane Airport. End of tour.

◆

15. NEZ PERCE NATIONAL HISTORIC PARK LOOP

Gayle Newman

Distance: 279 miles
Terrain: flat to hilly to mountainous
Total cumulative elevation gain: 12,128 feet
Recommended time of year: May–September
Recommended starting time: 8:00 A.M.
Allow: 6–7 days
Points of interest: Luna House Museum, Lewiston; Spaulding Mission and National Historical Park Museum; Lenore Archeological Site; Clearwater County Museum, Orofino; Lewis and Clark Canoe and Long camps; Pierce Court House; White Bird Battle Ground; Nez Perce Historical Society Museum, Nez Perce; Winchester State Park; St. Joseph's Mission

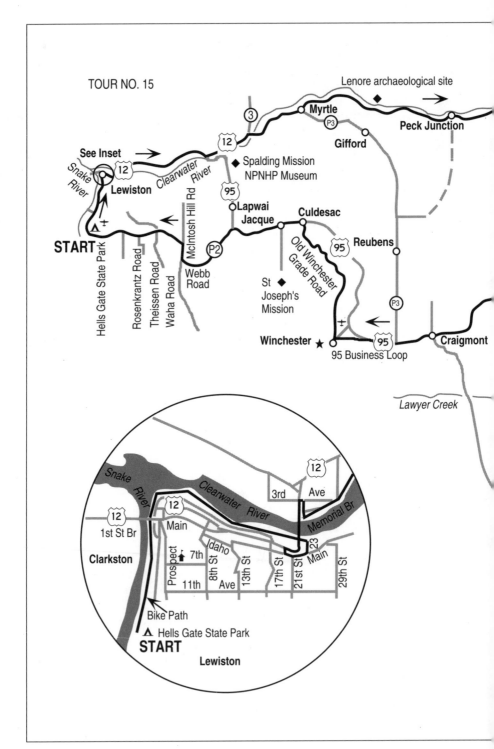

TOUR NO. 15

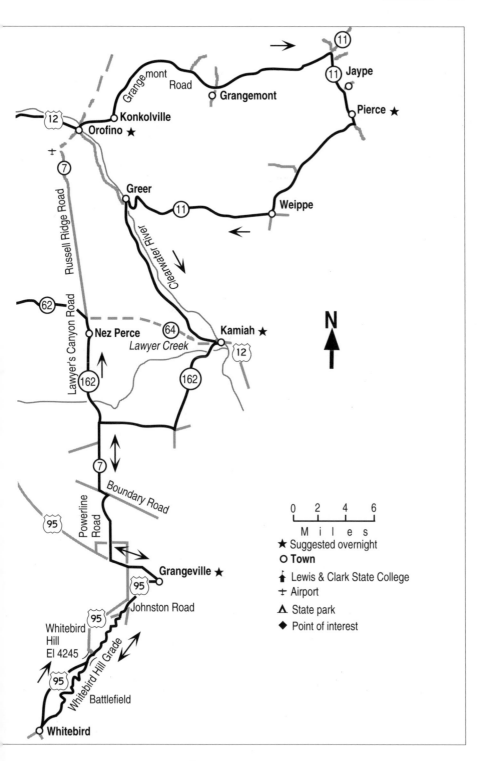

◆ ◆ ◆

PUBLIC TRANSPORTATION

Air: commercial airlines serve Lewiston; inquire if bicycles can be carried as baggage; to access the route, follow directions to parking in Hells Gate State Park and pick up the main route at the beginning or at Mile 31.0 on Day Seven
Train: none available

PRACTICAL INFORMATION

Key contacts: North Central Idaho Travel Association, 800-473-3543; Lewiston Chamber of Commerce, 208-743-3531; Hells Gate State Park, 208-799-5015; Orofino Chamber of Commerce, 208-476-4335; Pierce Chamber of Commerce, 208-464-2349; Kamiah Chamber of Commerce, 208-935-2290; Grangeville Chamber of Commerce, 208-983-0460; Winchester Chamber of Commerce, 208-924-5358; Winchester State Park, 208-924-7563

STARTING POINT

Hells Gate State Park near Lewiston: From Idaho follow Route 12 through downtown Lewiston, continue along the Snake River on Snake River Avenue, following the signs for the park. From Washington State, cross the Snake River on Route 12 and follow the signs for Hells Gate State Park, turning south on Snake River Avenue. In approximately 4 miles, turn right into the park. Register your car and purchase a permit, then turn right into the first parking lot at the north end of the park. The tour begins at the north end of this lot.

Experience living history. Revel in the majesty of the Snake, Clearwater, and Salmon rivers, high prairies, thickly forested hills, spectacular canyons, and ravines along this 279-mile route. As the week unfolds, so will an appreciation of the Nez Perce's reluctance to part from their homelands. An archaeological dig on the Clearwater River dates occupation back 10,000 consecutive years. Ancient ties to the land explain why the Nez Perce call themselves "Nee-Me-Poo," meaning "the people," even though they became better known as "Nez Perce."

Roaming east to the Bitterroots and as far west as the Cascades, the peaceful, nomadic Nez Perce tribe fished the rivers, hunted the forests, and dug camas bulbs on the prairies. On this tour, visit nineteen of the thirty-eight sites across Idaho, Oregon, Washington, and Montana that make up the Nez Perce National Historic Park.

Begin at Tsceminicum, Nez Perce for "meeting of the waters." The confluence of the Snake and Clearwater rivers in Lewiston is a focal point of the Nez Perce culture. Follow the banks of the Clearwater River, tracing Lewis and Clark's famous 1805 water voyage. The Clearwater River has cut through 2,000 feet of the Columbia Plateau's basalt lava flows to form this beautiful canyon. To acquire the historical base for the balance of the tour, take a short side trip to the Spaulding Mission and the Nez Perce National Historic Park headquarters. End the day in Orofino.

On Day Two, climb along Whiskey Creek, then enter Pierce, a rough-hewn logging town. Once the scene of the 1860 gold rush, Pierce later was the center of the fierce battle to control the region's timber. Discovery of gold intensified demands for Nez Perce lands and ultimately led to the 1877 Nez Perce War.

On Day Three pass just east of where Lewis and Clark and a band of the Nez Perce chanced to meet on September 20, 1805. The explorers camped with the

Nez Perce, resting for the next leg of their journey west, then left their horses and supplies for safekeeping. Upon their return the following year, Lewis and Clark camped near Kamiah for four weeks before they could cross the Bitterroot Mountains. Called "Camp Chopunnish" by Lewis and Clark and "Long Camp" by the Nez Perce, this was one of the most lengthy of Lewis and Clark's camps.

Before halting your bicycle wheels on Day Three, make them whir in a dramatic drop back to the banks of the Clearwater River at Greer. The 1914 bridge makes crossing the river a snap, but from 1861 to 1914, it was ferry service only. The Clearwater River grows feistier here as it squeezes down a narrowed basalt canyon. Many geologists believe this is the western edge of the continental margin. See the evidence in the dark gray diorite rock exposed along the walls of the Clearwater Canyon between Orofino and Kamiah.

End the day in Kamiah where Nez Perce legend says the tribe originated. Explore the "Heart of the Monster," a rock formation south of town that is the mythological site of Nez Perce creation. Nearby, visit Idaho's oldest Protestant church in continuous use, organized by five women missionaries in 1871. Across the river from Kamiah is where Lewis and Clark established their Long Camp.

On Day Four, climb up out of the forested Clearwater River Valley to the high camas prairies, rolling through ravine after ravine on the way to Grangeville. Lay over in Grangeville on Day Five for a 38-mile loop into the White Bird Battlefield. The White Bird Battle precipitated the notorious 1,170-mile "Flight of the Nez Perce." Chief Joseph's haunting words, "I will fight no more forever," seem to echo through the canyon.

On Day Six return to the Lapwai Valley via Nez Perce, Craigmont, and Winchester, towns formed from the remains of Nez Perce reservation lands carved up and handed out to settlers in 1895. Named in 1900 for the Winchester Rifle, the town has a nearby state park that originally was the site of the Craig Lumber Company. The lumber company created Lapwai Lake when it dammed Lapwai Creek for a mill pond. In 1963 the sawmill closed because mature timber had been logged away. Stay overnight in Winchester or in Winchester State Park on Lapwai Lake.

Complete this living history adventure on Day Seven by visiting St. Joseph's Mission and the Lapwai Fort. Climb out of the Lapwai Valley to the rolling range land near Lewiston. Inspired by the land and the legacy of the Nez Perce, pedal on to Hells Gate State Park and the tour's end.

MILEAGE LOG

DAY ONE: HELLS GATE STATE PARK TO OROFINO—47.6 MILES

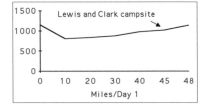

0.0   Hells Gate State Park, north end of the north parking lot. Ride north on the bike path toward Lewiston, with the Snake River on your left.

2.0   Pass under the Southway Bridge.

3.8   Pass under the First Street Bridge.

3.9   Tsceminicum—"The Meeting of the Waters" in Nez Perce. The Clearwater and Snake rivers meet here.

Visit Lewis and Clark Historical Center and see Nancy N. Dreher's sculpture representing Earth Mother, who nurtures all forms of life. Luna House

Museum, located across the overpass on the corner of C Street and Third Street, features pioneer artifacts, a self-guided walking tour of downtown Lewiston, and an extensive collection of historical photographs.

5.5   Left to continue east along the river, at the stop sign marking the end of the paved bike path.

5.6   Pass under US Highway 12/Memorial Bridge and immediately turn right on **Twenty-third Street** (unmarked), crossing the railroad tracks and riding uphill.

5.7   Right on **East Main Street** at a T intersection.

   5.7   Side Trip: To reach Potlatch Corporation's 2-hour lumbermill tours, turn left on East Main Street and left again on Mill Road. The tours are offered Monday through Friday at 1:00 P.M., plus a 9:00 A.M. tour in the summer. Backtrack to rejoin the main route.

5.8   Stay right, heading east on **US Highway 12**. Ride up the separated bike lane and cross the Clearwater River on the Memorial Bridge.

6.4   Right on **Third Avenue North** at the intersection, and immediately right again on **East Twenty-second North,** which doubles back toward the river.

6.5   Ride straight into a gravel parking lot as the road turns to the left.

6.6   Ride to the end of the Clearwater Park parking lot. Turn left on the **Clearwater Bike Path**, riding east with the Clearwater River on the right. You can try log rolling in the practice pond on the left.

11.0   Continue east on **US Highway 12** as the bike path ends.

   14.3   Side Trip: To visit the Spaulding Mission and the Nez Perce National Historic Park Museum and headquarters, turn right, following signs for US Highway 95 South, crossing over the river. The parking lot is on the left in 1.4 miles. Exceptionally knowledgeable and friendly park rangers assist as you explore the remains of Spaulding Mission to fit more pieces of the Nez Perce story together. Backtrack to rejoin the main route.

15.8   Pass the Spaulding Mission Site historical marker. The mission, established in 1836 by Henry and Eliza Spaulding, is across the river.

19.8   Gibbs Eddy. The Clearwater River was a log highway until 1971 when the Dworshak Dam was built. Log drives began on the North Fork and ended, 90 miles later, in Lewiston. On Day Three in the town of Pierce, see a logging *bateau* used to herd the logs.

22.3   Pass a turnoff for Myrtle (no services) on the left.

31.2   Rattlesnake Point rest area (rest rooms, water). A historical marker tells of 1967–1971 Lenore archaeological excavations that verified prehistoric occupation for 10,000 years on this site.

32.4   Pass Slaterville Steamboat Port. It lasted exactly 7 days. Seth Slater quickly discovered steamboats could not maneuver on the Clearwater River.

38.2   Peck Junction (store).

44.0   Enter Orofino (all services). Orofino began as a trading post in 1895. Ferry service began the same year. In 1899 the Northern Pacific Railroad completed a line from Lewiston.

45.1   Lewis and Clark camped here in the fall of 1805 and built canoes for their trip down the Clearwater River.

47.4   Left and cross the bridge for Orofino's city center.

47.6   Intersection at the end of the bridge, with Route 7 and Michigan Avenue. Continue straight on **Michigan Avenue** toward the city center.

DAY TWO: OROFINO TO PIERCE—31.4 MILES

0.0   Orofino, intersection of Michigan Avenue and Route 7. Ride north through town on **Michigan Avenue**.

2.5   Enter Konkolville (restaurant).

3.1   Pass Orofino Creek Road (unmarked) on the right.

3.2   Pass under a train trestle.

3.3   Bear left at the fork on **Grangemont Road** and begin a steep climb up Whiskey Creek.

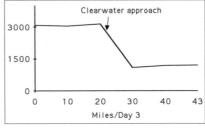

13.3   Pass access to Grangemont (no services) on the right.

25.8   Right on **Route 11** toward Pierce at a T intersection in Hollywood. Nearby is the Bertha Hill Lookout. Constructed in 1902, it was the first fire lookout in the United States.

27.5   Pass Jaype. Named for John Phillip Weyerhaeuser Jr., Jaype is the site of the Potlatch Plywood Mill. The plywood mill's pride is a building covering seven acres. **Caution:** Many logging roads enter the highway at this point.

28.2   Cross railroad tracks.

31.1   Enter Pierce (all services). Elias Pierce discovered gold near here in 1860, starting a rush that ultimately led to the Battle of the Nez Perce in 1877. The Pierce gold rush lasted only two years.

31.4   Cross the bridge into the heart of town. Pierce Courthouse, Idaho's oldest government building, is one block east of Main Street.

DAY THREE: PIERCE TO KAMIAH—43.1 MILES

0.0   Pierce, intersection of Moscript Street and Main Street. Ride south on **Main Street**.

0.6   Stay right. French Mountain Road is to the left. Cross a bridge over Orofino Creek. Near this location is Canal Gulch, where the first gold was actually discovered in 1860. Oro Fino, a boom town, came and went two years later when the gold played out.

1.8   Pass a historical marker denoting the change in Pierce's demographics after the gold rush. At one point the population consisted of 150 Chinese and 15 to 20 Caucasians. In 1885 a Caucasian merchant was brutally murdered in Pierce. Masked vigilantes from surrounding towns usurped the law and hung five Chinese residents without a trial. The whitewashing of this atrocity reached clear to the governor's office.

10.5   Enter Weippe.

10.8   Continue straight at this unmarked intersection.

11.3   Weippe city center (restaurant, rest rooms, water). Follow the road as it takes a sharp right turn. Several other roads enter from the left.

11.9   Pass a historical marker relating the chance 1805 meeting of Lewis and Clark and the Nez Perce Indians 3 miles east of here. The Weippe Prairie is a traditional fall gathering place for the Nez Perce who collected camas bulbs, an important food source. The Nez Perce held council near here after the Battle of the Clearwater in 1877.

21.3   Start down to the Clearwater River. **Caution:** There are multiple switchbacks with limited vision on the turns.

28.6   Enter Greer (store). The road turns left and crosses the river.

28.9   Left on **US Highway 12** at the stop sign. For the next 14 miles the shoulder comes and goes. **Caution:** Heavy traffic travels at high speeds. Use extreme caution.

43.1   Enter Kamiah (all services), named for the discarded bark of the Kame Hemp, used to make ropes and mats. City center is straight ahead.

DAY FOUR: KAMIAH TO GRANGEVILLE—32.6 MILES

0.0   Kamiah, intersection of US Highway 12 and Route 162/64. Ride west on **Route 162/64** away from the river.

0.1   Right on **Fifth Street,** following the signs for Route 162/64.

0.2   Left on **Pine Street**, following the signs for Route 162.

2.7   Cross Lawyer Creek. Begin a gentle uphill climb. Lawyer Creek and Lawyer Canyon are named for Nez Perce Chief Lawyer, accused of betraying his people by signing the controversial 1863 treaty.

10.2   Crest the Camas Prairie.

12.5   Pass a geological marker: The soil on the Camas Prairie lies atop Columbia Plateau lava flows. The Kamiah Buttes rising above these lava flows could be up to 40 million years old.

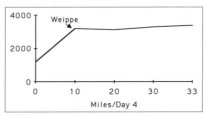

15.1   Left on **Route 7** toward Grangeville at a T intersection.

20.4   The road turns sharply left, passing Boundary Road (also named Reservation Line Road) on the right. At this point Route 7 and Boundary Road are the same.

22.5   Follow Route 7 as it turns sharply right. Boundary Road/Reservation Line Road continues straight ahead.

26.6   Continue straight as Route 7 becomes **Powerline Road**.

30.7   Left on **US Highway 95 South** at the stop sign.

31.8   Enter Grangeville (all services). The Charity Grange Hall Number 15, perhaps the first in the Northwest, was established here in 1876. The road to the grange hall became the main street of the new town of Grangeville.

32.1   Pass under a railroad trestle.

32.6   Left on **Main Street** toward city center.

The Clearwater River area has been home to the Nez Perce people for 10,000 consecutive years. (Photo: Jeanne McHale)

Day Five: White Bird Battlefield Loop—37.6 miles

0.0   Grangeville, Main Street and US Highway 95. Turn left on **US Highway 95 South.**

2.6   Left on **Johnston Road.**

4.6   Bear left at the fork, and begin an intense uphill climb.

8.9   Crest White Bird Hill.

9.9   Left on **US Highway 95 South** at the T intersection.

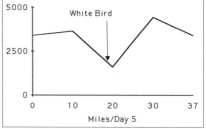

10.8 Left on **Old US Highway 95** at the entrance to the White Bird Battlefield Auto Tour, a feature of Nez Perce National Historic Park. Pick up a guide at the way station to explore the battlefield and events precipitating the fight. This is tour stop number 1. Each stop is marked by a red post. On June 17, 1877, the White Bird Battle was the opening scene of the Nez Perce War. **Caution:** Visibility is poor rounding the many switchbacks down White Bird Hill.

12.2 Stop number 2, "Calvary Advance."

17.2 Stop number 3, "Fighting Begins."

17.8 Stop number 4, "Troop Deployment."

18.3 Stop number 5, "Indian Attack."

19.0 Enter the town of White Bird (store, rest rooms, water).

19.7 Right on **US Highway 95 North,** riding back up White Bird Hill.

24.0 Stop number 6, the Wayside Exhibit Shelter.

26.0   Stop number 7, the Calvary Retreat Viewpoint.
26.8   Pass the entrance to the White Bird Battlefield Tour on the right.
27.7   Right on an unmarked road, retracing the route to Grangeville.
28.7   Crest White Bird Hill (4,425 feet).
33.5   Bear right at the fork.
35.0   Right on **US Highway 95 North** at the stop sign.
37.6   Right on **Main Street** in Grangeville.

DAY SIX: GRANGEVILLE TO WINCHESTER—48 MILES

0.0   Grangeville, intersection of C and Main streets. Ride west on **Main Street** toward US Highway 95.

0.1   Right on **US Highway 95 North**.

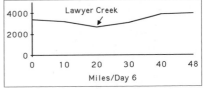

0.4   Pass under the railroad trestle.

1.9   Right on **Route 7**/Powerline Road, retracing the Day Four route.

10.1   Curve left on Route 7 to pass Boundary Road entering from the right.

12.2   Follow Route 7 as it turns sharply right. Boundary Road continues straight ahead.

17.5   Continue straight toward Nez Perce, passing the junction with Route 162 to Kamiah on the right. Route 162 and Route 7 follow the same route from here to Nez Perce.

19.9   Cross Lawyer Creek at the canyon bottom, and start climbing again.

24.6   After passing the Nez Perce Cemetery on the right, enter Nez Perce (store). Staked out in the 1890s, the Nez Perce townsite awaited the subdivision of the Nez Perce Reservation in 1895. Thousands of settlers lined up for the lots.

25.0   Right on **Eighth Avenue**, then left on **Oak Street**.

25.4   Left on **Fourth Avenue**/Route 62/7. (Route 162 becomes Route 62 at this juncture. Route 64 is to the right.)

25.5   Follow **Route 62/7** right as Fourth Avenue becomes Pine Street and heads north out of town toward Craigmont.

25.8   Follow Route 62/7 as it turns right, passing Walnut Street (unmarked) on the left.

27.2   Bear left at the fork to continue on Route 62 toward Craigmont. Route 7/Russell Ridge Road continues straight ahead. Craigmont was formed in 1920 when the towns of Ilo and Vollmer merged, ending a sixteen-year feud.

37.4   *Sharp* right to enter Craigmont on Route 62, which becomes **Boulevard Avenue**.

37.5   Ride under the railroad trestle, following the signs for **US Highway 95 North Business Loop**.

37.6   Continue straight through town at the intersection, following the signs for US Highway 95 North Business Loop.

38.1   Exit Craigmont on US Highway 95 North Business Loop.

38.5   Right on **US Highway 95 North** at the stop sign.

45.3   Left on **US Highway 95 Business Loop** to Winchester.

47.6   Pass a turnoff on the left for Winchester State Park (camping, rest rooms, water). Continue straight ahead for the town center.

48.0   Winchester town center (all services).

DAY SEVEN: WINCHESTER TO HELLS GATE STATE PARK—38.3 MILES

0.0   Winchester, intersection of US Highway 95 Business Loop and the turnoff to Winchester State Park. Ride north on **US Highway 95 Business Loop** through Winchester.

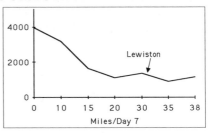

0.4   Go through the town center, passing the Business Loop for US Highway 95 on the right. Continue straight ahead on **Old Winchester Road**.

15.1   Left on **US Highway 95 North**.

15.6   Pass the turnoff on the right for Culdesac (store).

17.4   Enter Jacque (limited services). Just ahead on the left is the turnoff for St. Joseph's Mission, 4 miles up the road. Dedicated in 1874, it was the first Catholic mission to the Nez Perce.

21.3   Left on **P2**/Webb Road toward Lewiston, beginning a 4.8-mile climb. The town of Lapwai is 2.2 miles further ahead, north on US Highway 95.

27.3   Stay with P2/Webb Road as it turns right. Waha Road comes in from the left.

28.6   Follow P2 Road left. McIntosh Hill Road is straight ahead.

30.6   Enter Lewiston (all services). Pass the Lewiston Roundup rodeo grounds on the left.

31.0   Pass Thiessen Road on the left.

31.1   Left on **Lower Tammany Creek Road** (unmarked at this point) as Tammany Creek Road bends to the right.

37.5   Road name changes to **Snake River Avenue**.

38.3   Left into Hells Gate State Park. End of tour.

◆

16. SUN VALLEY LOOP

Gayle Newman

Distance: 278 miles
Terrain: flat to mountainous
Total cumulative elevation gain: 6,872 feet
Recommended time of year: late June–September
Recommended starting time: 8:00 A.M.
Allow: 5 days; layover days recommended
Points of interest: Goodale's Cutoff of the Oregon Trail; Craters of the Moon National Monument; Mount Borah earthquake fault; historic Challis mining

district; Sawtooth National Recreation Area; Yankee Fork mining district; Sunbeam Hot Springs; Stanley, a living ghost town; Redfish Lake; Sun Valley Resort; Ore Wagon Museum, Ketchum; Blaine County Historical Museum, Hailey

◆ ◆ ◆

PUBLIC TRANSPORTATION
Air: commercial airlines serve Hailey, just south of the Sun Valley city limits; verify that bicycle can go as baggage
Train: Amtrak serves Shoshone, but no baggage is loaded or unloaded; ship your bicycle ahead

PRACTICAL INFORMATION
Key contacts: Arco Chamber of Commerce, 208-527-8294; Challis Chamber of Commerce and Visitor Center, 208-879-2771; Challis Ranger Station, 208-879-4321; Stanley Chamber of Commerce and Visitor Center, 208-774-3411; Sawtooth National Recreation Area Headquarters, 208-726-7672; Sun Valley–Ketchum Visitor Information, 800-634-3347; Ketchum Ranger District, 208-622-5371

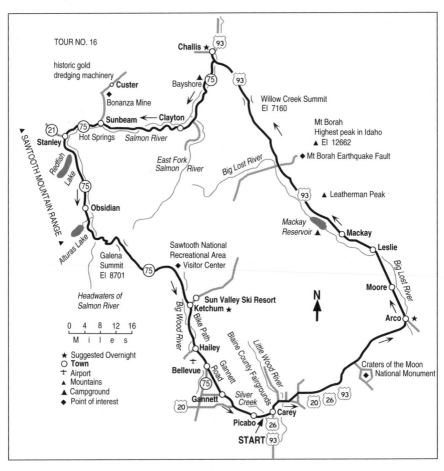

STARTING POINT

Blaine County Fairgrounds, Carey, Idaho: From I-84 eastbound take Exit 95 at Mountain Home, heading west on US Highway 20 to Carey. Turn left at the stop sign and proceed to the fairgrounds on the left in 0.7 mile. From I-84 westbound take Exit 173 in Twin Falls, heading north on US Highway 93 to Carey. Blaine County Fairgrounds is on the left. Park and secure your car behind the buildings in the rear of the fairgrounds. Leave a sign in your car window indicating "BT" (Bicycle Tour). Blaine County Fair and Blaine County representatives accept no liability or responsibility for parked cars or their contents.

Loop through the heart of Idaho on a 278-mile tour with something to satisfy every cyclist. Hobnob with the famous in Sun Valley, explore Idaho's 1880s mining boom, soak in a natural hot spring, and discover the Snake River plain's volcanic past. To extend the tour's 5 days into 9 or more, add layovers to the recommended overnights in Arco, Challis, Stanley, and Sun Valley–Ketchum. These resort areas are great for sightseeing, ghost town exploring, and relaxing, but definitely reserve lodging and camping in advance.

On Day One, cycle the northern edge of the Snake River plain through dramatic landscapes, ranging from hills blanketed with sagebrush to twisted outcroppings of exposed volcanic rock. At Goodale's Cutoff, consider the hardy Oregon Trail pioneers who detoured through here to avoid Indian confrontations. Goodale's Cutoff departs the Oregon Trail at Fort Hall, rejoining it 20 miles west of here, south of the Boise River.

Midway to Arco, enter another world. Craters of the Moon National Monument is a "weird lunar landscape" where Apollo astronauts were trained. On 7 miles of paved road, loop through 84 square miles of testimony to 13,000 years of violent volcanic forces. From here, drop 600 feet into Arco, the atomic city. Harboring vestiges of the "Old West" and an intoxication with technology, Arco has a unique personality. It is both the first city in the world to be electrified by nuclear power and home to Experimental Breeder Reactor Number 1, the world's first nuclear energy plant. This national historic landmark is 18 miles east of town and open in summer for self-guided tours.

On Day Two head north out of Arco, going up the Big Lost River through a broad valley between the White Knob Mountains and the Lost River Range. So named because it disappears south of Arco, the Big Lost River sinks into the porous basalt on the Snake River plain to flow underground, resurfacing west of Twin Falls as part of Thousand Springs. Pass through the small, scenic town of Mackay. An 1880s copper discovery in the nearby White Knob Mountains spurred Mackay's namesake, George Mackay, to build a smelter here. Two years later the smelter was carted off to California to satisfy a bankruptcy claim. The district survived the loss to become Idaho's largest copper producer from 1900 to 1930.

Pass Mount Borah, the highest peak in Idaho, rising up 12,662 feet to the east of the route. In 1983 after an earthquake registering 7.3 on the Richter scale, Mount Borah's peak grew 1 foot and the surrounding valley dropped 4 to 5 feet. Along the base of the mountain, notice a 6-foot-high cliff formed during the earthquake. End the day's climbing at Willow Creek Summit (7,160 feet) and enjoy more views of the Borah Earthquake Zone before slipping through the narrow, scenic Grandview Canyon into Challis.

Circled by mountains, Challis was founded in 1876 as a supply center for the Salmon River mines. Many buildings still in use date back to the 1800s. In the visitor center, just south of town, get an excellent introduction to the nearby fascinating Land of the Yankee Fork Historic Mining Area.

Leave Challis on Day Three to roll on Route 75 through the Salmon River Valley. These waters have carried sockeye salmon, Shoshone Indians, Lewis and Clark, Hudson's Bay Company trappers, early miners, and adventure-seeking rafters. Called the River of No Return, the Salmon's steep and narrow canyons permitted only downriver travel until jet boats arrived in the 1950s. Stop for a soak in the river's natural hot pools. Your clue to the most popular spot is a Roosevelt-era bath house near the river.

Relive Idaho's 1880s mining boom in Bayshore, Clayton, Sunbeam, and Yankee Fork mining districts. Sunbeam Dam is one relic. Constructed in 1910 at Yankee Fork by the Sunbeam Consolidated Gold Mining Company, the dam supplied electricity for the mine. Partially destroyed since 1934, it decimated the famous 800-mile sockeye salmon run. Prospect the heart of the mining district, now primarily the well-preserved ghost towns of Bonanza and Custer, by arranging transportation with the Stanley Chamber of Commerce. The ghost towns are along a rough gravel road that can be accessed near Sunbeam.

As the third day of touring approaches its end in Stanley, thrill at the sight of the jagged Sawtooth Mountains crowning the Stanley Basin. Stanley looks much as it has for nearly a century. Experience the charm in dirt roads and stubby log buildings set in picturesque surroundings. Although known for many years by the Shoshone Indians, the Stanley Basin was named for John Stanley, who discovered placer gold here in 1863.

On Day Four pick up a recorded route description at the Stanley Ranger Station. Stop to listen and enjoy the cassette amid the scenery between Stanley and Ketchum, dropping it off at the Sawtooth National Recreation Area Visitor Center just prior to entering the urban area. See remains of Sawtooth City, an 1880 mining camp, and the Vienna silver and lead mining district. The day's highlight and hurdle is the 8,701-foot Galena Summit that separates the Windriver Valley from the Sawtooth Valley. The highway follows what once was the Sawtooth Grade Toll Road, which served the Sawtooth mines. It was predated by a deeply grooved track scouted by Shoshone Indians and later used by fur trappers. Survey the scenery from the Galena overlook, just before the summit, identifying the three mountain ranges (Sawtooths, Boulder, and White Cloud) and sighting the headwaters of the Salmon River. Then coast through the Wood River Valley, passing the Pioneer Mountains to the east and the Smoky Mountains to the west. End the day in Sun Valley–Ketchum.

Transformation of Sun Valley–Ketchum into a world-famous, four-season resort began in 1936. Averill Harriman, board chairman, insisted the Union Pacific Railroad purchase a 3,888-acre ranch and construct the country's first ski resort. See remains of the world's first chair lift on Dollar Mountain. Enjoy the variety of recreational and cultural activities offered here year-round. Pedal the more than 20 miles of bike paths and trails connecting Sun Valley, Ketchum, and Bellevue. Visit the grave of author Ernest Hemingway, the first of many celebrities to grace this valley. The grave lies in the Ketchum town cemetery, not far off the tour's main route, and the Hemingway Memorial is along Trail Creek, east of the original Sun Valley Lodge.

On Day Five head south along the Wood River Trail to Hailey, home of Ezra Pound, famed twentieth-century poet. In Hailey walk among historic buildings and visit the Blaine County Historical Museum, then pedal 5 miles south to the trail's end in Bellevue. Continue on the road toward Carey, stopping to enjoy the Silver Creek Nature Conservancy and Silver Creek, a classic catch-and-release trout stream. Formed by artesian springs, Silver Creek is a desert habitat oasis and a haven for wildlife. Watch for sandhill cranes, long-billed curlew, blue herons, and the many other species of birds that migrate through the area.

MILEAGE LOG

DAY ONE: CAREY TO ARCO—43.2 MILES

0.0   Carey, Blaine County Fairgrounds. Turn left out of the parking lot to head north on **Main Street**, which becomes **Route 20 East**.

13.0   Pass a historical marker for Goodale's Cutoff of the Oregon Trail.

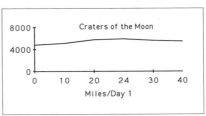

24.3   Craters of the Moon National Monument is on the right.

42.2   Enter Arco (all services).

43.2   Main intersection in Arco, junction with Route 93 on the left. Route 20 and 26 continue right. Lodging is to the right.

DAY TWO: ARCO TO CHALLIS—79.6 MILES

0.0   Arco, main intersection. Proceed north on **Route 93** toward Challis.

7.4   Enter Moore (store to the left).

16.0   Cross the Big Lost River.

18.0   Enter Leslie (no services).

25.6   Enter Mackay (store). Continue straight through town.

30.5   Pass Mackay Reservoir (campground, rest rooms) on the left.

35.7   Pass a historical marker noting the Lost River was originally named for an Iroquois Indian, Thackery Goddin, who first explored the river in 1819. The river was rich in beaver until it was trapped out in 1824.

39.9   Pass Vance Canyon off to the right.

48.3   Pass a historical marker for the Mount Borah Earthquake Fault, located 2.5 miles down the gravel road to the right.

55.7   Willow Creek Summit (7,160 feet).

65.7   Enter Grandview Canyon above Challis. There is a great photo opportunity at the turnout on the right, just after entering the canyon.

77.0   Cross the Salmon River.

77.4   Pass a junction with Route 75 to the left. Lodging is available from here to Challis.

78.3   Pass a historical marker about Michael Bourden, a Hudson's Bay Company trapper. He discovered this valley while searching for beaver in 1822.

79.3   Enter Challis (all services).

79.6   Left on **Golf Course Road** to explore historic Challis.

The Sun Valley Loop slips through narrow, scenic Grandview Canyon near Challis. (Photo: Ken Winkenweder)

Day Three: Challis to Stanley—54.6 miles

0.0   Challis, junction of Route 93 and Route 75. Proceed west on **Route 75** toward Stanley.

0.4   Pass a historical marker noting the Bison Jump Site discovered at the base of these cliffs. A bison herd was driven off a cliff in this infrequently used hunting method.

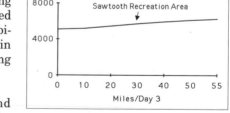

5.6   Cross the Salmon River.

7.0   Pass Big Bend Campground (rest rooms, water) on the left.

7.3   Pass Bayshore Campground (rest rooms, water) entrance on the right.

17.2   Pass the Big Fork Salmon Road on the left and cross the river.

17.3   Cross the river again and begin a gentle climb.

21.3   Enter Clayton (store), where lead and silver were discovered in 1864, 12 miles north of town on Bayshore Creek. In 1872 a smelter was located here by Joel Clayton.

29.0   Enter the Sawtooth National Recreation Area.

29.4   Pass a rest area (rest rooms, water) on the left.

33.5   Pass float boat access on the left. **Caution:** There is traffic congestion in this area.

33.8   Enter Torrey (store, rest rooms, water).

35.2 Pass a picnic site (no services) on the right.

38.9 Pass a scenic overlook on the left, where you can view salmon spawning beds.

39.7 Pass O'Brian Campground (rest rooms, water) to the left (on the other side of the river).

41.6 Pass Yankee Fork Crossing. There is a great overlook to the left.

41.7 Pass the Sunbeam Village turnoff (store, rest rooms, water) on the right and the remains of the Sunbeam Dam on the left. Between here and Stanley are at least four more campgrounds. Sunbeam Hot Springs are on the left, just beyond the turnoff. Enjoy a refreshing dip in a natural hot spring in the river. The nearby bath house was built by the Roosevelt-era Civilian Conservation Corps.

53.1 Enter Lower Stanley. Between here and Stanley proper, you pass many lodging options.

54.3 Enter Stanley (all services).

54.6 Route 75 passes through a junction with Route 21 to the right. Turn right for the Stanley town center.

Day Four: Stanley to Sun Valley–Ketchum–60.5 miles

0.0 Stanley, junction of Routes 21 and 75. Proceed south on **Route 75** toward Sun Valley.

2.5 Pass the Stanley Ranger Station on the right, where you can borrow a descriptive cassette for the route into Sun Valley.

4.2 Pass Red Fish Lake Resort and the Visitor Center turnoff on the right. The lake, 3 miles away, offers views of Mount Heybourn. Redfish Lake, named by Indians, once was spawning grounds each fall for thousands of red sockeye salmon.

5.7 Pass a fish hatchery (daily tours) turnoff on the right.

10.4 Enter Obsidian (no services).

20.7 Pass the Alturas Lake turnoff on the right.

22.3 Pass a historical marker noting that Sawtooth City formed when gold was discovered on Beaver Creek in 1879. After many delays and difficulties harvesting the gold, work stopped permanently in 1892.

25.0 Pass a historical marker to the Vienna lead and silver mining district, up Smiley creek on the left. Continue climbing up a broad valley to Galena Summit.

30.3 Pass a scenic overlook on the right.

31.2 Galena Summit (8,701 feet).

33.0 Pass a historical marker noting that Alexander Ross, searching for beaver with the Hudson's Bay Company, came over the pass in 1824.

45.2 Pass several campgrounds in the next 5 miles.

52.8 Cross the Big Wood River. Return borrowed cassettes in the Sawtooth National Recreation Area Visitor Center on the left.

57.8 Right on **Hulen Meadows Road** and left immediately on the **Wood River Trail**.

60.5   Follow the bike path through town. Turn left on **Fourth Street** toward the Ketchum town center (all services) before continuing at an angle across the street.

    60.5 Side Trip: To see Hemingway's grave, turn left on Main Street/ Highway 75 for three blocks. At the fork follow Highway 75 right. Immediately ahead on the right is the Ketchum Cemetery.

Sunrise at Redfish Lake (Photo: Ken Winkenweder)

Day Five: Sun Valley–Ketchum to Carey–39.9 miles

0.0 Ketchum Visitor Center. Ride downhill on **Fourth Street** away from Route 75/Main Street.

0.2 Left on **Second Avenue.** Stay on Second Avenue, following the bike route signs.

0.8 Right, just before Route 75, on the **Wood River Trail**.

1.7 Cross Elkhorn Road. Turn right toward Hailey at a T intersection on the bike path.

2.3 Cross the Big Wood River.

2.8 Follow the bike path as it crosses over to the east side of the highway.

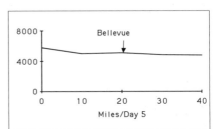

11.5 Enter Hailey (restaurant, store, rest rooms, water).

15.9 Enter Bellevue (restaurant, store, rest rooms, water).

17.5 End of the trail. Turn left on **Gannett Road** (unmarked) at a T intersection. Route 75 and downtown Bellevue are immediately right.

24.7 Enter Gannett (store, cafe on a seasonal basis).

25.0 Follow the road as it turns 90 degrees left.

29.3 Left on **Route 20 East** toward Carey at a stop sign at the T intersection.

32.3 Enter Picabo (store).

35.8 Cross Silver Creek. The Silver Creek Nature Conservancy is to the right.

39.2 Left on **Route 20 East** at the stop sign to enter Carey.

39.9 Left into Blaine County Fairgrounds parking lot. End of tour.

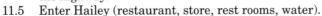

17. PIONEER HISTORIC BYWAY AND BEAR LAKE LOOP

Gayle Newman

Distance: 321 miles
Terrain: flat to mountainous
Total cumulative elevation gain: 8,164 feet
Recommended time of year: June–mid-October
Recommended starting time: 8:00 A.M.
Allow: 6 days
Points of interest: Soda Springs and Hooper Springs geysers; the Oregon Trail; Hudspeth's Cutoff; Niter Ice Caves, Grace; Franklin, the oldest town in Idaho; Bear Lake Hot Springs; John Bagley's Mansion, Montpelier; Minnetonka Cave; Bear Lake State Park; Lander's Cutoff; Periodic Springs, Afton; Henry's Store, Henry

TOUR NO. 17

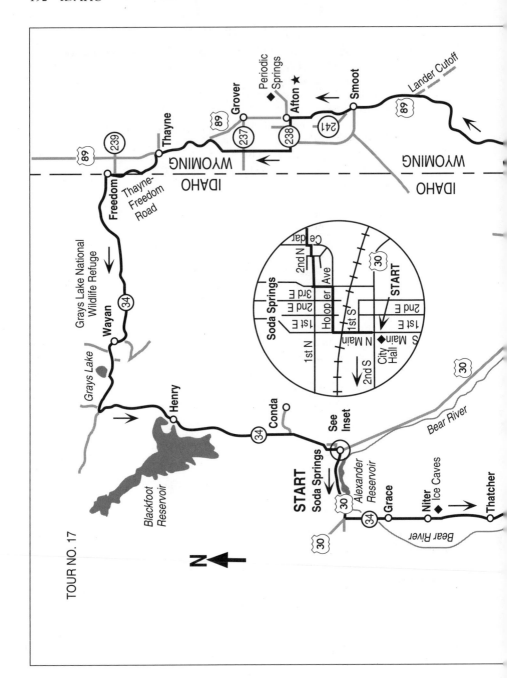

N

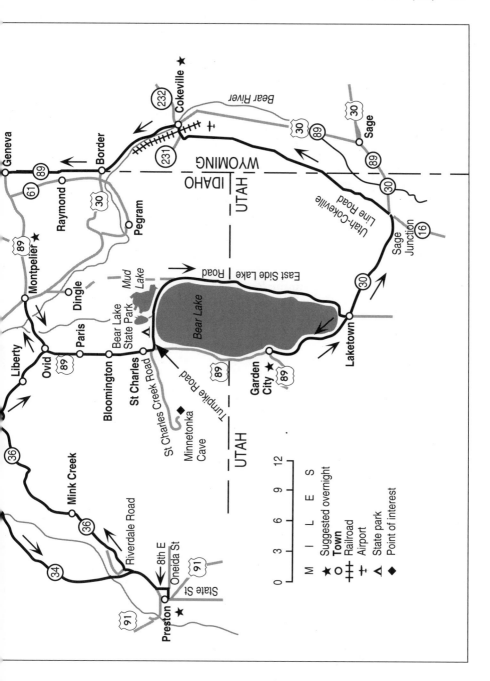

◆ ◆ ◆

PUBLIC TRANSPORTATION

Air: commercial airlines serve Pocatello, 27 miles via Highway 30 from Soda Springs, but verify that the bicycle can go as baggage or ship it ahead
Train: Amtrak serves Pocatello, but no baggage is loaded or unloaded there; ship the bicycle ahead

PRACTICAL INFORMATION

Key contacts: Soda Springs Tourist Information, 208-547-4470; Soda Springs City Hall (parking), 208-547-2600; Preston Chamber of Commerce, 208-852-2703; Montpelier Chamber of Commerce, 208-945-2072; Bear Lake Information, 800-448-BEAR; Cokeville Chamber of Commerce, 307-279-3223; Star Valley Chamber of Commerce, 307-886-3156; Cache National Forest (Utah), 801-753-2772; Caribou National Forest, 208-847-0375; Southeast Idaho Travel Council, 800-423-8597 or 208-776-5273

STARTING POINT

City Hall in Soda Springs, Idaho: From I-15 south of Pocatello, take Exit 47 and continue east on US Highway 30 to Soda Springs. City Hall is at North Main and Second South, on the right at the entrance to town. Request permission to park your car.

Intersect and retrace the Oregon Trail and its branches on this 6-day, 321-mile tour in the Three Corners Region of Idaho, Utah, and Wyoming. Cycling over Salt River Pass, Tincup Pass, and Emigration Canyon in Idaho's southeastern corner seems like jet travel compared to pioneers averaging 15 miles per day in ox-driven wagons on the Oregon Trail. Pedaling a water bottle, energy bars, and a few snacks from one town to the next is easy contrasted with hauling 10 gallons of water, 75 pounds of coffee, 200 pounds of beans, 800 pounds of flour, and more.

This little-traveled corner of the west offers plenty of opportunities for reflecting on the contrasts all around you. Between the interludes of quiet, forested canyons and mountain passes, miles of range roll past. Birds now travel through this same area that only 200 years ago witnessed one of this country's largest migrations of people.

Start the tour with free sparkling soda water from Hooper Springs. Emigrants on the Oregon Trail looked forward to baths and the refreshing, naturally carbonated drinking water available here. Many of the historic springs are subdued now, flooded by the 1924 construction of Soda Springs Dam. On the way out of town you can stop to see deep ruts worn into the Oregon Trail, then turn toward Preston, watching for Soda Point, known to pioneers as Sheep Rock. A noted landmark on the Oregon Trail, Soda Point designated Hudspeth's Cutoff and the turn toward Fort Hall.

Next come the Niter Ice Caves, the Bear River Range, and Gem Valley. On the other side of this 10-mile climb, pass a delta created after the Ice-Age overflow of the Great Salt Lake, and enter Preston, the day's destination. Explore the Preston area, known as Worm Creek until 1881, which supplied wild hay to neighboring Franklin, Idaho's oldest town. Franklin was settled in 1860 as a planned Mormon expansion colony. Idaho's first railroad, the Utah Northern, stopped here in 1873. Visit the Relic Hall Museum on East Main Street, one of several buildings in Franklin's historic district worth a stop.

Another interesting landmark lies 2.5 miles west of Preston on US Highway 91. See the Bear River Battle Site where in 1863 approximately 400 Shoshone Indians were slain in a single day. Among the biggest battles in the takeover of the West, it was larger than Wounded Knee, Little Big Horn, or Sand Creek.

On Day Two go up and over the Bear River Range toward Montpelier. Wind through aspen groves in the Cache National Forest, watching for bear and deer. Descend from the pass along Emigration Creek through Emigration Canyon to Liberty, a Mormon settlement dating back to 1864. Enter Montpelier on Washington Street, which at one time divided the Mormon "uptown" and the gentile "downtown."

Virtually every town passed on Days Two and Three—from Franklin to Ovid, from Montpelier to St. Charles—resulted from planned Mormon expansions beyond Salt Lake City. Early on Day Three, visit Paris, settled in 1862 as the first Bear Valley community. The Bear Lake Stake Tabernacle in Paris is on the National Register of Historic Places. You can take a self-guided tour past splendid wooden houses and the community's oldest brick buildings.

In St. Charles follow Bear Lake's eastern shore past its brilliant turquoise waters. The unusual color may be due to the lake's large quantities of soluble carbonates or to the sky reflecting off the green plants covering its shallow bottom. Discover the Bonneville Cisco, a white fish native only to this body of water. Known locally as the Bear Lake sardine, it is less than seven inches long and weighs about two ounces. Until fishing for it was outlawed in 1920, a commercial fishery harvested the Bonneville Cisco. Cross into Utah and end the day in Garden City at Bear Lake's southern end.

On Day Four pedal southeast through a corner of Utah into Wyoming. Known as Star Valley, this area is a land of sharp contrasts: the Salt River and Wyoming mountain ranges, sage-covered plains, and fertile valleys. Many towns in Star Valley sprang up after the federal government banned polygamy in 1882. When Idaho attempted to enforce the ban, a migration east, to more lenient Wyoming, resulted. The day's destination is Cokeville, Wyoming.

Ride north from Cokeville on Day Five. Parallel the Oregon Trail from Cokeville to Border, a rum-running station during Prohibition, then climb the Salt River Pass. From the pass the Salt River flows north to the Snake River, but is not salty, as its name implies. There are bedrock salt deposits and saline springs nearby. Coast down the pass to end the day in Afton, entering town through an antler arch.

On Day Six return to Idaho in Freedom, where the state line splits the town. Follow the Pioneer Historic Byway, climbing through the Caribou National Forest. The route parallels Lander's Cutoff, an alternate that rejoins the Oregon Trail further west at Fort Hall. Ride through aspen groves, turning south near Grays Lake Wildlife Refuge where sandhill cranes nest. Farther along, at the Blackfoot Reservoir, Henry's Store, established in 1892, still operates. Large phosphate mines mark the return to Soda Springs. Finish pedaling in Soda Springs, but consider a soak in Lava Hot Springs (20 miles west on the Portneuf River). Join the long history of people who have used the springs for healing and renewal, including the Shoshone, the Bannocks, and early pioneers.

The Pioneer Historic Byway and Bear Lake Loop retraces part of the Oregon Trail. (Photo: Gayle Newman)

MILEAGE LOG

DAY ONE: SODA SPRINGS TO PRESTON—50.5 MILES

0.0   Soda Springs City Hall. Turn left on **Second South Street**/US Highway 30 West.

0.6   Pass the Soda Springs Golf Course. **Note:** To see Oregon Trail wagon ruts, turn left into the golf course parking lot. Pick up directions and a key to the access gate in the golf course office. If the golf course is busy, visitors to the wagon rut site may not be accommodated.

6.6   Left on **Route 34 South**. Soda Point, south of US Highway 30, was a well-known landmark on the Oregon Trail. It marked Hudspeth's Cut-

off, named for Benomi Hudspeth, who led a party due west from here
in 1849.

11.1   Enter Grace (store).

14.6   Pass the Niter Ice Caves, just
off the road a few hundred feet
on the left.

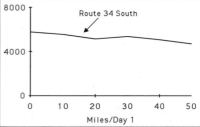

16.2   Enter Niter (limited services).
Continue on Route 34 South toward Thatcher.

25.6   Pass a historical marker: Range
wars started when farms began
to displace range land. In this valley, armed ranchers blocked farming
for six years. A farm community finally formed in 1872.

43.8   Pass the junction with Route 36 on the left.

44.0   Pass a geological site that once was the northern edge of Lake Bonneville.
Formed when the Great Salt Lake swelled during the last Ice Age, Lake
Bonneville retreated and left delta sediments. The Bear River now cuts
through the sediment originally deposited as red clay.

48.1   Left (0.2 mile before the "ENTERING PRESTON" sign) on **Eighth East Street**
(unmarked).

49.5   Right on **Oneida Street** at a T intersection.

50.4   Continue straight across First East Street.

50.5   Preston city center (restaurants, motels to the left), intersection of
Oneida Street and State Street.

DAY TWO: PRESTON TO MONTPELIER—45.4 MILES

0.0   Preston, city park at the corner of First East and Oneida streets. Proceed east on **Oneida Street**.

0.9   Left on **Eighth East Street** (unmarked).

2.3   Right on **Route 34**, heading north at a T intersection.

4.7   Start down a 7 percent grade.

5.4   Right on **Riverdale** Road, halfway down the hill.

6.4   Bear right at the fork.

8.9   Bear left at the fork.

10.0   Right on **Route 36 East** at a
stop sign.

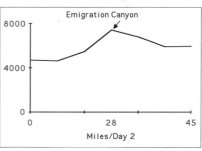

13.4   Stay left to pass the Mink Creek
turnoff on the right.

13.5   Enter Cache National Forest.

28.4   Crest the pass (7,424 feet) above
Emigration Canyon. Start a 6 percent downhill grade.

30.0   Leave Cache National Forest.

36.1   Enter Liberty (no services), founded in 1864.

40.2   Enter Ovid (no services), founded in 1864. Turn left on **US Highway 89**
toward Montpelier.

44.9   Enter Montpelier (all services). Continue straight across the bridge over
the railroad tracks. Montpelier, founded in 1864, was on the Oregon
Trail.

45.1   Pass the Montpelier Bank site, robbed by Butch Cassidy in 1896.

45.4   Ninth and Washington streets, Montpelier. Washington Street once sepa-
       rated the two distinct districts.

DAY THREE: MONTPELIER TO GARDEN CITY, UTAH—54 MILES

0.0   Montpelier, Ninth and Washington streets. Ride west on **Washington
      Street** back through the city center.

5.2   Stay left with **US Highway 89**, passing the Route 36 junction on the right.

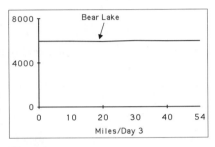

8.5   Enter Paris (store), the first settlement in Bear Valley.

11.3 Enter Bloomington (no services). The first European female con-
      verted to the Church of the Lat-ter Day Saints arrived in Utah in 1868, bringing other British converts with her. They settled in Bloomington.

16.1 Enter St. Charles (all services), birthplace of Gutzon Borglum, a sculp-
      tor best known for the faces he carved on Mount Rushmore.

16.5 Pass the Minnetonka Cave (1-hour tours mid-June–Labor Day) turnoff
      on the right. The limestone cavern is 9 miles up this paved road.

16.6 Left on **Turnpike Road** (unmarked), following signs to North Bear Lake
      and Bear Lake State Park.

19.7 Pass Bear Lake on the right. Rich in beaver, the lake was used exten-
      sively by early mountain men.

21.4 Pass Bear Lake State Park (sandy beach access, rest rooms, wildlife
      refuge). Mud Lake is to the left.

23.2 Pass Bear Lake Hot Springs on the right. The water is piped to an in-
      door pool.

23.3 Follow Turnpike Road as it turns sharply right and is renamed **East
      Side Lake Road**. (Pass the gravel road from Dingle on the left). In the
      next 20 miles the route passes numerous campgrounds.

29.0 Pass access to Bear Lake State Park (rest rooms, water). Continue ped-
      aling south toward Utah.

43.9 Laketown, Utah (restaurant). Turn right on **US Highway 30 East** to-
      ward Garden City at a stop sign.

54.0 Enter Garden City, Utah (all services).

DAY FOUR: GARDEN CITY, UTAH TO COKEVILLE, WYOMING—37.4 MILES

0.0   Garden City, Utah. Backtrack on Day Three's route 10.1 miles
      on **US Highway 30 East** to-ward Laketown.

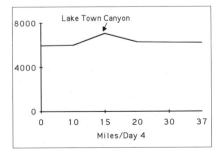

10.1 Laketown junction. Continue straight toward Wyoming on **US
      Highway 30 East**. Start uphill through Old Lake Town Canyon.

14.5 Crest Lake Town Canyon (6,341 feet).

The Pioneer Historic Byway and Bear Lake Loop covers a little-traveled corner of the West. (Photo: Gayle Newman)

21.9   Left at Sage Junction on **Utah–Cokeville Line Road**, riding north to Cokeville.

29.7   Enter Wyoming.

33.9   Pass Cokeville Municipal Airport on the right.

36.5   Follow the road as it turns right, passing Road 231 on the left. Enter Cokeville, adjacent to the Oregon Trail.

37.4   Intersection of US Highways 30/89 and Road 231/232 in Cokeville town center (all services). Today's Cokeville is a ranching center, but it owes its name to early settlers who mined coal east of town for coke.

DAY FIVE: COKEVILLE, WYOMING TO AFTON, WYOMING—52.5 MILES

0.0   Cokeville, junction in town center with Road 231/232 and US Highways 30/89. Continue north on **US Highways 30/89**.

10.2   Right at Border junction, continuing on **US Highway 89** toward Afton.

20.4   Right toward Afton on **US Highway 89**. Straight ahead is the town of Geneva (all services).

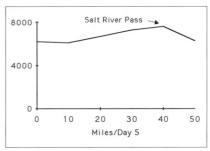

36.3   Crest Salt River Pass (7,630 feet). The pass separates drainages of the Thomas Fork and Bear River, and the Salt River.

39.5   Pass a historical marker: Lander's Cutoff, the first federal road west of the Missouri River, was named for Frederick W. Lander, who founded the trail in 1858.

44.9   Enter Smoot (limited services). Continue straight through town.

46.1   Pass the junction with Road 241 to Osmond on the left.

51.5   Enter Afton, home to one of the world's few chinchilla fur farms.

52.1   Pass Second Avenue on the right.

52.1 Side Trip: To see Periodic Springs, a sacred place of healing for the Shoshone, turn right on Second Avenue and ride 6 miles up the Swift Creek Canyon. The springs gush out of an opening in the cliffs at semi-regular intervals. Early fall is the best viewing time because the intervals are more frequent—approximately every 18 minutes. Backtrack to rejoin the main route.

52.5   Corner of Fourth Avenue and Washington, Afton town center (all services).

DAY SIX: AFTON, WYOMING TO SODA SPRINGS—80.8 MILES

0.0   Afton, corner of Fourth Avenue and Washington. Ride south on **Washington Street**/US Highway 89, as if heading back to Cokeville.

0.3   Right on **Road 238**.

4.1   Pass a junction with Road 237.

12.3   Left on **US Highway 89** at the stop sign.

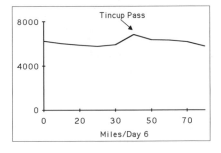

17.5   Enter Thayne (all services), home of the Star Valley Cheese Factory. Continue straight through town. Henry Thayne was the community's first postmaster and merchant. In the 1920s he invented winter cutter racing in which horses pull riders in chariots on frozen tracks.

18.4   Left on **Lincoln Road**/Thayne–Freedom Road/City Road 125.

24.2   Enter Freedom (store), the oldest town in the Star Valley, founded in 1879. Go straight, passing Road 239 on the right. Freedom's main street straddles the Wyoming–Idaho border.

25.2   Left on **Route 34**. Follow the signs to Soda Springs. Enter Caribou National Forest.

39.7   Crest Tincup Pass (6,829 feet). Exit Caribou National Forest.

44.4   Pass the cutoff to Wayan (no services), named for Wayne and Ann, the couple who ran the post office.

44.7   Pass a historical marker: Half-Iroquois John Grey discovered this valley in 1818 while trapping beaver. Caribou Mountain rises up 9,800 feet to the north, and Caribou City was located 3 miles northeast of it. Discovery of gold on Caribou Mountain in 1870 spurred a rush from Utah.

46.4   Bear left, passing the entrance to Grays Lake National Wildlife Refuge on the right. The wildlife refuge headquarters is 2.5 miles down this road. In September more than 4,000 sandhill cranes visit this area.

49.3   Follow Route 34 as it makes a hairpin turn to the left.

60.0   First views of the Blackfoot Reservoir.

61.3 Enter Henry (store). Henry's Store was established in 1892.

74.6 Pass the turnoff for Conda, where large phosphate beds are located. Phosphate mining is the backbone of Soda Spring's economy.

78.4 Enter Soda Springs (all services).

79.5 Following the bike path signs, turn right on **First North Street**. Cross Cedar where First North Street jogs left and then right. Continue on First North Street.

79.9 Left on **Third East Street**, and then right on **Hooper Avenue**.

80.5 Left on **North Main Street** at a T intersection where a spur of the future bike path goes right.

    80.5 Side Trip: To sample the different flavors of naturally carbonated spring water, turn right on the bike-path spur. Pass the Merry-Go-Round Spring, Lover's Delight Spring, and Hooper's Spring in Hooper Park on this 2.4-mile round trip. Backtrack to rejoin the main route at North Main Street.

80.7 Pass through an older section of Soda Springs. One block left is Thomas Corrigan Park with two historical locomotives: Galloping Goose and Dinky Engine, and the Pioneer Historical Museum. To the right one block is Geyser Park, home to the world's only "captive geyser."

80.8 Right on **Second South Street** and turn left immediately into the city hall parking lot. End of tour.

◆

18. YELLOWSTONE AND GRAND TETON NATIONAL PARKS

Gayle Newman

Distance: 334 miles
Terrain: flat to mountainous; not recommended for novice cyclists
Total cumulative elevation: 7,709 feet
Recommended time of year: July–October
Recommended starting time: 5:30–6:00 A.M. in the parks
Allow: 7–10 days; layover days recommended; 6-day shortcut
Points of interest: Upper and Lower Mesa Falls; Island Park caldera; Henry's Lake; Yellowstone National Park; Grand Teton National Park; Jackson Hole Resort; Snake River Grand Canyon

PUBLIC TRANSPORTATION
Air: none available
Train: none available

PRACTICAL INFORMATION
Key contacts: Ashton Chamber of Commerce, 208-652-3987; Yellowstone National Park Office, 307-344-7381; Flagg Ranch, 307-733-2811; Grand Teton National Park Office, 307-739-3300; Jackson Hole Chamber of Commerce, 307-733-3316

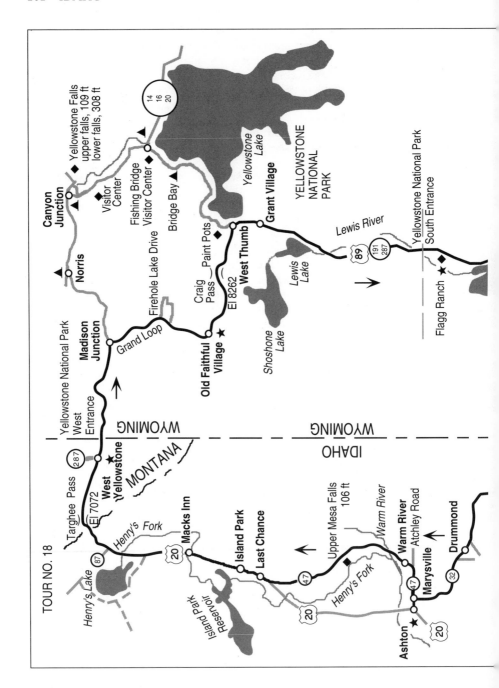

TOUR NO. 18

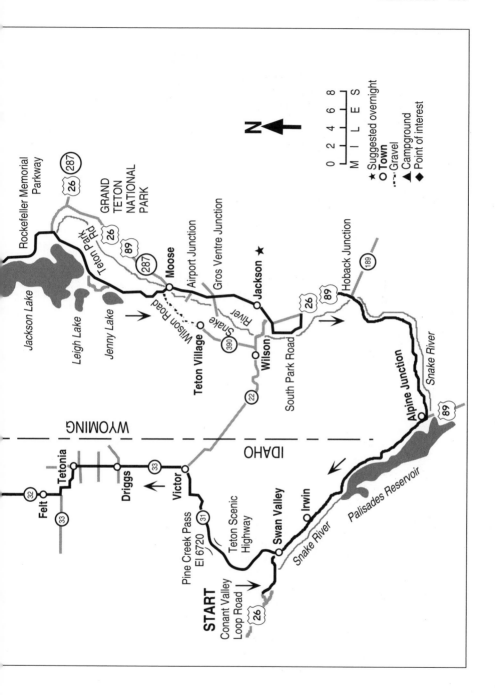

Note: This tour requires advance planning. To make it the delightful experience it can be:

- Start out as early in the day as possible—5:30 to 6:00 A.M. Peak traffic hours through the parks are mid-morning to late afternoon.
- Be aware that park roads can be narrow and rough. Watch especially for vehicles with extended mirrors.
- Check on road and snow conditions in advance. During May and June the roads in Yellowstone National Park may be snow-free, but high snow banks are a safety hazard.
- Be prepared for freezing temperatures. Summer weather at high altitudes is deceiving. Temperatures may reach 67° Fahrenheit during the day and plunge to 25° at night.
- Plan shorter cycling days with longer-than-normal stops. Touring at high elevations requires special planning.

Advice for campers:

- Camping is not available at Old Faithful. To reach another overnight stop on Day Three, see the alternative route described in the mileage log.
- Campgrounds fill up early in the day and are relatively far apart. However, a limited number of sites are reserved for bikers and hikers at most campgrounds in the parks.
- Opening and closing dates vary by campground.
- Make reservations through Mistix for June through Labor Day for Yellowstone's Bridge Bay Campground, on an alternative route for Day Four.

STARTING POINT

Conant Valley Sportsman's Access, west of the Yellowstone Park entrance: From Idaho Falls, take US Highway 26 east for 39 miles. Just after dropping down into Conant Valley, watch for the "ENTERING SWAN VALLEY" sign. Turn left just beyond the sign on Conant Valley Loop Road. At the stop sign turn left, then right, into the Conant Valley Sportsman's Access parking lot. No permission is necessary to park and secure your car in this lot.

Adventure, challenge, and elevation soar a mile high on this 334-mile, three-state tour. Circle through Yellowstone and Grand Teton national parks, where wildlife viewing is as effortless as sitting in the saddle. In the shadow of the majestic Teton Mountain Range, pedal past sights like Firehole Canyon, Lower Geyser Basin, nesting pelicans, grazing elk, and Henry's Fork of the Snake River. This is a land of open ranges and abundant wildlife. Get used to negotiating right-of-way with buffalo and cattle.

On Day One, leave Swan Valley to tackle the first hurdle, Pine Creek Pass. Ascend through ponderosa pine groves into the relatively barren Teton Valley, known to settlers originally as Pierre's Hole. This 6,000-foot "valley" is named for Pierre Tevanitagon, an Iroquois fur trapper for the Hudson's Bay Company. From the early 1800s, mountain men and Nez Perce and Flathead Indians gathered annually here to barter and replenish supplies. The Rendezvous is re-enacted every summer in Driggs. The route also passes through Victor, Tetonia, Felt, and Drummond. Accented with antlers, wooden boardwalks, saloons, and cowboys, these distinctly Western towns lie before the backdrop of the Tetons, which sit like pyramids in the distance. End the day in Ashton.

The earth's largest concentration of geysers, mud pots, fumaroles, and hot springs is in Yellowstone National Park. (Photo: Aventure Cycling Assn. [Greg Siple])

On Day Two follow Henry's Fork of the Snake River out of the Teton Valley. The route climbs steeply through forest to Upper and Lower Mesa Falls. Henry's Fork rushes toward the walkway at Upper Mesa Falls, then plunges 114 feet to cut its way through the wilderness. The landmark here is the Big Falls Inn, a turn-of-the-century way stop for visitors journeying into Yellowstone National Park. Leave the inn to continue to Henry's Lake. From there to West Yellowstone, Montana, follow the route Chief Joseph's Nez Perce band took after the Battle of Big Hole. Brimming with outfitters, guides, and everything a tourist might need, West Yellowstone thrives on the millions of travelers to or from the park. Its sulfurous fumes can be an affront to the senses, but West Yellowstone is a perfect overnight stop before riding through the park.

Begin Day Three at Yellowstone's west entrance on the Montana–Wyoming border. In these 3,472 square miles lies the earth's largest concentration of thermal phenomena. Geysers, mud pots, fumaroles, and hot springs bubble, gurgle, steam, and spout all along the route. Formed in 1872 as the world's first national park, Yellowstone is most famous for its wildlife, a fantastic array of more than 60 species of mammals and 200 species of birds. Many can be seen from the bicycle saddle, but be sure to avoid close encounters with Yellowstone's most-remembered mammal species, the black bear. End the day at Old Faithful, which offers a famous lodge as well as cabin accommodations. After your overnight there, continue south on Day Four to the West Thumb on Yellowstone Lake, crossing the Continental Divide three times at or above 8,000 feet.

On Day Five the Grand Teton Range dominates the skyline. Every turn from Yellowstone to Jackson mesmerizes with a changing view of chiseled granite peaks. Twelve glaciers continuously carve these stone towers. Watch for nesting pelicans as the route passes Jenny Lake Dam. Just before leaving Grand Teton National Park, stop at the Chapel of the Transfiguration where you can gaze out the window at the perfectly framed mountains. Pedal another 13 miles to the bustling resort town of Jackson, Wyoming, a great site for a layover day. Many sights in Grand Teton National Park are nearby and other options lie within a day's hike or bike ride.

On Day Six say goodbye to the Tetons to coast down into the Grand Canyon of the Snake River. Along the way scramble down to the river bank for a peaceful respite among ponderosa pine and an aria of rushing water. Complete the day's journey in Alpine Junction, Wyoming, or cut the last day from the tour by pedaling over Teton Pass to the Swan Valley.

Even as the tour comes to a close on Day Seven, you continue to reel past stunning beauty. Just beyond Alpine Junction, re-enter Idaho and survey the outstanding view from right to left. Begin with the Targhee National Forest sloping down to the roadway, then move to a panorama of Palisades Reservoir with the Caribou National Forest spread beyond it. Soon the 15-mile northeastern shoreline of the reservoir's spectacular coves and bays add to the show. As pedal strokes end in Conant Valley, a natural high remains, bringing to a close your memorable week of mile-tall challenges, adventure, and elevation in Grand Teton and Yellowstone national parks.

MILEAGE LOG
DAY ONE: CONANT VALLEY SPORTSMAN'S ACCESS TO ASHTON—72.7 MILES

0.0   Conant Valley Sportsman's Access. Turn left out of the parking lot on **Conant Valley Loop Road**.

1.0   Left on **US Highway 26 East** at the stop sign.

2.0   Cross the Snake River.

2.9   **Caution:** No shoulder for the next 2 miles.

5.0   Enter Swan Valley (all services).

5.2   Left on **Route 31**, heading north on the Teton Scenic Highway.

5.9   Start climbing over Pine Creek Pass.

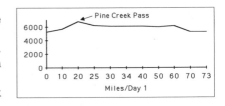

10.2   Enter open rangeland. Watch for cattle on the road.

19.4   Summit of Pine Creek Pass (6,720 feet).

20.8   First view of the Teton Range.

25.6   Enter Victor (all services). A Mormon settlement founded in 1899, this is a way stop for travelers to Yellowstone National Park. It is named for Claude Victor, who carried the mail over Teton Pass in the 1800s.

26.0   Left on **Route 33** at a stop sign, heading north toward Driggs.

31.6   Pass a historical marker noting the Teton Valley was named Pierre's Hole for Pierre Tevanitagon, an Iroquois trapper for the Hudson's Bay Company.

33.8   Enter Driggs (all services), founded in 1889 when a large group of Mormon settlers immigrated from Salt Lake City.

34.3   Pass a turnoff to Grand Targhee Ski Area.

42.1   Enter Tetonia (store).

44.3   Right on **Route 32**, heading north toward Ashton and Yellowstone.

47.4   Enter Felt (no services).

63.0   Pass Drummond (store) on the right.

72.5   Left on **Route 47** at a stop sign, heading into Ashton.

72.7   Enter Ashton (all services). Founded in 1906 when the Oregon Short Line Railroad (OSL) shifted 2 miles west from Marysville, this town is named for Bill Ashton, chief OSL engineer. The railroad was completed to Wyoming in 1907.

DAY TWO: ASHTON TO WEST YELLOWSTONE, MONTANA—63.1 MILES

0.0   Ashton, junction of Routes 47 and 32 on the east edge of town. Proceed straight ahead on **Route 47**, the Mesa Falls Scenic Byway.

0.6   Enter Marysville (no services).

3.9   Curve left, following Route 47, passing Atchley Road, which continues straight ahead.

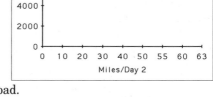

7.8   Cross the Warm River and bear left at the fork. Start climbing.

10.3   Scenic overlook. Warm River is down below.

13.6   Lower Mesa Falls is on the left. An overlook is 0.1 mile off the road.

14.3   Pass Upper Mesa Falls on the left. The historic Big Falls Inn is 0.9 mile off the main route. Walking paths lead to the falls.

27.2   Right on **US Highway 20** at a junction with a stop sign.

29.8   Enter Last Chance (all services).

34.5   Cross Buffalo Creek. A U.S. Forest Service Center is to the right.

34.8   Enter Island Park (all services). Island Park is a large caldera, 18 miles by 23 miles in diameter, formed millions of years ago when a volcano's magma chamber collapsed. A 1,200-foot scarp is visible on its southern and western rims.

40.0   Enter Macks Inn (all services). Cross Henry's Fork of the Snake River, a popular takeoff point for float trips.

48.8   Pass Henry's Lake turnoff on the left. The lake is 2 miles off the main road. Chief Joseph's band of Nez Perce camped several times at Henry's Lake. Formed by glacial action, Henry's Lake is noted for its trout fishing.

49.5   Pass the junction with Route 87 on the left.

53.6   Targhee Pass (7,072 feet). Enter Montana. Tarhgee, head chief of all Bannocks, met the governors of Utah and Idaho here in 1860, in an effort to preserve peace. The Shoshone also used this route on their annual buffalo-hunting excursions.

Cyclists cross a bridge on an alternative route in the Yellowstone and Grand Teton National Parks tour. (Photo: Adventure Cycling Assn.[Greg Siple])

62.1   Enter West Yellowstone, Montana (all services). Continue straight ahead for the town center.

   62.1 Alternative: For less traffic, turn right on Iris Street.

62.4   Left on **Yellowstone Avenue**.

63.1   Continue straight past the stop sign at Canyon Street toward the entrance to Yellowstone National Park.

   63.1 Alternative: For those who wish to camp rather than stay in West Yellowstone, continue into the park to Day Three, Mile 13.5 (see below), and follow the alternative route described.

DAY THREE: WEST YELLOWSTONE, MONTANA TO OLD FAITHFUL VILLAGE, WYOMING—30.8 MILES

0.0   West Yellowstone, entrance to Yellowstone National Park. Continue into the park.

2.2   Enter Wyoming.

13.5   Right on the **Grand Loop** at the Madison Junction stop sign toward Old Faithful and the West Thumb on Yellowstone Lake.

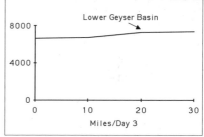

   13.5 Alternative: This alternative route allows for camping on Day One, but it takes you on a 3-day detour from the main route. Turn left at Madison Junction, and follow signs 14 miles to Norris Junction (camping) or 12 miles farther to Canyon Junction (camping, lodging). On Day Two, continue in the park, riding southeast 28 miles to Fishing Bridge (camping, lodging) on Yellowstone Lake or to Bridge Bay Campground just beyond (camping). On Day Three ride southwest to West Thumb on Yellowstone Lake and rejoin the main route's mileage log at Day Four, Mile 19.4.

14.1   Pass the Firehole Lake Drive turnoff.

21.5   Pass the Lower Geyser Basin on the right.

22.6   Pass Firehole Lake Drive on the left.

23.6   Pass Midway Geyser Basin.

29.2   Right on the overpass toward Old Faithful.

30.8   Enter Old Faithful Village (all services).

DAY FOUR: OLD FAITHFUL VILLAGE, WYOMING TO FLAGG RANCH, WYOMING—42.5 MILES

0.0   Old Faithful Village, Old Faithful Inn parking lot. Backtrack on the Day Three route 1.6 miles to Grand Loop Road.

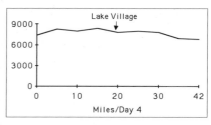

1.6   Cross Grand Loop Road on the overpass, following it as it loops around to the right, merging on **Grand Loop Road** toward the West Thumb.

7.5   Cross the Continental Divide on Craig Pass (8,262 feet).

15.2   Cross the Continental Divide (8,391 feet).
19.4   Pass Lake Village (store, rest rooms, water) on the left.
21.1   Pass Grant Village (store, rest rooms, water) on the left.
23.4   Cross the Continental Divide (7,988 feet).
40.5   Pass the south entrance to Yellowstone National Park.
42.5   Right into the Flagg Ranch, Wyoming.

DAY FIVE: FLAGG RANCH, WYOMING TO JACKSON HOLE, WYOMING—53.6 MILES

0.0   Flagg Ranch, turnoff on the Rockefeller Memorial Parkway. Ride south on **Rockefeller Memorial Parkway** toward Jackson Hole.
4.9   Enter Grand Teton National Park.
15.6   Pass the turnoff to Colter Bay (all services) on the right.
20.0   Pass the entrance to Jackson Lake Lodge on the right.
21.1   Right on **Teton Park Road** at the Jackson Lake Junction.
22.3   Pass Jenny Lake Dam. Watch for nesting pelicans.
25.2   Pass the turnoff to Signal Mountain Summit on the left.
31.1   Pass the North Jenny Lake Loop Drive on the right.
34.0   Pass the Jenny Lake Junction turnoff on the right.
40.7   Pass the Chapel of the Transfiguration on the left. You can go inside for a framed view of the mountains from the window.
40.9   Leave Grand Teton National Park.
41.2   Pass the Wilson Road turnoff on the right.

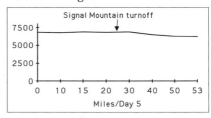

    41.2   Alternative: Turn right on Wilson Road for 6 miles to reach Teton Village (many lodging options). All but 1.5 miles are paved at this writing. Backtrack to rejoin the main route.
41.8   Right on the **Jackson Hole Highway**/Rockefeller Memorial Parkway at the stop sign.
45.4   Pass the airport junction, continuing straight ahead.
47.3   Pass Gros Ventre Junction, continuing straight ahead.
53.4   Enter the Jackson Hole city limits (all services).
53.6   Pass the Jackson Hole Visitor Center on the left, immediately after the road turns left into town.

DAY SIX: JACKSON HOLE, WYOMING TO ALPINE JUNCTION, WYOMING—38.9 MILES

0.0   Jackson Hole Visitor Center. Turn left out of the parking lot toward the town center.
0.1   Right on **Perry Avenue**.
0.2   Left at the dead end on **Glenwood Street**.
0.3   Right on **Mercill Avenue** at the stop sign and follow the road to the left.
0.4   Right at Miller Park on **Gill Avenue**.

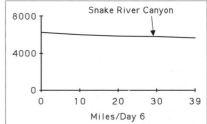

0.5   Left on **Jackson Street**.

0.6   Right at the stop sign on **West Broadway**.

1.8   Pass the junction with Route 22 toward Wilson and Teton Village.

    1.8 Shortcut: To shave a day off the tour and/or try a different route, turn right on Route 22, and follow it 5 miles to Wilson, then continue up and over Teton Pass (8,429 feet) and enter Idaho. In Idaho, Route 22 becomes Route 33. Turn left on Route 31 in Victor, 23 miles from Wilson, and then retrace the Day One mileage log 25.6 miles from Victor back to Conant Valley Sportman's Access for a Day Six total of 48.6 miles.

2.4   Right on **South Park Loop**.

3.5   Left on **South Park Road**.

4.0   Pass a junction with an unmarked road.

8.7   Right on **US Highway 26** at the T intersection.

16.1   Hoback Junction (store). Turn right on **US Highway 26 West**/Highway 89 South toward Alpine Junction. For the next 20 miles the route follows the Snake River Grand Canyon.

38.9   Alpine Junction (all services).

A waterfall creates an aria of rushing water on the Yellowstone and Grand Teton National Parks tour. (Photo: Gayle Newman)

DAY SEVEN: ALPINE JUNCTION, WYOMING TO CONANT VALLEY SPORTSMAN'S ACCESS—32.9 MILES

0.0   Alpine Junction. Ride west on **US Highway 26**.

2.4   Enter Idaho. Start climbing. Pass the Palisades Reservoir on the left.

15.5   Pass the Palisades Dam on the left.

23.2   Enter Irwin (store).

24.3   Enter the outskirts of Swan Valley.

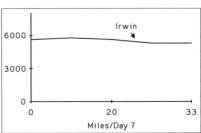

27.7   Pass the junction with Route 31 on the right, continuing straight through town.

30.9   Cross the Snake River.

31.9   Right on the **Conant Valley Loop Road**.

32.9   Right into Conant Valley Sportsman's Access parking lot. End of tour.

MONTANA

◆

19. FLATHEAD VALLEY LOOP

Chuck Haney

Distance: 90 miles
Terrain: mostly flat with some short hills, increasing toward Glacier National Park
Total cumulative elevation gain: 2,957 feet
Recommended time of year: May–September
Recommended starting time: 9:00 A.M.
Allow: 2 days; 1-day side trip/connector to tour 20, Glacier National Park Loop
Points of interest: Stumptown Historical Society Museum, Whitefish; Whitefish State Park; Conrad Mission, Kalispell; Flathead Lake; Jewel Basin hiking area, Bigfork; Glacier National Park

PUBLIC TRANSPORTATION
Air: commercial airlines serve Kalispell, from where you can pick up the tour on Day One, Mile 46.9
Train: there is Amtrak service into Whitefish

PRACTICAL INFORMATION
Key contacts: Whitefish Chamber of Commerce, 406-862-3501; Glacier Country (Kalispell), 800-338-5072; Flathead Convention and Visitors Bureau, 800-543-3105

STARTING POINT
Whitefish, Municipal Building at Second Street and Baker Street (one of two traffic lights in Whitefish): Request permission to park overnight here or at a local bicycle shop.

Trade 2 days of mostly flat pedaling for sensational scenery, splendid rural surroundings, and charming, historic communities. You can have company on this 90-mile tour by choosing Labor Day Weekend when up to 300 participants in the Flathead Valley Bicycle Club-sponsored Huckleberry 100 buzz around the route. Enjoy mountain backdrops on all sides, rural touches, creeks and wild rivers, wildlife, and, of course, Flathead Lake. The loop captures the pure essence of this special valley. Extend the 2-day tour, and more than double the delights, with a 1-day side trip to West Glacier, from where you can either return to Whitefish or begin tour 20, Glacier National Park Loop.

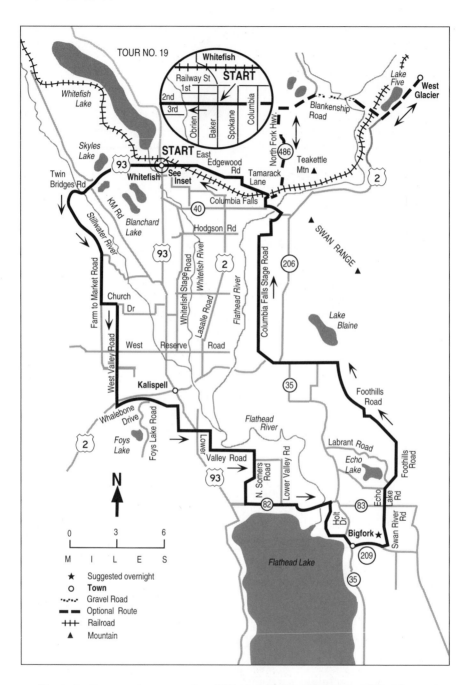

Begin in the resort community of Whitefish. Nestled against Big Mountain, Whitefish is a jumping-off point for excellent mountain biking. Originally nicknamed "Stump Town," Whitefish incorporated in 1905. Its growth on Whitefish Lake was hindered by stumps left by loggers. Being a bad guy in those days meant not only landing in jail, but also hard labor removing the stubborn stumps.

Start on US Highway 93, pedaling past the Whitefish Lake Golf Course and the Whitefish State Park turnoff. Cross the Stillwater River, watching for deer, and pass abundant small farms and ranches. Head toward Kalispell via the "Farm to Market Road," aptly named for its pioneer role in linking local products with the valley's largest town.

Continue south as beef farms give way to large dairies, then pump up the short but steep Sheepherder's Hill to revel in the valley view. Continue on to solve the mystery of giant whalebones that symbolize a simple story. A retired sailor brought them from the Oregon coast as a reminder of the sea.

In Kalispell, head toward Airport Road. Originally occupied by the Kootenai and Kalispell Indians, this area flourished as a trading center in the late 1800s. In the 1890s, with construction of the Great Northern Railway, came the real push. South of the present-day community, Demersville residents dreamed of a boom with steamer ships on Flathead Lake and railroads on both ends of the waterway. Steamers were no longer needed when railroad owners, working with Charles Conrad, laid out Kalispell. Ten years later, the railroad moved north to Columbia Falls and Whitefish. You can visit the Conrad Mansion, however. It is one of the major attractions in Kalispell.

Out of Kalispell continue on Cemetery Road. This is a resting place for early Montana pioneers, but there is no repose for touring cyclists. The narrow shoulder and brisk traffic demand constant attention while skirting along the Flathead River about its business as it flows into Flathead Lake. Farms and wetlands along the route teem with waterfowl. You may notice osprey perched high in man-made nesting sites along Highway 82. Later, be wary of low-flying golf balls from the Eagle Bend Golf Course. Thank goodness for helmets that allow a focus on the much more interesting rock outcroppings along Flathead Lake, the largest natural freshwater lake west of the Mississippi River.

Enter the artsy community of Bigfork. You can get literal here and find a big fork of food to end an interesting day of Flathead Valley touring. Linger amid glorious scenery and the bustle of tourism. Situated at the fork of the Flathead, Upper Flathead, and Swan rivers, Bigfork is thought to have been named by Indians who passed the appellation on to E. L. Sliter, a 1902 homesteader.

On Day Two, scoot back into Whitefish along a loop route different from that of Day One. Begin in the foothills of the Rockies toward Whitefish and Glacier National Park, following the Swan River. Cruise past wild turkeys gobbling in meadows shaded by the scenic Swan Range, then twist and turn on a smooth stretch of gravel.

Beyond the tiny Mountain View School, the valley spreads out below. Drop down to it and the Columbia Falls Stage Road. Enjoy outstanding views revealing the Swan Range enveloped in a green mosaic woven with the blue thread of the Flathead River. Stagecoaches really did use this pleasant 10-mile straight stretch of now-paved road, but Columbia Falls does not have a falls. When founded in 1889, Columbia Falls was designated Columbia in honor of the mountain just east of town, but Post Office officials in Washington, D.C., rejected the name. Befuddled, the local postmaster, for reasons no one really understands, merely added "Falls" to the name, and it stuck.

At the main street of Columbia Falls, you can divert a few blocks off the route to visit one of Montana's oldest churches, St. Richard's at 1210 Ninth Street West. Then, turn on the North Fork Highway and either continue the direct route into Whitefish or take the additional 1-day side trip to West Glacier.

Rural tracks near Kalispell are reminders of the past. In the 1890s a hoped-for transportation boom never happened. (Photo: Chuck Haney)

From the side trip you can either backtrack to Whitefish to end your Flathead Valley excursion, or begin tour 20, Glacier National Park Loop. Both the main route and the side trip have a short distance of gravel, but prepare for another 2-mile stretch into Whitefish (hey, this *is* Montana). After that, whisper into town through lovely horse ranch country.

For the side trip to West Glacier heading into Glacier National Park, stay with the North Fork Highway past the aluminum factory. From there, climb gradually on a road with a good shoulder and very little traffic, enjoying magnificent views. One of the nicest paved roads in the valley, this is especially scenic in autumn when stately gold tamaracks mark the way. Next negotiate the Blankenship Road gravel section. It covers 4.3 miles and dictates slower riding or wider tires. Pass the confluence of the North and Middle Forks of the

Flathead River, which with the South Fork forms the nation's longest Wild and Scenic River system. It stretches 219 miles across some of Montana's most ruggedly beautiful country.

After the Lake Five Resort area, link with US Highway 2 and the community of West Glacier. Then continue into Glacier National Park for at least 4 more days of cycle touring (tour 20, Glacier National Park Loop) or backtrack to Whitefish to complete your tour of the scenic Flathead Valley.

MILEAGE LOG
DAY ONE: WHITEFISH TO BIGFORK—46.9 MILES

0.0   Whitefish, intersection of Second and Baker streets. Follow **Second Street** west and north. After leaving town, it becomes **US Highway 93.**

4.3   Left on **Twin Bridges Road.**

6.4   Left on **Farm to Market Road.**

14.3   Left on **Church Drive.**

15.3   Right on **West Valley Road.**

18.3   Cross West Reserve Road.

19.3   Cross Farm to Market Road.

20.3   Cross Three Mile Drive.

20.5   Climb Sheepherder's Hill.

21.9   Cross US Highway 2, and turn left on **Whalebone Drive.** Approximately a mile down the road to the right are Oregon whalebones in a private yard.

24.1   Left on **Foys Lake Road.**

25.1   Right on **Valley View Drive.**

26.4   Right on **Eleventh Street.**

26.7   Right on **First Avenue.**

27.1   Right on **Airport Road.**

28.3   Left on **Cemetery Road.**

29.3   Cross US Highway 93, staying straight.

30.4   Bear right as road curves to become **Lower Valley Road.**

34.8   Continue straight as road name changes to **North Somers Road.**

36.8   Left to remain on North Somers.

38.3   Left on **Highway 82.**

42.9   Cross the Flathead River, and turn right on **Holt Drive.**

44.3   Right, then curve left to the golf course.

46.9   Cross Highway 35. Enter Bigfork (all services).

DAY TWO: BIGFORK TO WHITEFISH—43 MILES

0.0   Bigfork. Head south on **Highway 35.**

0.2   Left on **Highway 209.**

2.5   Left on **Swan River Road,** crossing an old steel bridge.

5.0   Cross Highway 83. Road name changes to **Echo Lake Road.**

7.2   Take the right fork on **Foothills Road.**

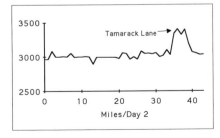

14.5   Pass Mountain View School.
20.3   Pass the junction of Highways 206 and 35, continuing on **Highway 35 West**.
21.3   Right on **Columbia Falls Stage Road**.
29.7   Follow the road as it curves right.
30.6   Left to stay with Columbia Falls Stage Road.
31.5   Right on **River Road**.
32.3   Left on **US Highway 2/40**.
33.2   Right on **Nucleus Avenue**.
33.7   Right on **North Fork Highway**/State Road 486.

33.7 Side Trip: Continue on **North Fork Highway** toward Glacier National Park.
42.2   Right on **Blankenship Road**, gravel for 4.3 miles.
46.5   Left on **Belton Stage Road** at the T intersection.
46.8   Right past Lake Five Resort.
47.0   Left on **US Highway 2**.
49.0   Left on **Park Entrance Road** to enter West Glacier (all services). Backtrack to rejoin the main route, or begin tour 20, Glacier National Park Loop.

34.0   Left across railroad tracks on **Tamarack Lane**.
34.8   Left up a short, steep hill on Tamarack Lane.
35.8   Pass the Meadow Lake Golf Course.
37.3   Left at a dead-end sign to stay with Tamarack Lane.
38.3   Right on **East Edgewood Road**.
42.2   Left on **Second Street**, and cross the railroad tracks.
43.0   Baker Street in Whitefish. End of tour.

20. GLACIER NATIONAL PARK LOOP

Chuck Haney

Distance: 209 miles
Terrain: gentle to strenuous with a nice downhill each day; not recommended for novice cyclists
Total cumulative elevation gain: 11,572 feet
Recommended time of year: late June–early September
Recommended starting time: 6:00–7:00 A.M.
Allow: 4 days; layover days recommended
Points of Interest: Lake McDonald; McDonald Lodge; Wild Goose Island; Museum of the Plains Indians, Browning; Marias Pass; Izaak Walton Inn

PUBLIC TRANSPORTATION
Air: commercial airlines serve Kalispell; connect to this route by using parts of tour 19, Flathead Valley Loop, or by driving/cycling US Highways 93, 2, or 89 from Kalispell to West Glacier
Train: Amtrak serves Whitefish and West Glacier

PRACTICAL INFORMATION

Key contacts: Glacier Park Ranger Station, 406-888-5441; Glacier Park Reservations, 800-332-9351; Glacier Country Information (Kalispell), 800-338-5072

STARTING POINT

West Glacier, immediately north of Highway 2 on the Going to the Sun Road: Check with the Glacier Park Ranger Station for one of the several options for overnight parking in West Glacier.

Capture the shining jewel of Northwest bicycling by pedaling Glacier National Park. When conditions are right, it is the most spectacular place on the planet to ride a bike. Within the park there are only two paved roads, but what roads they are. There is more diversity on this 209-mile loop than one can possibly fathom.

From the park's west entrance at West Glacier, ride 12 usually traffic-free miles on the Camas Road to the North Fork of the Flathead River. Intersect there with the North Fork Highway 486. The more famous of the two roads, the fabulous Going to the Sun Road, opened in 1932 after eleven years of construction wizardry. Marvel at the upper sections chiseled out of the mountainsides, an engineering feat connecting the 52 scenic miles between West Glacier and St. Mary.

On this 4-day tour, travel the entire length of the Going to the Sun Road, then leave a wet, green climate to spill out on the wide-open prairie where awesome views of the Rocky Mountains await. Spend 2 nights in St. Mary, looping on the second day without baggage across the Blackfeet Reservation to Browning. Finally, follow the wild Middle Fork of the Flathead River back to West Glacier.

On Day One, get a really early morning start from the village of West Glacier. Due to narrow roads and high traffic volumes, two sections are closed to bicyclists from 11:00 A.M. to 4:00 P.M., from the park's summer opening through Labor Day. From Apgar to Lake McDonald Lodge and between Logan Creek and Logan Pass, these closures are strictly enforced. Also, carry layers of clothing for adjusting to the mountain environment.

Spin past the park's west entrance and onto the Going to the Sun Road, riding some of Montana's finest and smoothest pavement. At Apgar Village and Campground, continue along the photogenic shores of 10-mile-long Lake McDonald, originally Terry Lake. Duncan McDonald, the son of the first white settler in the valley, carved his name in a tree nearby, apparently causing passersby to think the lake bore his name. Now it does. Cycle flat terrain past Sprague Creek Campground and historic Lake McDonald Lodge with its 1936 jammer buses out front. Each red "mountain limo" carries seventeen people on park tours.

The Great Northern Railway built enormous log hotels in the park between 1911 and 1915, luring visitors from the east. Hiking chalets, complete with overnight accommodations and catered meals, also were constructed. Environmental concerns and the chalets' state of disrepair prompted their closure to the public in 1993. They are expected to reopen in 1996.

Continue into the thickening forest as white water in McDonald Creek gushes forth. Avalanche Creek Campground beckons with hiking among giant cedar trees and opportunities as abundant as the wildlife to spy bear, moose, deer, elk, or mountain lion. Instead answer the call to Logan Pass. Feel the burn as the grade steepens at Logan Creek. Mind the pedals as the 4 to 5 percent grade continues up to the 6,600-foot pass. With proper gearing you can get into a nice rhythm, then concentrate on the stunning scenery. Watch for numerous summer wildflowers, cascading waterfalls, spectacular mountain vistas, and, if you are lucky, mountain goats near the road.

At 24 miles, near the hairpin turn called the Loop, feel the road narrow as it clings precariously to the mountainside. With the Garden Wall on your left, dig in for 8 more uphill miles. Survey the scenic spires most of the way to the top of Logan Pass where the Visitors Center offers you water and rest rooms. Welcome the shelter in bad weather, but do not expect refreshments. Several outstanding hikes take off from the trailheads here.

Smile and recharge tired muscles on the exhilarating 10-mile dive to the shores of St. Mary Lake. Plunge 2,100 feet down the smooth lakeshore pavement past the Rising Sun Campground and into a noticeably different climate

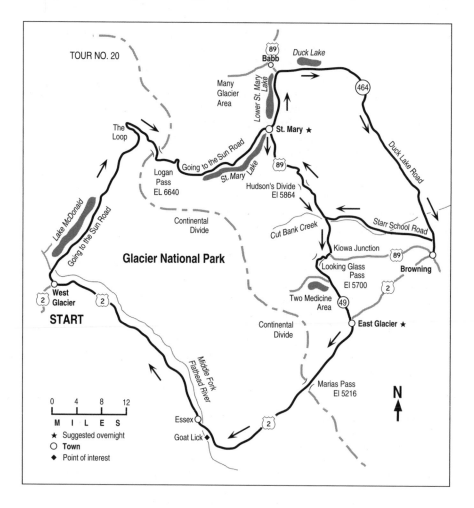

and terrain. On the way check out the most-photographed spot in the park, Wild Goose Island. Small mammals, such as ground squirrels and chipmunks, scamper about, but you may also see coyotes, elk, eagles, and hawks. The St. Mary Campground is a good place to listen for coyote calls, so end the first day of riding there or a mile farther along the route in the village of St. Mary.

Lay over in St. Mary for the loop into Browning on Day Two, returning to St. Mary for a second night. Ride into a different world on the Montana prairie, taking pleasure in the rolling, sparsely traveled asphalt ribbon, complete with a moving picture of the massive Rocky Mountain front. Take an intermission at Browning, to soak up Blackfeet culture and history in the Museum of the Plains Indians, then continue to enjoy the show. Pass Duck Lake, quacked up to be excellent for fishing and wind surfing, and roll past cattle ranches spread out like pancakes on a vast plate. Coyotes and soaring birds stalk their prey and in early summer prairie wildflowers explode with color. Then ascend Hudson's Divide Pass. At nearby Triple Divide, all water flows to either the Atlantic or Pacific oceans, or north to Hudson's Bay. In certain years the multitude of wildflowers along the divide can be mind-blowing. From the top, marvel at more big-sky vistas of the prairie and the mountains, then drop 6 miles back into St. Mary.

Remember Day Two's downhill run while ascending Divide Pass on Day Three. In the mere 31 miles to East Glacier, two major climbs and several smaller ones form a series of hurdles. After Divide Pass, twist and turn along the Rocky Mountain foothills to Kiowa Junction. Narrow and winding, the second big climb, up 5,700-foot Looking Glass Pass, affords great views down into the Two Medicine Valley of Glacier. Grind 3.5 miles, then crest the summit. On the screaming descent, whiz by the Two Medicine entrance to Glacier National Park (a great side trip), cross the Two Medicine River, and zip into East Glacier under a canopy of aspens.

Although East Glacier has many places to lodge or camp, the summer season changes the picture, making it tough to find a spot anywhere near the park. Reserve your place in advance or arrive early in the day. Stock up on provisions and enjoy the restaurants in East Glacier, but do not be lured by Amtrak's tempting rail ride back to West Glacier or the Flathead Valley.

Cycle on Day Four on US Highway 2 to West Glacier. Even if the wind is howling in 5,216-foot Marias Pass, accept the challenge of a gradual incline on the slim, 12-mile road to the top. On the pass there are rest rooms, water, and camping facilities, but the best part is the road. Smile as it widens out and falls for most of the next 43 miles. US Highway 2 hugs the boundaries of Glacier National Park and the Flathead National Forest, paralleling the railroad track and the wild Middle Fork of the Flathead River. You can look for rafts on the river and for mountain goats enjoying the mineral treats on the cliff beside it. At Mile 27, watch for the goat lick. Blushing pavement signifies the spot or is the asphalt turning red from the heat of your blistering cycling pace?

Enjoy food and services available about every 20 miles along this road. The Izaak Walton Inn in Essex also offers history in a rustic facility known for its early railroad memorabilia. On the final few miles back into West Glacier, the road narrows as if to squeeze the last wonderful moments from four spectacular cycling days in Glacier Country.

*Capture the shining jewel of Northwest bicycling by pedaling Glacier National
Park.* (Photo: Chuck Haney)

MILEAGE LOG

DAY ONE: WEST GLACIER TO ST. MARY—50 MILES

0.0   West Glacier. Proceed east toward the Glacier National Park entrance.

1.0   Right on **Going to the Sun Road**.

16.0 Pass Avalanche Creek Campground (camping, water) on the right.

20.0 Pass Logan Creek and begin climbing.

24.0 Hairpin turn on "the Loop."

32.0 Logan Pass Visitors Center (water, rest rooms), Continental Divide (6,640 feet).

49.0 St. Mary Campground (camping, water, restaurant nearby).

50.0 Village of St. Mary (all services).

DAY TWO: ST. MARY–BROWNING LOOP–71 MILES

0.0   Town of St. Mary. Head north on **US Highway 89** toward Babb and the
      Canadian border.

7.3   Right on **Duck Lake Road/Highway 464.**

39.0 Pass Starr School Road on the right.

40.0 Browning (all services).

    40.0 Side Trip: Turn right on **US Highway 2.** Continue a mile to the
      Museum of the Plains Indi-
      ans. After your visit, back-
      track to rejoin the main
      route.

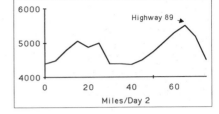

40.0 From Browning, backtrack on
      US Highway 2 to **Duck Lake
      Road/Highway 464.** Turn left.

42.0 Left on **Starr School Road.**

56.0 Right on **US Highway 89.**

65.0 Hudson's Divide Pass (5,864 feet) and Triple Divide (8,011 feet) nearby.

71.0 Village of St. Mary (all services).

*From Logan Pass to the shores of St. Mary Lake is an exhilarating 10-mile
dive.* (Photo: Shari Hogshead)

DAY THREE: ST. MARY TO EAST GLACIER—31 MILES

0.0   Village of St. Mary. Turn right (south) on **US Highway 89**.

6.0   Hudson's Divide (5,864 feet). Triple Divide is nearby.

19.0   Right on **Highway 49** at Kiowa Junction.

22.5   Looking Glass Pass (5,700 feet).

31.0   East Glacier (all services).

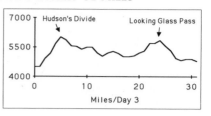

DAY FOUR: EAST GLACIER TO WEST GLACIER—57 MILES

0.0   East Glacier, intersection of Highway 49 and US Highway 2. Turn right on **US Highway 2**.

12.0   Marias Pass (5,216 feet) summit area (camping, rest rooms, water).

27.0   Pass the goat lick. (Look for the red pavement.)

30.0   Essex (restaurant), home of the historic Izaak Walton Inn and its railroad memorabilia.

57.0   West Glacier. End of tour.

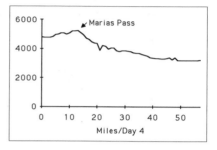

APPENDICES

◆

APPENDIX A: Tour Junctions

◆

APPENDIX B: Tour Lengths

TOUR	DAY	MILES
1. Puget Sound and Island Adventure	7	214
2. North Cascades Highway	2	130
3. Leavenworth Loops	2	82
4. Wenatchee Apple Loop	2	98
5. Grand Coulee and Potholes Sunshine Loops	3–4	189–236
6. Northern Exposure Loop	3	209
7. Two-State Canyons Loop	8	368
8. Central Washington Bluebird Loop	3	156
9. Pacific Ocean Beach Excursion	3	152
10. Central Oregon Coast to Cascades Loop	9	504

Tour	Day	Miles
11. South Coast and Redwoods Loop	9	440
12. The Great Basin and Cascades Loop	9	492
13. Wallowas and Blue Mountains Loop	8	428
14. The Idaho Panhandle	9	450
15. Nez Perce National Historic Park Loop	6–7	279
16. Sun Valley Loop	5	278
17. Pioneer Historic Byway and Bear Lake Loop	6	321
18. Yellowstone and Grand Teton National Parks	7–10	334
19. Flathead Valley Loop	2	90
20. Glacier National Park Loop	4	209

◆

APPENDIX C: Suggestions for Linking the Tours

1. Puget Sound and Island Adventure: Connect to tour 2, North Cascades Highway, via Highway 20 between Anacortes and Diablo. Connect to Seattle via ferry from Victoria, British Columbia.

2. North Cascades Highway: Use Highway 153 and US Highway 97A between Winthrop and Chelan to connect to tour 4, Wenatchee Apple Loop, or take Highway 20 to Anacortes and tour 1, Puget Sound and Island Adventure.

3. Leavenworth Loops: Use US Highway 97 near Cashmere to connect to Old Blewett Highway and link to tour 6, Northern Exposure Loop, near Ellensburg.

4. Wenatchee Apple Loop: Connect to tour 2, North Cascades Highway, via US Highway 97A and Highway 153 between Chelan and Winthrop, or to tour 6, Northern Exposure Loop, via US Highway 97 and the Old Blewett Highway to Ellensburg. To link to tour 5, Grand Coulee and Potholes Sunshine Loops, travel US Highway 2.

5. Grand Coulee and Potholes Sunshine Loops: Connect to Vantage on tour 6, Northern Exposure Loop, via Highway 26 (east of Royal City) and the I-90 bridge over the Columbia River.

6. Northern Exposure Loop: Use the I-90 shoulder to cycle into Seattle. Watch for the Nelson Siding Road, Alpental Road, and other backroads westbound, or ride the freeway shoulder all the way.

7. Two-State Canyons Loop: Connect to tour 13, Wallowas and Blue Mountains Loop, at Weston on Oregon Highway 11, noting that the two tours cover the same route from Weston to Joseph, or to tour 15, Nez Perce National Historic Park Loop, via Clarkston for 2 miles on Highway 128 to Lewiston, Idaho.

8. Central Washington Bluebird Loop: Connect to tour 6, Northern Exposure Loop, via the Yakima Valley Highway/Highway 12. Between Union Gap and Selah, ride the Yakima Greenway bicycle trail.

9. Pacific Ocean Beach Excursion: See *Bicycling the Backroads of Southwest Washington,* 3d ed., or *Bicycling the Pacific Coast,* 2d ed. (The Mountaineers, 1994 and 1990) for connecting routes to Longview and north along the coastline.

10. Central Oregon Coast to Cascades Loop: Connect to tour 11, South Coast and Redwoods Loop, on US Highway 101 between Reedsport and Coos

Bay or connect to tour 12, The Great Basin and Cascades Loop, on Highway 242 from Belknap Hot Springs, or Highways 126/20 from Clear Lake to Sisters, and then to Bend. For additional tours in Oregon, see *Bicycling the Backroads of Northwest Oregon,* 2d ed. (The Mountaineers, 1992).

11. South Coast and Redwoods Loop: Connect from tour 10, Central Oregon Coast to Cascades Loop, via US Highway 101 on the coast between Coos Bay and Reedsport, and to tour 12, The Great Basin and Cascades Loop, via Highway 62 from Trail toward Crater Lake.

12. The Great Basin and Cascades Loop: Connect to tour 11, South Coast and Redwoods Loop, on Highway 62 from Union Creek to Trail.

13. Wallowas and Blue Mountains Loop: To connect to tour 12, The Great Basin and Cascades Loop, from Sumpter on Highway 7 continue west to US Highway 26 to Prineville, then Highway 126 and US Highway 97 to Bend.

14. The Idaho Panhandle: Connect to tour 15, Nez Perce National Historic Park Loop, via Highways 3, 6, 9, and 3 from St. Maries to Myrtle.

15. Nez Perce National Historic Park Loop: To connect to tour 16, Sun Valley Loop, take US Highway 95 from Grangeville south to New Meadows, then follow Highway 55 to Banks and Highway 21 to Stanley. There may be a few miles of gravel on Highway 21.

16. Sun Valley Loop: Connect to tour 17, Pioneer Historic Byway and Bear Lake Loop, via US Highway 20 from Arco to Idaho Falls, then follow driving instructions to the tour's start.

17. Pioneer Historic Byway and Bear Lake Loop: Connect to tour 18, Yellowstone and Grand Teton National Parks, via US Highway 89 from Alpine Junction.

18. Yellowstone and Grand Teton National Parks: Connect to tour 17, Pioneer Historic Byway and Bear Lake Loop, via Highway 34 from Freedom, Wyoming, to US Highway 89 at Alpine Junction.

19. Flathead Valley Loop: Follow the side-trip route in the tour for connecting to tour 20, Glacier National Park Loop.

20. Glacier National Park Loop: See linking instructions in the tour.

◆

APPENDIX D: Key Contacts

Adventure Cycling Association
Box 8308
Missoula, MT 59807
406-721-1776

Amtrak
800-872-7245 (800-USA-RAIL)

British Columbia Tourism (and accommodation reservations)
800-663-6000

Eastern Oregon Visitors Association
800-332-1843

Idaho Travel Council
800-635-7820 or 208-334-2470

League of American Bicyclists
190 W. Ostend Street, Suite 120
Baltimore, MD 21230-3755
410-539-3399

Mistix (campground reservations in national parks)
800-365-2267

Oregon State Parks
800-452-5687 or 503-731-3411

Oregon Tourism
800-547-7842 (out of state)

Pacific Bed & Breakfast Agency
(national network brochure)
206-784-0539

Travel Montana
800-541-1477 or 406-444-2654

U.S. Forest Service Reservations
800-280-2267

Washington State Department of Tourism
800-544-1800

Washington State Ferry Service
800-84-FERRY

Washington State Parks and Recreation Commission
7150 Clearwater Lane, Box 42650
Olympia, WA 98504-2650
360-753-2027

APPENDIX E:
Bicycle Touring Checklist

PACKS

handlebar bag or rack pack
rear and/or front panniers
waist pack or knapsack

FIRST AID

antiseptic
adhesive strips
large gauze pads
tape
scissors or knife
aspirin or ibuprofen
aloe vera gel
phone cash or card

BIKE ACCESSORIES

helmet
cycle computer
attachment straps or shock cords
pump strap(s)
water bottles
lights
small tool kit
tubes (2)
extra tire (for remote areas)
handcleaner and cloth
pump
patch kit
tire irons
spokes to fit wheel (tape to frame)
freewheel remover tool
lock
bell

MISCELLANEOUS

flashlight
extra battery
camera, film, accessories
maps
wallet (identification)
credit cards
currency
sewing kit

pencil and notebook
keys
sunglasses
compass (remote areas)

PERSONAL GEAR

mirror
razor
toothbrush
toothpaste
comb or brush
insect repellent
sunscreen
lip salve
toilet tissue
towel and washcloth
soap and shampoo
talcum powder (to prevent chafing)
reading material

CLOTHING

cycling shorts and tights
cycling jerseys
cycling gloves
cycling socks
cycling shoes
walking shoes
underwear
dress-up clothing
sweater
handkerchiefs
raincoat and rain pants
fingered gloves
rain booties (thin)
hat, bandanna, ear band
swim suit
polypropylene or wool shirt
emergency clothing layer

CAMPING EXTRAS

clothespins and nylon cord
cookware and utensils
stove fuel with extra fuel

camp stove
can opener
dish detergent
garbage/sandwich bags
waterproof matches
cup and eating utensils
laundry detergent
stuff sacks

SHELTER

tent and/or tarp and rain fly
ground cloth
sleeping bag/sack and stuff sack
sleeping pad

SHIPPING SUPPLIES

strapping tape
black marking pen
wrenches to fit pedals, allen heads,
    and headset
derailleur protector

INDEX

ABOUT THE AUTHORS

JEAN HENDERSON
Author/Editor

Bicycling is a lifestyle for Jean Henderson, who rides most weekends with fellow members of The Mountaineers. Co-author of *Bicycling the Backroads of Northwest Oregon*, 2d ed., she and Ken Winkenweder, map creator for that book and this one, reside in Seattle. They have pedaled in the Northwest and in Europe. They also teach folk dancing and enjoy hiking and skiing.

ROGER AASEN
Author of the North Cascades Highway Tour

An avid cyclist, Aasen enjoys both road and mountain-bike tours. A Seattle native who now resides in Kirkland, Washington, Aasen is a member of The Mountaineers Bicycling Committee and a regular volunteer for other organizations. Among other outdoor activities he enjoys are hiking, kayaking, and snowshoeing.

SUSIE STEPHENS
Author of the Northern Exposure Loop

An avid cyclist, Stephens has toured Japan, Baja, the U.S. West Coast, and many parts of Washington by bicycle. A resident of Seattle, she promotes bicycle safety, transportation, planning, and education in her career as executive director of the Northwest Bicycle Federation.

ALLEN THROOP AND THE MID-VALLEY BICYCLE CLUB
Author of the Oregon Tours

When not bicycling on weekends, Allen Throop, a resident of Corvallis, Oregon, is generally cross-country skiing, hiking, backpacking, or canoeing. An avid bicycle tourist since 1987, he has commuted by bicycle even longer. Throop has written sections of route guides for canoeing in Oregon and hiking in Tasmania.

MID-VALLEY BICYCLE CLUB, CORVALLIS
Creators of the Oregon Tours

The Oregon tours, ridden originally by club members of the Mid-Valley Bicycle Club on their annual 9-day adventures, have been modified somewhat to facilitate use by individuals. Members who created the tours, reviewed the early drafts, and supported Throop in bringing the information into book form include: Henry Throop, Chuck and Nancy Meitle, Marilyn Smith, Andrew Herstrom, Richard Burgess, Penny Fulton, Jerry Rooney, Bruce Hecht, and Heather Throop. Behind Allen all the way, as the stoker on their tandem, was Janet Throop.

GAYLE NEWMAN
Author of the Idaho Tours

Newman calls cycling the Zen approach to sightseeing that involves all the senses. She does not consider herself a hard-core cyclist, but has explored backroads and byways out of a love of the sport. A Seattle native who holds a degree in social welfare from the University of Washington, Newman lives with her husband, Ken, in Moscow, Idaho. She also loves to backpack, read, and write.

CHUCK HANEY
Author of the Montana Tours

Haney is a bicycle mechanic/photographer who has lived in Whitefish, Montana since 1990 with his wife and children. He has written two bicycling guidebooks, and specializes in sports, landscape, agriculture, and wildlife photography. Haney is the past president of the Flathead Valley Bicycle Club and founder and ride director of the "Huckleberry 100 Tour."

◆

THE MOUNTAINEERS, founded in 1906, is a nonprofit outdoor activity and conservation club, whose mission is "to explore, study, preserve, and enjoy the natural beauty of the outdoors...." Based in Seattle, Washington, the club is now the third-largest such organization in the United States, with 14,000 members and four branches throughout Washington State.

The Mountaineers sponsors both classes and year-round outdoor activities in the Pacific Northwest, which include hiking, mountain climbing, ski-touring, snowshoeing, bicycling, camping, kayaking and canoeing, nature study, sailing, and adventure travel. The club's conservation division supports environmental causes through educational activities, sponsoring legislation, and presenting informational programs. All club activities are led by skilled, experienced volunteers, who are dedicated to promoting safe and responsible enjoyment and preservation of the outdoors.

The Mountaineers Books, an active, nonprofit publishing program of the club, produces guidebooks, instructional texts, historical works, natural history guides, and works on environmental conservation. All books produced by The Mountaineers are aimed at fulfilling the club's mission.

If you would like to participate in these organized outdoor activities or the club's programs, consider a membership in The Mountaineers. For information and an application, write or call The Mountaineers, Club Headquarters, 300 Third Avenue West, Seattle, Washington 98119; (206) 284-6310.

Send or call for our catalog of more than 300 outdoor titles:
The Mountaineers Books
1011 SW Klickitat Way, Suite 107
Seattle, WA 98134
1(800)553-4453